Filipino Peasant Women

Exploitation and Resistance

Ligaya Lindio-McGovern

PENN

University of Pennsylvania Press

Philadelphia

D0209901

HQ
1757
L55
1997

10 9 8 7 6 5 4 3 2 1

Published by
University of Pennsylvania Press
Philadelphia, Pennsylvania 19104-4011

Library of Congress Cataloging-in-Publication Data

Lindio-McGovern, Ligaya.
    Filipino peasant women : exploitation and resistance / Ligaya
Lindio-McGovern.
        p.   cm.
    Includes bibliographical references and index.
    ISBN 0-8122-3410-3 (alk. paper). — ISBN 0-8122-1624-5 (pbk. :
alk. paper)
    1. Women peasants—Philippines.   2. Women peasants—Philippines—
Political activity.   3. Women agricultural laborers—Philippines.
4. Women in rural development—Philippines.   I. Title.
HQ1757.L55   1997
305.48'9624—dc21   97-19617
                                                            CIP

To

the Filipino peasant women of KAMMI and AMIHAN,
   who continue to struggle for social
   justice and women's liberation
   in the Philippines

Jim and Paul,
   in whose lives Philippine history plays a part

Monica Macasinag and Teofilo Lindio,
   my parents, for their sixty-fifth year of marriage

Contents

Foreword

The situation of the Filipino peasant woman is a prime example of the invisibility of women. In one Philippine talk show where women of different social sectors were invited, the host who introduced his woman peasant guest exclaimed, "I did not know there are women farmers!" This invisibility stems from the fact that statisticians do not count the women who do more than 50 percent of the farm work; they are seen as "merely helping" their farmer husbands.

Ligaya Lindio-McGovern is to be commended for choosing Filipino peasant women as the subjects of her book, and especially for including resistance in the perspective of her study. Many articles and treatises have been written on the exploitation of peasant women, but there are few who document their struggle against oppression.

Lindio-McGovern's methodology is likewise commendable: she immersed herself in the lives of her subjects. It is, of course, a great advantage that she comes from the peasant class, a reality that cannot be learned in books or even by immersion; and the fact that she is of the same ethnicity and can speak their language gave her an understanding that would not be accessible to a foreigner.

Although the daily lives of peasant women were the focus of the study, Lindio-McGovern includes an important chapter on the various theories of women and development that helps us understand why the author chooses empowerment as the lens through which to evaluate development in relation to Third World women.

Lindio-McGovern includes a thorough historical discussion of the Philippine economy which provides the necessary context for the modern Filipino peasant woman. Moving from the general situation of peasant women to a study of a specific peasant women's organization (Kababaihang Magbubukid ng Mindoro [KAMMI], Peasant Women of Mindoro), Lindio-McGovern bolsters her analysis with examples and concrete incidents. One gets a vivid picture of the problems faced by peasant women, both as peasants and as women: landlessness, job insecurity, usury, and a general lack of recognition of their productive social and economic roles. Filipino peasant women are unable to hold certificates of land transfer and are relegated to doing work in the field in addition to domestic work even as they fulfill their role in the social reproduction of the system that makes them poor.

The two chapters on the politics of resistance of KAMMI and its mother organization, AMIHAN, provide important documentation showing that Filipino peasant women are not victims of exploitation. Rather, they have mobilized their strength to resist through organization; land occupation; collective forms of work; consumer cooperatives; the use of traditional rice seeds, natural fertilizers, pesticides, and indigenous herbal medicine; collective income-generating projects; day care center development; education; and consciousness-raising.

Among these forms of resistance, the most innovative is that of land occupation, a form of people's land reform premised on the sound principle that land should belong to the tiller, not to an absentee landlord. There is certainly something very wrong with a situation in which landlords—who own so much land elsewhere—leave large tracts idle while people living near them are starving because they have no land to cultivate. The efforts of the members of KAMMI and other farmers to make use of idle land is certainly justifiable; the actions of the military and the landlords who try to profit from the work these people have done are reprehensible. It is tragic that many of these forms of resistance have failed, owing to the government's lack of interest in implementing genuine land reform and landlords' use of force.

One of the most interesting chapters of the study is the painstaking documentation of the work performed by KAMMI and AMIHAN in education and consciousness-raising. The sessions given by different resource persons are not only faithfully summarized, but the very process of training, as well as the interactions between resource persons and trainees, is recorded, analyzed, and evaluated. The content of the sessions appears comprehensive, and the interaction is lively and at times critical. The impression is that this is a liberating pedagogy, not a banking methodology, although there are some exceptions depending on the resource person.

AMIHAN's politics of resistance attest to the national scope of the struggle of peasant women against oppressive forces. It is remarkable that this struggle is not merely reactive but proactive, with AMIHAN formulating alternative development policies. Another noteworthy element of the book is its discussion of the difficulties between AMIHAN and its male counterpart organization, the KMP, which underlines the need for politically progressive men to be gender aware.

This work demonstrates the effectiveness of the author's innovative methodology, which she terms "organic feminist inquiry." I highly recommend the use of this methodology to study the exploitation and resistance in other sectors, such as female workers and poor urban women. I recommend, too, that other Filipino women conduct similar studies of Philippine realities. For in the past, it has been all too common for foreign scholars writing about Filipino issues to take credit for ideas they obtained from interviews with Filipinos.

Finally, I am sure the Filipino peasant women who were the subjects of this study are grateful to Lindio-McGovern for drawing them out of their invisibility and for documenting their struggles and their vision of a more just and more humane society.

Sr. Mary John Mananzan
GABRIELA National Chairperson

Preface

My interest in studying Filipino peasant women springs from a combination of factors: personal, political, and academic. On the personal level, it is my peasant class origin that draws my interest. I wanted to understand more about my roots. I also wanted to understand more profoundly why the producers of food often have little, or sometimes nothing, to eat. My own experience of poverty in the Philippines, where I grew up, posed a lot of questions for me during my college years. On the political level, I wanted to make an intellectual contribution to the Philippine movement after becoming involved in grassroots organizational work among Filipino activists in the United States who supported the struggle for social justice in the Philippines. My political involvement made me see the importance of engaging in continuing research, even if we feel we already "know" the situation. I realized that serious involvement in social change also means understanding in detail what we want to change, if we are to think about alternative policies. Although my involvement required profound intellectual analysis of the situation in the Philippines, I felt the need to hear the voices of the poor directly, for it is in their name that many of the official spokespersons of the national liberation movement advocated such changes as "genuine agrarian reform." But what does "genuine agrarian reform" mean from the perspective of poor peasant women?

It is in this moment of quiet questioning that my political experience became linked with my academic awakening. My exposure to women's studies in the academy made me question the standard ways in which we analyze issues. My feminist awakening made me realize how naive I had been to allow unquestioningly a male Filipino activist, with whom I was then working in Chicago in 1984, to suppress my voice by telling me not to bring the "feminist issue" into our political work. My engagement in this project is partly a response to the need to bring out the voices and experiences of poor women in the movement for change in the Philippines as well as in social/development analysis. In 1988 I came across a magazine about AMIHAN, the National Federation of Peasant Women in the Philippines. Since I had not heard much about peasant women's organizations, nor were they discussed in development literature I had read, I decided to research the issue.

While working on the final version of this book, I went back to the Philippines in May and June of 1996 in order to observe new developments firsthand and to revisit the two peasant women's organizations featured in this study: AMIHAN and KAMMI (Kababaihang Magbubukid ng Mindoro, translated as Peasant Women of Mindoro), one of AMIHAN's local chapters on the island of Mindoro. The demands for genuine agrarian and other reforms that the peasant women raised seemed even more urgent than they had in 1989, when I first came in personal contact with these two organizations.

The present study documents and analyzes AMIHAN's and KAMMI's politics of resistance on the national and local levels as they are shaped by the social, political, and economic contexts of everyday lives. Although unknown to many, women's struggles, arduous and often exacting a price, are becoming an important part of the social construction of Philippine reality. Their struggles also defy the stereotype of Third World peasant women as unpoliticized and passive victims of development and underdevelopment. Their story urgently needs telling.

This book is appropriate not only for scholars and graduate students but also for activists, community organizers, and feminists interested in understanding the development processes that exploit, oppress, and repress Filipino peasant women and their forms of resistance. I have tried to make it useful for upper-level undergraduate courses on women and development, the sociology of development, international or global perspectives on women, social movements and social change, third world women, and fieldwork. Some readers may know little about the Philippines; for them I have provided a historical overview of the colonial experience of Filipino women. Most readers will not have had face-to-face encounters with Filipino peasant women; for them I include some detailed personal accounts of situations and activities I observed during my fieldwork. Such details are often omitted from publications; I hope they may be of interest to the casual reader, and of use to those who wish to do comparative studies relying mainly on secondary data.

To protect my informants, I have given them pseudonyms and have avoided mentioning specific names of their villages.

I am grateful to the many people who helped me in my research for this project. I especially thank the peasant women of AMIHAN and KAMMI who participated in this study, for providing generous hospitality in their villages, for trusting me, and for touching my life. I also thank the past and present staff of the AMIHAN national office, who facilitated my entry into the field, especially Rina Anastacio and Lourdes Calma; and Tess Oliveros and Lita Mariano, who helped me during my second visit. I also thank the past and present staff of the Mindoro Institute for Development, who greatly facilitated my fieldwork, especially Maricris Beth, Mavic, Malu, Lynn, and Chris. The GABRIELA international representative at the time I was making preparations for this project, Rachel Sancho, helped me to establish initial contact with AMIHAN. I also would like to thank the few members of GABRIELA who agreed to be interviewed.

I benefited from the comments and suggestions of Judy Wittner, Kathleen McCourt, Philip Nyden of Loyola University of Chicago, and Richard Dello Buono of Rosary College in Illinois during the early stages of this research. I am grateful to my colleague at Indiana University–Kokomo, Jon Kofas, for his suggestions on how to improve some parts of the final version of the book, and to political science professor Kenneth Bauzon of St. Joseph's College in Brooklyn, New York, for reading sections of the manuscript and making helpful comments. I also thank the office of the Task Force Detainees of the Philippines in Quezon City for providing me with materials documenting their work. Several of my students read portions of the manuscript and helped me to see its usefulness; Michael Adams and Wilma Pilkin deserve special mention. I also greatly appreciate the suggestions of the reviewers of the University of Pennsylvania Press and my editor, Patricia Smith, whose conversations with me were helpful in revising the manuscript. I give special thanks to Sr. Mary John Mananzan, president of St. Scholatica's College and founder of the Institute of Women's Studies in Manila, for taking time from her busy schedule to write the foreword for this book. I cannot take for granted the support I received from members of my family in the Philippines who helped me to get around, especially Romulo, Sally, Regino, and Ramon, and Ma and Pa who prayed that I be safe in the field; my father-in-law and late mother-in-law, who extended care to my young son, Paul, while I was in the Philippines; and Jim, my husband, and Paul for giving me the time I needed to complete this book.

Introduction

The Ramos Regime:
Development Policy, Repression, and Resistance

From Ferdinand Marcos's Presidential Decree 27, which in 1972 proclaimed the whole Philippines a land reform area,[1] through Corazon Aquino's Comprehensive Agrarian Reform Program (CARP), which in 1986 was propagated as the centerpiece of her administration, to incumbent President Fidel Ramos's Philippines 2000, which aims to bring the Philippines up to the level of the new industrializing countries (NICs), the demand of peasant women for genuine agrarian reform has remained unheeded. AMIHAN contends that the current government's Medium Term Philippine Development Plan (MTPDP), popularly known as Philippines 2000, further undermines not only the peasants' struggle for land but also their emancipation from the national and global structures that cause their poverty and exploit them as peasants and as women. Thus, on June 6, 1996, AMIHAN mobilized a public demonstration in Manila and called for peasant women to persistently and more militantly struggle (*puspusang makibaka*) for true agrarian reform. AMIHAN distributed a flier critical of the government's development policy because of its failure to redistribute land to landless peasants. In this flier, written in Pilipino, AMIHAN criticized the Ramos government for making the situation of the peasants—and peasant women in particular—"more precarious" than it was under the Aquino administration. It gave the following reasons: Ramos's Philippines 2000 program (1) is rapidly converting the "few remaining lands" on which peasants make a livelihood into industrial and commercial zones, subdivisions, resorts, and golf courses; (2) is "taking back" the certificates of land transfer, emancipation patents, and certificates of land ownership that were awarded to some peasants under the Marcos and Aquino administrations; (3) will convert two-thirds of the 5.1 million hectares of rice and corn lands to production of export crops, such as cut flowers, asparagus,

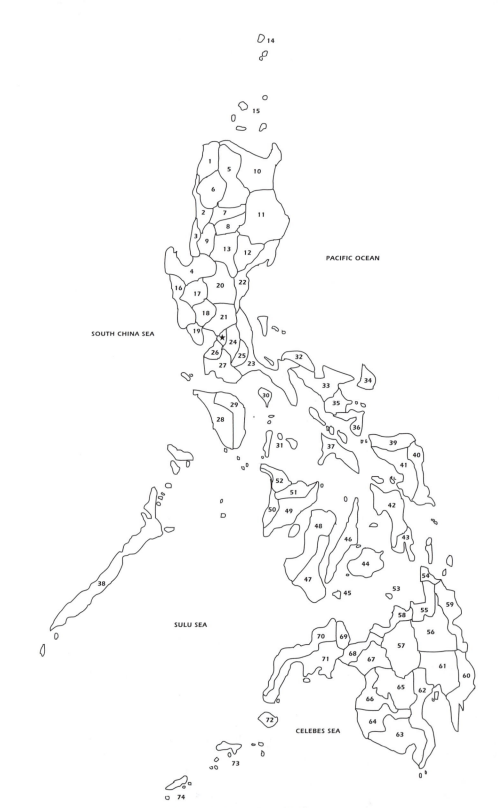

Figure 1. Map of the Philippines.

Key to Figure 1. Map of the Philippines

Luzon Region

1 Ilocus Norte
2 Ilocus Sur
3 La Union
4 Pangasinan
5 Kalinga Apayao
6 Abra
7 Mountain Province
8 Ifugao
9 Benguet
10 Cagayan
11 Isabela
12 Quirino
13 Nueva Viscaya
14 Batanes
15 Babuyan Is.
16 Zambales
17 Tarlac
18 Pampanga
19 Bulacan
20 Nueva Ecija
21 Bataan
22 Aurora
23 Quezon Province
24 Rizal
25 Laguna
26 Cavite
27 Batangas
28 Occidental Mindoro
29 Oriental Mindoro
30 Marinduque
31 Romblon

Southern Tagalog Region

32 Camarines Norte
33 Camarines Sur
34 Catanduanes
35 Albay
36 Sorsogon
37 Masbate

Bicol Region

38 Palawan (Southern Tagalog Region)
* Manila (national capital)

Visayas Region

39 Northern Samar
40 Eastern Samar
41 Western Samar
42 Leyte
43 Southern Leyte
44 Bohol
45 Siquijor
46 Cebu
47 Negros Oriental
48 Negros Occidental
49 Iloilo
50 Antique
51 Capiz
52 Aklan

Mindanao Region

53 Camiguin
54 Surigao del Norte
55 Agusan del Norte
56 Agusan del Sur
57 Bukidnon
58 Misamis Oriental
59 Surigao del Sur
60 Davao Oriental
61 Davao
62 Davao del Sur
63 South Cotabato
64 Sultan Kudarat
65 North Cotabato
66 Maguindanao
67 Lanao del Sur
68 Lanao del Norte
69 Misamis Occidental
70 Zamboanga del Norte
71 Zamboanga del Sur
72 Basilan
73 Sulu
74 Tawi-Tawi

and other commodities for the foreign market; and (4) will lead to the "reconcentration" of lands among a few landowners and foreign multinational corporations.

AMIHAN contended that under Philippines 2000, the conversion of prime agricultural lands to full-scale commercial use for export further concentrates land—even those areas slated for land reform by CARP (see Chapter 5)—among a few landowners. As these landlords rapidly convert their holdings, they are finding ways to displace their tenants and to recover lands that were already designated by the Department of Agrarian Reform (DAR) for distribution to tenants.[2] AMIHAN's contention is supported by the following information: In 1993, the DAR canceled 10,598 certificates of land transfer and 9,133 emancipation patents, taking back 24,731 hectares of land from 18,348 farmer-beneficiaries.[3]

The DAR's conversion plan will exclude 6.1 million hectares from land reform.[4] This is facilitated by Republic Act 1778, recently passed by the Philippine Congress, which exempts fishponds, prawn farms, and aquaculture, livestock, and poultry farms from being covered by CARP reforms. Under RA 1778, many landlords are converting their estates into prawn farms and fishponds, dislocating many tenants and farm workers.[5]

As land conversion gears up, it will continue to displace more and more peasant families from their source of livelihood, thereby greatly increasing poverty and misery. CALABARZON, which includes the provinces of Cauite, Laguna, Batangas, Rizal, and Quezon, is now being converted into a huge industrial zone to attract foreign investors; this may displace 100,000 local peasant families. In Misamis Oriental, 640,000 coconut farmers have been displaced by the conversion of 84,000 hectares of coconut land, and in central Mindanao, 23 percent of the population are expected to be directly affected by land conversions.[6]

Massive land-use conversions are absorbing ancestral lands of indigenous peoples, igniting strong resistance in these communities. During my second visit to Mindoro, I learned that the Mangyan indigeous communities will lose their upland ancestral farmlands to the chromite mining project of a Japanese multinational corporation. On the way to Santa Cruz, I saw huge tracts of lowland rice fields that will be inundated if the mining project is not halted. This land had once been unusable. When part of a river dried up, landless peasants occupied the area and made productive fields. The Mangyans and surrounding communities held a series of demonstrations along the mountain slopes and adjacent river, surrounded by the military. The Mangyan chief spoke to the provincial governor, who had been invited to come to one of these demonstrations. When the governor questioned why the Mangyans were rejecting progress, the Mangyan chief unequivocally argued that although they did want progress, the government's concept of progress was different from

theirs. For the Mangyans, losing their lands, the source of their livelihood, is not progress.[7]

Such resistance among indigenous Filipinos is taking place in other
parts of the country as well: in the Quezon-Aurora mountains, the Agtas
are against the building of dams; in Panay, the Sulods are protesting
military encroachment into their land; and in Mindanao, the Lumads
are resisting logging firms' deforestation and other land-use conversions
affecting their ancestral lands.[8]

The Medium Term Agricultural Development Plan (MTADP) of the
Ramos administration will transform 65 percent of rice and corn lands
into nonstaple export crop production and the rest into pasture for
cattle breeding (Tungcul 1996). This will contribute to rice shortage, as
evidenced by the mid-1995 crisis, in which people could not find rice in
the markets. As well, this policy will escalate the price of rice, which even
now is unaffordable to the many poor. During my second visit to Mindoro, a member of KAMMI told me, "We peasants are victims of the increase in the price of rice. We are the ones producing rice, but we don't
have money to buy rice."

The price of development in Philippines 2000 is being borne by the
ordinary people, who benefit least from or are marginalized by that
development. This is shown by the implementation on January 1, 1996,
of the Expanded Value Added Tax (E-VAT), a regressive tax measure
widely opposed by the grass roots. This tax has raised the price of prime
commodities, making life harder for the low-income majority (Philippine Human Rights Information Center 1996, 4).

AMIHAN also contends that Philippines 2000 will further increase the
control of transnational corporations over public and private lands.[9] The
landholdings of Dole Philippines increased from 35,000 hectares in 1985
to 90,000 hectares in 1995, while those of the Philippine Packing Corporation increased from 24,000 hectares in 1985 to 44,000 hectares in
1995, and those of Guthrie doubled from 16,000 hectares in 1985 to
32,000 hectares in 1995.[10] The Investors Lease Act of 1993, RA 7652,
which extends foreign corporations' lease period on public lands to 50–
75 years, will further limit landless peasants' access to these lands (Nera-
Lauron 1994). And because the big landlords can more profitably lease
or sell their lands to multinational corporations, poor landless peasants
will be further marginalized. Peasant women's struggle for change is thus
complex, because they must contend with the global structures that are
intricately interlocked with national and local power structures.

Counterinsurgency operations and human rights violations of the
Marcos and Aquino administrations still continue. As of November 20,
1995, there were 218 political detainees across the country, and as of
February 5, 1996, there were still 201 political prisoners in fifty-five

detention centers throughout the Philippines.[11] Human rights activists have observed a subtle trend in how the state acts against political dissent: dissenters are now charged with or convicted of common criminal offenses.[12] This criminalization of political dissent, activists say, allows the government to deny the existence of political prisoners.

Other developments also indicate continuing military repression: (1) the budget for the Citizens Armed Forces Geographical Units (CAFGUs)—the government's paramilitary units usually deployed in rural areas—has been increased; (2) military and paramilitary troops in some parts of the country—for example, in the Bicol region, Samar, and Panay Island—have also increased; and (3) military operations have resulted in 1,031 forced evacuations in fifty-nine provinces.[13] As of 1995, the counterinsurgency had displaced approximately 1.8 million people.[14] And as of 1993, forced evacuations had turned 75,234 Filipino children into refugees within their own country.[15]

As in past administrations, human rights advocates still face risks. For example, on February 27, 1996, the *Philippine Daily Inquirer* reported the murder of Ferdie Reyes, a journalist and human rights lawyer in Dipolog City. According to witnesses, Reyes was shot by a soldier, although no suspect has been identified because people are afraid to testify.[16]

Yet, despite the hurdles posed by elite-controlled development processes and policies, AMIHAN and its local chapters like KAMMI have persisted not only in resisting exploitation and oppression but also in trying alternative approaches toward securing a more liberating development.[17]

Defining Development and Third World Women

In this work I attempt to understand and explain the politics of underdevelopment and resistance in the Philippines, using the experience of organized Filipino peasant women as a starting point, since the majority of women in the Philippines are poor peasants. My approach has been influenced by Gita Sen and Caren Grown, who argue that "when we start from the perspective of poor Third World women, we give a much needed reorientation to development analysis" (Sen and Grown 1987, 18). Since poor Third World women comprise the majority of the poor, who suffer both economic and social disadvantages, including gendered forms of domination, there is every reason to make their experience the "vantage point" (Sen and Grown 1987, 23) from which to examine the politics of development and underdevelopment in the Third World. My approach has also been influenced by Dorothy Smith's concept of "institutional ethnography," in which the problematic issue of a feminist inquiry begins from and is established by women in their everyday lives.

Smith situates these questions and problems within the larger structures in which the women's lives are enmeshed (Smith 1987). I did not conduct my research merely in order to test Smith's concept, however, because I wanted to be open to what might emerge in my own face-to-face encounters with Filipino peasant women.

Although there is current debate on the use of the words *development, underdevelopment,* and *Third World,* I will limit myself here to briefly explaining my use of these terms. I use *development* to refer to the way the political economy is organized, its political and economic policies and the interests they serve, and the dominant ideology and principles on which these economic and political policies are based. The Philippine development promoted by past and present governments widened the gap between the rich and the poor. I use the term *underdevelopment* to refer to the process of exploitation that results from a development promoting primarily the interests of a local owning class or foreign investors. "Underdevelopment" and "exploitation" are thus interchangeable here. Development is exploitative when a few are enriched through economic relations that fundamentally impoverish those at the bottom of the class and gender hierarchy. Interlocking internal and external forces in this exploitation make this underdevelopment quite complex, but also possible to change. I do not use "underdevelopment" to imply that the Third World must follow First World capitalist development in order to improve the conditions of the poor. Underdevelopment is conceived here within a critical perspective: it is a consequence of First World imperial capitalist penetration of Third World economies, initially through colonialism, transforming their precolonial communal production and property relations, taking out resources, and using human labor of the Third World in a manner more beneficial to the First World. I use the term *Third World* as a conceptual category for nations whose political economies have been dominated by other countries through colonialism, neocolonialism, and modern forms of imperialism, with their allied force, militarism. These are nations whose political economies have been largely linked to the capitalist globalization of the economies of imperial powers, among which are the United States, Britain, and Japan. There are, however, ongoing forms of resistance in the Third World, in which people are searching for political and economic alternatives that would empower the grass roots. This process of resistance makes the concept "Third World" dialectical and dynamic.

The way in which Third World women, and especially poor women, experience the politics of development and underdevelopment provides a context in which to redefine a concept of Third World development that is more liberating for not only women but men and children as well. Women's forms of resistance point toward the possibilities for change, an alternative agenda for development that is sensitive to the particular situation of women, and a politics of change that recognizes the important role of women.

The experience of Third World women is exemplified by that of the Filipino peasant women I focus on in this book. Although a comparative study of Southeast Asian women is much needed, I have chosen to focus on the everyday lives of organized Filipino peasant women and on the politics of their resistance within the context of underdevelopment. I have done so because there is little current literature on Filipino women and development. And since the majority of Filipino women are peasants, an understanding of their lives is necessary to grasp the impact of Philippine development on Filipino women.

Methodology and Theoretical Frames

The peasant women who were my informants were members of AMIHAN. To understand the local politics of peasant women, I focused on one of AMIHAN's chapters, KAMMI (Kababaihang Magbubukid ng Mindoro). KAMMI is the provincial federation of peasant women's village organizations in Mindoro, a province in the southern Tagalog region of Luzon. Although the experience of Filipino peasant women linked to AMIHAN is not representative of that of all Filipino peasant women, I chose to study these women because AMIHAN advocates a development agenda that is an alternative to what is officially promoted in the Philippines.

To gather primary data about peasant women's experience, I conducted fieldwork in the Philippines from May to August, 1989. As an insider, sharing both the language and the peasant-class origins of my informants, I had advantages over foreign anthropologists or sociologists (Altorki and El-Solh 1988). These advantages quickly facilitated my fieldwork (see Appendix A). For forty-eight days I stayed in Occidental Mindoro, where I talked to thirty peasant women who belonged to KAMMI, observed and participated in their activities, visited some of their homes, and on several occasions spent one or more nights with them. To better understand the structures that impact on peasant women's lives, I also interviewed a rice trader and several people in the National Food Authority regional office in Mindoro. To understand the national politics of AMIHAN, I participated in the activities of its National Council and interviewed four of its leaders, mainly in the Manila area before and after my stay in Mindoro. During the rest of my fieldwork, I interviewed women associated with GABRIELA, the nongovernmental national coalition of women's organizations in the Philippines to which AMIHAN is also federated, and gathered relevant literature in the Third World Studies Center in the University of the Philippines, at the Asian Social Institute, at the Women's Resource Center, at the Department of Agrarian Reform, at the regional office of the National Food Authority (NFA) in Mindoro, and at the Mindoro Institute for Development, also in Mindoro.

When I went back to the Philippines from May 3 to June 20, 1996, I revisited AMIHAN in Manila and KAMMI in Mindoro to get updated information about them. I interviewed two national leaders of AMIHAN, who I thought would be key informants, and one local organizer from Quezon. I also stayed in Mindoro for several days and talked to available members of KAMMI. I visited Calintaan, where I had been in 1989, and Santa Cruz, where I had not been before. I talked to some of the women I had met in 1989 as well as some new members. My companion, an AMIHAN national leader, visited San Carlos and shared with me information she gathered there. I also gathered documents and literature from AMIHAN and KAMMI.

The methodology of my research is significant for its contribution to an area in which very little study has been done: fieldwork in a militarized zone. The militarization in Mindoro, as in other parts of the country, posed difficulties in my research. To deal with this political context as well as the cultural context of peasant women's lives, I developed what I call *organic feminist inquiry* (see a discussion of its elements in Appendix A). Current literature on feminist issues deals largely with Western contexts of research; Third World women, who face the detrimental impact of militarization in their everyday lives, have been little studied (Reinharz 1992, 1983; Smith 1987; Lather 1988; Stanley and Wise 1990; Harding 1987). That I was able to conduct my fieldwork successfully in a militarized area where westerners had difficulty gaining entry makes the information I present here all the more valuable.

No book has yet been written which views the everyday lives of Filipino peasant women and the politics of their resistance within the national and international context of development and underdevelopment. Third World peasant women are often presented simply as victims of underdevelopment. If we ignore their politics of resistance, not only do we miss an opportunity to learn from them, but we also preclude their experience as a source for rethinking the place of women in Third World development. Development analysis must take into account the forms of resistance that Third World women wage, because their struggles offer us alternative perspectives on development. Though I sometimes hear it said that there is no alternative development in the Third World except that which is legitimated by the conservative government, one need look no further than the politics of resistance of Filipino peasant women to contradict this view.

Because I wanted to examine the politics of development, underdevelopment, and resistance in the Philippines from the point of view of

Filipino peasant women, I chose not to try to test some grand theory of political economy evolved from a Western context, nor did I want to limit myself strictly to a pre-defined framework. I chose instead to begin my analysis of development from the experience of Filipino peasant women. This approach—which sets my work apart from mainstream literature on Third World development—helped me reorient development analysis and allowed me to be open to what was emerging in my fieldwork (see further discussion of this in Appendix A).

Although I focus on AMIHAN and one of its local chapters, KAMMI, these are not the only organizations in the Philippines with agendas for political change. From the period of the Marcos dictatorship to the present, organized resistance has come from different sectors operating on two fronts: the underground and the aboveground. The Communist Party and New People's Army (the revolutionary army in the Philippines) are underground revolutionary forces; I chose not to study them for obvious reasons. Among the organizations that operate aboveground is the KMP (Kilusang Magbubukid ng Pilipinas, or Peasant Movement in the Philippines), a progressive grassroots national federation of farmers open to both men and women. The KMP was founded before AMIHAN was formally launched. An aboveground women's organization with an agenda of political change is GABRIELA, the National Federation of Women's Organizations in the Philippines. It consists of approximately 105 women's groups, of which AMIHAN is one. The main thrusts of GABRIELA are to coordinate women's groups nationally in advancing an agenda of feminist change, to bring a feminist perspective and the women's agenda into the national liberation movement, and to influence the national liberation movement to make Filipino women's liberation central to its concerns. It advocates that the national liberation movement cease treating the exploitation and liberation of Filipino women as the concerns of only women's groups, since such a view marginalizes women's or gender issues on the national level.[18]

KMK (Kilusan ng Manggagawang Kababaihan, or Movement of Women Workers) is, like AMIHAN, a grassroots women's organization federated with GABRIELA. It comprises mostly urban women workers, some of whom have jobs in industrial and agribusiness transnational corporations. Like AMIHAN, KMK is a national federation with headquarters in metropolitan Manila. Its major goal is to empower women workers through organization so they can collectively work for their rights as both women and workers. Like AMIHAN, KMK has a national agenda for political change that becomes the rallying point of various women workers' organizations affiliated with it. While a comparative study of AMIHAN and KMK would be valuable, it is unfortunately beyond the scope of the present work.

GABRIELA, AMIHAN, and KMK are aboveground women's organizations; on the underground terrain of the Philippine women's struggle is MAKIBAKA (Malayang Kilusan ng Bagong Kababaihan, "Free Movement of New Women"). Started by radical female students in the 1960s, MAKIBAKA was forced underground after the Marcos dictatorship harassed and killed its leaders. MAKIBAKA's goal is to make the woman question a part of the national liberation struggle and to link the women's movement to the revolutionary movement in the Philippines. MAKIBAKA believes there can be no genuine liberation and revolutionary struggle if there is no emancipation of women during and after the revolution.[19]

Embedded in the body of literature on women in Third World development and underdevelopment are various, sometimes competing, perspectives, all with implications for policy. In Chapter 1, I present an overview of some of these perspectives, not because they are frameworks to be tested in later discussions, but because some development policies relevant to the lives of Filipino peasant women are premised in one or more of them. I found that the forms of resistance of the Filipino peasant women involved in my research negate some of the premises of, for example, the integrationist perspective on women in development; they relate instead to other emerging alternative perspectives. I do not include a discussion of postmodernism and poststructuralism, although there is current debate on these perspectives, because they have little to contribute to discussions of Third World women (San Juan 1992).

In Chapter 2 I provide a brief historical overview of colonization in the Philippines, and attempt to draw from limited historical data the particular experience of Filipino women.[20] I saw the need for this chapter only after writing Chapter 3, in which I examine the dynamics of underdevelopment and exploitation in the lives of the peasant women of KAMMI. For I was left with the question, Did the current system of land ownership in the Philippines exist in the precolonial past? In seeking the answer I came to understand that the poor and landless Filipino peasant has been historically and socially constructed. This historical perspective enhanced my understanding of peasant women's resistance as an effort to reshape Philippine historical legacies in a way that will help liberate not only themselves but others as well. Chapter 2 is intentionally brief, since the focus of the book is not a historical analysis of the Philippine political economy. For a more thorough historical examination of Philippine political economy and gender, I refer the reader to Elizabeth Uy Eviota's work *The Political Economy of Gender: Women and the Sexual Division of Labour in the Philippines.*

In Chapter 3, I attempt to understand the politics of underdevelopment in the Philippines from the experience of the Filipino peasant women who are members of KAMMI. I examine their everyday lives and view from their vantage point the structures of power that keep them poor. To begin analysis of Philippine development and underdevelopment with their experiences is my way of letting them speak.

In Chapter 4 I examine the local politics of resistance of KAMMI. I use "politics" broadly here, to include the forms of resistance peasant women engage in in order to change the structures, ideas, and ideologies that affect their everyday lives; the issues they raise and how they articulate their views, perspectives, and analysis; how they come together to define and solve their problems; their strategies for collective action and their claim to have a common voice; and their everyday conversations about the social situation surrounding them. I examine the ways in which "politics" responds or relates to the larger structures in which the peasant women's everyday lives are enmeshed (analyzed in Chapter 3). My purpose in this chapter is not to evaluate KAMMI's organization, agenda, or actions based on some external criteria or political theory evolved from Western or First World experience, but rather to see them from the perspective of the women members.

Since the peasant movement led by AMIHAN has developed a larger structure to coordinate various local efforts, in Chapter 5 I look at the national politics of this organization, with emphasis on the development issues that AMIHAN raises nationally, how the organization articulates these issues publicly, and its alternative agenda for development. I focus on AMIHAN's National Council, since it is composed of representatives from its provincial and regional chapters.

I conclude this book by examining the implications of the exploitation and resistance experienced by peasant women on reconceptualizing and reorienting development analysis and perspectives on Third World women.

One argument in the ongoing debate on methodology in feminist research calls for researchers to report their own experiences in the field as well as how their research affected them personally (Reinharz 1992). This methodology is intended to bridge the gap between the researcher and the subject of study, whom some would prefer to call a "research collaborator." Thus, in Appendix A I discuss methodological issues and difficulties I encountered during my fieldwork and how I dealt with them by evolving *organic feminist inquiry*. I do this not only to contribute to the continuing debate on feminist research methods, but also because the difficulties I experienced in doing fieldwork in a militarized area constitute legitimate data.

Repression is a part of the politics of underdevelopment and exploitation in the Philippines, as it is in other Third World countries. Where militarization is most intense, repression has limited scholars' access to

(Bauzon 1991, 1992), and human rights advocates' documentation of, women in rural areas. Some human rights researchers I met during my fieldwork said there were times when they could not enter villages to conduct their work because of military operations. Research on women in militarized zones thus becomes a political act, since it makes the situation of the oppressed known. Research becomes part of the process of change when it increases awareness of the power structures and exploitation that repression seeks to maintain. When I told one of the members of KAMMI that I was interested in knowing about peasant women's problems and what they were doing to solve them, she was pleased and said, "Now we will be known" ("Makikilala na tayo"). I took her comment as a form of resistance to women's invisibility and to the lack of public awareness of their situation. This book is my way of making their situation "known."

Chapter One
Perspectives on Third World Women and the Politics of Underdevelopment

[A] narrow definition of development confounds rather than elucidates women's role in society. Development cannot be defined in purely economic terms; it has also political, social, and ideological ramifications. Moreover, development interpreted broadly should include an expansion of choices, that make life with dignity possible, and greater participation for all peoples—independently of gender, ethnicity, or race—in the decision-making processes that affect them.
—Maria Patricia Fernandez Kelly (1986)

The Integrationist View of Women in Third World Development

In the early 1970s the idea of "integrating women into development" became part of the debate in mainstream studies of development (Rood-kowsky 1984). Pioneered by Ester Boserup in her book *The Woman's Role in Economic Development* (1970), this Western concept was promoted by multilateral development and aid agencies.

The "integrationist view" (Anand 1984) held that women in the Third World would overcome poverty and inequality if they were made part of the market wage economy. Such integration would ensure income for women and make possible their participation in the development process. Based on the modernization model of development, which contends that developing nations can eliminate poverty if they are integrated into the international market economy, the notion of "integrating women into development" looks upon women as an untapped resource, the use of which could help a country to achieve economic "growth." "Growth" was to be measured in terms of increased exports and GNP, which was expected to trickle down to the poor (Youssef 1976; Anand 1984). This model assumed that Third World countries were poor because their populations were growing faster than "growth" could trickle down, or because resources were inadequate and technology was not sufficiently modern.

The integrationist concept of development failed not only to recognize the actual productivity of Third World women but to question the nature of development into which women were to be integrated (Karl 1984a,e). The view assumed that Third World women could improve their lot mainly through education and employment within the capitalist economy (Anand 1984).

"Integrationists" believed that Third World women were passive and acquiescent regarding the course development was taking in their countries (Roodkowsky 1984, 16). Women, they thought, were unconcerned with the pressures and goals of development. Uncritically viewing development as economic growth within a capitalist framework, integrationists equated women's liberation with the accumulation of cash through wage labor and with mobility within a hierarchical occupational structure (Roodkowsky 1984). They did not consider how this development model produced poverty in the Third World, as documented by Andre Gunder Frank (1974, 1981) and Lenny Siegel (1979), or how the politics of development and underdevelopment affected the lives of Third World women.

A Critique of the Integrationist Approach

Lourdes Beneria and Gita Sen (1986) criticize the integrationist perspective on women in development. Focusing on Boserup's book, which is framed within the classical modernization paradigm, they challenge her belief that modernization is an inevitable economic process into which women must be integrated.

Beneria and Sen emphasize that "modernization [is] not a neutral process, but one that obey[s] the dictates of capitalist accumulation and profit-making" (Beneria and Sen 1986, 150). In their view, modernization generates and intensifies inequalities, taking advantage of existing gender hierarchies to place women in subordinate positions. Capitalist accumulation has a powerful tendency to separate the direct producers from the means of production and to make the conditions necessary for their survival more insecure and contingent. In rural areas, this may be manifested in new forms of class stratification between rich, capitalist landowners and poor, landless peasants. A focus on gender in development shows how the sexual division of labor serves this powerful tendency as well as how capital accumulation may define a new division of labor in which women are assigned a particular place (Beneria and Sen 1986, 149).

Beneria and Sen suggest that an analysis of women's subordination must consider their roles as both producers and reproducers, and show how households are exploited in the process of capitalist accumulation and expansion (Beneria and Sen 1986, 152–54). They argue that such analysis must take into account the interaction between women's productive and reproductive roles, not dichotomize these two spheres of women's lives. For example, under capitalist relations, household work, mainly relegated to women, is unpaid or unsubsidized, although such work not only maintains and reproduces the labor force but also upholds the values needed to keep the system intact. Capital accumulation rests not only on the exploitation of women's productive work, but also on the household and women's place in it.

In my view, what Beneria and Sen's analysis lacks is a consideration of how the state in Third World nations propels and sustains capitalist accumulation. A pattern becoming more and more visible in Third World development is the synchronization of military policies with the increased entry of international capital, both of which can have an impact on women's roles as producers and reproducers. The effects of this process on women must be examined in the politics of underdevelopment in the Third World.

A similar critique of the integrationist perspective on women in Third World development comes from Noeleen Heyzer (1986, viii). She begins her book on women in development with the following statement:

What is problematic is not the lack of integration of women into the development process, but the nature of women's integration, the concept of development itself, and the strategies put forth at different levels to bring about capital accumulation. All these have a specific impact on the position of women and on the relationship between men, women, and children.

Heyzer argues that the various forms and bases of women's subordination are linked to the larger structures that generate the inequalities and class positions which develop from the interaction of economic and sociocultural systems. We must therefore locate different groups of women within the concrete context of their daily lives. Heyzer's approach is more empirical than Beneria and Sen's. She documents how the integration of Southeast Asian economies into the peripheries of the world capitalist system has negatively affected poor women. For example, as agricultural production in these economies began to focus on export, production shifted from staple foods to cash crops, and women's poverty increased. The mechanization of cash crop production also displaced many peasant women from farm work. In such export-oriented plantation sectors as Malaysia, for example, the reproductive role of poor women is exploited as their children are used as unpaid or cheap labor.

While Heyzer provides a good overview of general patterns of capitalist development and their negative impact on Southeast Asian women, she sacrifices in-depth treatment of the particularities of the politics of underdevelopment in each of the four countries she studied: Malaysia, the Philippines, Indonesia, and Thailand. Despite this limitation, she recognizes the one neglected area of study on Southeast Asian women—their strategies and organizations for change (Heyzer 1986, 8). Thus, Heyzer ends her documentation with a chapter on nongovernmental organizations (NGOs) and grassroots women's movements in Southeast Asia. The emergence of these women's organizations indicates that Southeast Asian women are entering into the politics of development that affects them. These organizations share the underlying principle that significant long-term change in their individual and community situations can come only through changes in the larger political economy. For example, they work to alter structures discriminatory of women and serve as pressure groups for change in national policies that affect them. Poor women are taught to identify and discuss their problems, to understand how their problems are linked to the broader social systems, and to turn their new understanding into political action. This process of politicization seeks to develop not only women's awareness of the causes of their problems, but also their capabilities in dealing with these problems, and their understanding of how they can make society value their work. Heyzer considers political consciousness-raising important, since the social structures that people internalize may not change rapidly, even if the actual social conditions that helped produce them have changed (Heyzer 1986, 133). Politicization is an important process in these organizations, but also a difficult one, given the repressive response of governments hostile to such critical consciousness.

I agree with Heyzer's conclusions that the process of emancipation of Southeast Asian women from the forces that subordinate them requires organization and new social structures. Their organization must go beyond helping women simply to adapt survival strategies to an existing system; they must direct them toward social transformation. Heyzer nevertheless lacks an in-depth empirical investigation into the politics of the organizations she mentions, the historical context of their subordination and emancipation, and the political context of their social formation.

The Emerging Literature Within the Marxist-Feminist and Marxist-Feminist-Dependency Framework

Emerging literature on women in Third World development—in reaction to the integrationist perspective—contains Marxist-feminist or

Marxist-feminist-dependency underpinnings. Although in need of refinement, such theoretical frameworks can be useful in explaining gender and the politics of underdevelopment in the Third World. This current literature has more radical implications for policy and organization than one can draw from the integrationist perspective.

According to Leonora Angeles (1986), the Marxist-feminist perspective evolved out of the realization that Marxism as an analytical tool has the potential to help us understand how historical transformation affects the lives of men and women. Classical Marxism has no feminist perspective, however, because it analyzed women in relation to the economic system, but not the gendered power relations between men and women. Marxist-feminist analysis examines gender relations in ways that are distinct from but at the same time connected to capitalist relations. It locates the place of women in the power hierarchy, before and after the capitalist transformation of the mode of production. A socialist revolution does not automatically abolish gendered relations. Elizabeth Croll (1986, 252), for example, found in her study of socialist development in the Soviet Union, China, Cuba, and Tanzania that women "repeatedly assert that socialist development programs will not of their own accord bring about changes in gender relations, and it seems apparent that in the absence of a well-defined policy, female labor has intensified, which to a certain extent has subsidized economic development." Croll's analysis reveals that while economic plans in these societies encouraged women to contribute to economic development through involvement in productive work, these strategies paid little attention to decreasing women's household responsibilities and to reducing the sexual division of household labor. Policymakers believed such goals would prove costly.

Some Marxist-feminists integrate the dependency perspective into their analysis of Third World women's lives by taking into account how the peripheral position of Third World countries affects the position of women. In other words, they believe that women's place in the political economies of Third World countries is a consequence of their countries' dependent position in the world capitalist system. For example, the modernization of agriculture has not really benefited the majority of poor women and men (Anand 1984; Karl 1984b,c,d). The close link between developing countries and the capitalist world market has harmed women: food production for subsistence has been displaced by food production for export, and the self-sufficiency of subsistence farming has been undermined by foreign aid, resulting in rising Third World hunger.

Anita Anand (1984) points out the need for a new theory of development incorporating feminism, which will enable the poor and the powerless to develop strategies addressing the roots of underdevelopment and the institutionalized exploitation of women. Women must not integrate themselves into exploitative capitalist systems, but must instead organize and mobilize all women—locally, nationally, and internationally—as a first step toward radically changing power relations. Patriarchial structures and attitudes must be systematically deconstructed at the same time that national structures are being transformed. It is organized women who will play a significant role in achieving these ends.

Women have not been liberated by their integration into wage work within the context of the international division of labor and capital accumulation associated with the growth of transnational corporations (Karl 1984a; Enloe 1980, 1983b; Fuentes and Ehrenreich 1984; Safa 1986; Grossman 1979; Nash 1983; Perpiñan 1986). Employment of women in multinational corporations has not brought them significant economic benefits, even though it enables them to enter into the wage economy. And while it is true that these women are at least not jobless, they are nevertheless exploited as a source of cheap and easily controlled labor.

These corporations also stifle women's potential to obtain collective power by restricting their opportunities to organize. Patriarchy alone, without military reinforcement, is inadequate to sustain the control mechanisms necessary to reassure foreign investors that there exists a profitable climate for investment (Ong 1979; Enloe 1983b, 1985; Lim 1983). The state thus protects the interests of transnational corporations through military repression and legislation of policies that control labor organizations.

Some scholars have examined Third World women as reproducers and producers. Felicity Edholm, Olivia Harris, and Kate Young (1981) distinguish biological reproduction from social reproduction, which includes the daily and the generational reproduction of the labor force. While biological reproduction refers to the physical development of human beings, that of the labor force refers to the reproduction of the processes whereby people become and continue to be workers. The rationale behind this analytical distinction is that if the nonbiological processes that subordinate women can be identified then gender inequality and women's oppression is not inevitable but can be changed.

Beneria (1979) proposes the thesis that women's subordination is rooted in their special roles in the reproduction of the labor force. Most societies, she says, have assigned to women two aspects of the reproduction of the labor force: child care and the domestic activities associated with the daily maintenance of the labor force. Beneria stresses that it is important to analyze women's role in reproduction in order to understand the nature and extent of not only their participation in production but also the sexual division of labor. In most rural economies, domestic work and nondomestic work are highly integrated. Participation of women in agricultural marketing work is often considered an extension of their domestic work.

In my view, consideration of the reproductive role of women is an important theoretical step in studying women in Third World development. It helps us see how their private spaces can become locations of resistance. As well, it allows us to examine the link between household work and nonhousehold work in the proletarianization of the peasantry, and how women's household work and its concomitant ideological construction are exploited in maintaining the articulation of different modes of production and production for the world market. This is well illustrated by Maria Meis (1982), who found that the whole industry of lace making in Narsipur is sustained by the productive work of women lace makers within the confines of their homes. This confinement allows trading of their product to be controlled by men. There has thus emerged a new class of male traders who have enriched themselves through export of the lace produced by women. But the women remain poor while the industry prospers.

Other studies show how Third World women combine productive and reproductive roles through their involvement in the informal sector (Mason 1985; Bolles 1986). The unemployed are not supported by state welfare institutions, necessitating the development of an informal sector that fills consumers' need for low-cost goods and services, and thereby lowers the cost of reproducing the labor force (Babb 1986). Thus, women's work in the informal sector, which is often regarded as part of their domestic work, actually links women to the public sector of the economy (Bolles 1986, 74).

Most Marxist-feminists do not explicitly take into account how the different modes of production characterizing Third World political economies affect class and gender relations. As Patricia Stamp (1986) argues, in the European experience, the emergence of capitalism transformed pre-capitalist type of production (feudalism) and brought about the formation of a capitalist class structure composed of the proletariat and the bourgeoisie. In the experience of colonized societies (as most Third World nations are), however, the capitalist penetration of their political economies did not completely transform earlier forms of production. Pre-capitalist elements persist as they merge, in a distorted form, with capitalism. In this situation, the primary contradiction, Stamp says, is between capital and the peasantry. The exploitation of landless peasants, in which surplus is expropriated from them, subsidizes underdeveloped capital. Third World economic relations can be adequately understood only with some conception of how the social relations of gender are involved in this articulation of different modes of production.

Stamp's case study of the Kikuyu ethnic group in Africa shows that patriarchy is not a universal concept. The precolonial Kikuyu community had a communal mode of production that was basically classless in the sense that no group was free to appropriate or accumulate surplus produced by another group. Kikuyu women elders had a collective authority in various decisions, including disposition of lineage resources. Colonialism, with its imported sex-gender system, distorted this precolonial system, however. Men gained the power to appropriate the surplus from the women's petty commodity production. Under the colonial policy of land consolidation, which began in the 1950s and continued into the early 1960s, women lost their ownership of the means of production: land and its produce. The colonial government legally changed a lineage system of land ownership, which gave women the right to own land, to ownership by individual male heads of household. Men also then gained control over the produce of the land, relegating women to subsistence production. Although women continue to have control over subsistence production, their nonwage labor actually subsidizes the reproduction of labor power and capitalist cash crop production. It is this form of subsidy to capital that partly feeds the dynamics of capital accumulation. This analysis shows why gender is an important concept in analyzing the articulation of different modes of production in Third World political economies.

Cheryl Johnson (1986) also emphasizes that gender analysis in the context of Third World women's experience must be integrated with historical analysis of the legacy of colonial relationships. In her examination of the colonial experience of Yoruba women of southwestern Nigeria, Johnson discovered that colonial patriarchy not only exacerbated inequality between men and women, but also generated class divisions among women. Colonialism thus developed both male and female elite classes, while the majority of women and men were impoverished.

Development as Empowerment

While the Marxist-feminist-dependency framework conceptualizes women in Third World development from an economic perspective, another emerging body of literature asserts that women acquire power through development. Audrey Bronstein (1982) views development for women in terms of political empowerment. Such development, she says, must be defined in terms of women's

increasing ability to assume influence and control over all aspects of her environment—physical, economic, social, and political. . . . Peasant women are not in charge of their own lives. Unless they are empowered to examine and challenge where authority and power lie at home, in the village, and in their countries, there will be little real growth and change. Development must involve a reallo-cation of power. (ibid., 268)

For Bronstein, "conscientization" is the first and essential step toward the acquisition of power. Conscientization involves the process whereby women identify the human-made forces and mechanisms of their op-pression and discover within themselves the ability to learn and the power to effect change (ibid., 266–67). It is a process of politicization that is central to the liberation of Third World women, whose triple oppression (at work, in the family, and in the community) is contextu-alized in the history of the exploitation that has created continuing oppressive economic and political structures (ibid., 22). It is thus in Bronstein that we see a different conceptualization of not only Third World working-class women, but particularly peasant women. While the integrationist and Marxist-feminist-dependency perspectives basically de-pict Third World women as victims of the nature of Third World devel-opment, in Bronstein, these women are not just being acted upon by historical forces of underdevelopment. They are, in fact, working out their empowerment amidst the risks of repression, and they possess an emerging consciousness that I think must be considered in refining our concepts of gender and politics of underdevelopment. The lives of the peasant women of Bolivia, Peru, El Salvador, and Guatemala that Bron-stein studied are enmeshed in national and international structures of dependency and underdevelopment, but they are also resistant to these forces. This is also the experience of the Filipino peasant women upon whom I focus in this book.

Chapter Two
Philippine Colonization:
The Experience of Filipino Women

Many feminists now question what we claim to be our history. Our historiography which is dominated by men narrates history of men. Women are rarely mentioned.

—Maria Luisa Camagay (n.d.)

[A]ny solution to the problem of women's general lack of political and economic power . . . is not just a question of women vis-à-vis men in their respective societies, but also a question of the position of the societies in which women find themselves vis-à-vis their former colonizers.

—Cheryl Johnson-Odin (1986)

The Precolonial Philippine Political Economy and the *Status* of Filipino Women

The Economy

Before its colonial conquest, the Philippines had predominantly a subsistence economy (Salgado 1985, 3–4). Filipinos produced for their own needs from local resources. Living in subsistence villages, peasants, who also were part-time craftsmen, were relatively self-sufficient (Constantino 1975, 32).

Natural resources—food, forests, and minerals such as gold—are abundant in the Philippines. The precolonial Filipinos demonstrated technical ingenuity in extracting and producing finished products from these local resources to meet their needs. They grew cotton, from which they made clothing. They were excellent shipwrights. Their native vessels, *caracoas*, in fact surpassed the Spanish galleons in speed (Salgado 1985, 5).

In this precolonial economy, property was for the most part held communally. For instance, among the *barangays* (barrios or villages, a basic social unit), land and other means of production were rarely owned privately (Constantino 1975, 39). Men and women participated equally in the community ownership of land.

To acquire land, early Filipino communities generally used *kaingin*, a method by which the forest is cleared using slash-and-burn. Although now prohibited by the government, this practice is sometimes still found. For example, Ate Wona, a member of one of the village chapters of KAMMI, farms a small plot of lowland she said she acquired through *kaingin*.

In terms of inheritance rights, women also had equal access to parents' property and equal rights to use land, since lineage was traced bilaterally through male and female lines (Wurfel 1988, 3).

Despite this relative equality of women and men in the early communalism and kinship relations, however, there was already a sexual division of labor that put a greater burden on women. Women were just as integrated into production as men were, but in addition they were the primary bearers of reproductive tasks. In agriculture, it was in general the men who prepared the land while the women did the planting and harvesting (Mangahas 1987, 11). But in some cases when the men had to defend the community from enemy attack, women took on the larger tasks of agricultural production as well (Eviota 1985, 30–31).

Political Life

The political life of precolonial Filipinos was not rigidly stratified. The village was administered by a chief, who achieved his position by rendering service valuable to the survival of the community. He did not have absolute powers and could be deposed by the members of the barangay. Although he assumed more political responsibilities than others, in most cases he continued his work as a farmer or craftsman or both (Constantino 1975, 33). The chiefs therefore did not really constitute a separate politically elite class, such as we find in the Philippines today. There was "consultative decision-making among barangay elders," making the administrative system relatively democratic (Wurfel 1988, 3).

In this system of governing, however, women did not have the same access to positions of power as men. Although female members of the chief's family shared his privileges, a woman could inherit his position only if there were no male heirs (Colin 1903).[1]

Some women, because of special skills and knowledge, gained public influence and power as priestesses. These were the *babaylanes* or *catalonas*, whose knowledge of herbal medicines gave them power over the reproduction and health of the community. They not only cured the sick and presided over such rituals as weddings, births, and funerals, but also served as advisers to the chiefs by "foretelling the outcome of political events" (Mangahas 1987, 13).

Women and Peonage

The early Filipino communities had a practice of lending and borrowing called the peon system, in which a debtor had to render unpaid labor service when he or she was unable to repay what was owed. One therefore usually became a peon when one was unable to pay a private debt or legal fine. One could cease being a peon by paying one's debt. This debt-servitude practice made women a commodity for exchange. In a few cases, women (and children) were sold or given in reparation for damages (Chirino 1903).

Rice was the most commonly borrowed commodity, with payment and interest taking the same form. Interest was high because rice was considered an important commodity. If the rice grains were used as seedlings, it was expected that the return would double the investment. Lending rice was, after all, risky because of the possibility of loss due to natural calamities. In many cases, the surplus produced by the peons belonged to the community and was distributed in lean months (Constantino 1975, 33–34).

Today the practice of rendering labor service in payment for private debt can still be found. In Mindoro, Ate Lalay, a member of KAMMI, worked for a few days on the land of a male member of the community as payment for money she had borrowed from him. During my short stay in Albay, a province in the Bicol region, I met a thirteen-year-old village girl who was rendering domestic service for a few weeks in her relative's urban house as payment for her parents' debt. I learned later that the relative had then given the girl some money for her schooling; she had not felt right accepting her young relative's unpaid service because of their kinship relation.

Filipino Women and the Colonial Transformation of Philippine Political Economy

Spanish Colonization, 1521–1896

The 375 years of Spanish colonial domination, in which the Church and Spanish government colluded, dramatically transformed the Philippine political economy. Spanish colonialism brought about the breakdown of communalism, exacerbated gender inequality, disintegrated the subsistence economy, and took away from Filipinos control of their own labor and resources. Communal lands were eventually transformed into private property (Constantino 1975, 40). This was the beginning of a landlord system of land ownership, which resulted in the formation of a class of landless peasants.

The Filipinos virtually lost control over their land and its produce when the king of Spain decreed the introduction of *encomiendas*—large tracts of land (along with the Filipino inhabitants) that were awarded to Spanish friars and imperial soldiers. The Filipino people now no longer produced for their own consumption but for their colonial masters, since they had to pay tribute to the *encomienderos* in the form of crops and other agricultural products. Spanish colonial policy exempted the chiefs and their descendants from paying tribute, however. In fact, in most cases they were the ones who collected the tribute from their communities and turned it over to the encomienderos, who generally did not live inside the encomienda.

Registration and titling of lands were introduced to deal with conflicts. Titles were placed in the name of the male head of household, depriving women of direct ownership of and control over decisions concerning land (Mangahas 1987, 13).

Land titling—used to legalize private land ownership, especially among the colonizers—led to the landlessness of many Filipino peasants and paved the way to the legalized seizure of ancestral lands.[2] For example, the Maura Law of 1894 gave landholders one year to acquire titles to their land; that which remained untitled after the deadline was forfeited. Approximately 400,000 peasants lost their holdings through ignorance of this law; to their surprise they became tenants of big landowners. Many other peasants lost their land through the Pacto de Retroventa, a law requiring them to put up their land as collateral for loans (Philippine Peasant Institute 1989, 4).

Thus, colonial private ownership created a small landed social class who did not directly till the land. Those who did till the land—which they did not own—formed a class of agricultural workers who lost control of not only the use of the land but also their labor and produce. The Catholic Church became one of the largest landowners, with some friar estates so huge that they included entire towns or more (Salgado 1985, 12). Other landed classes that developed from the privatization of land ownership were the Spanish officials; the *principalia*, descendants of the precolonial village chiefs (*datus*) who collaborated with the colonial rulers; and the Chinese mestizos (of mixed Chinese and European ancestry), who acquired huge holdings that even the Spaniards envied (Salgado 1985; Constantino 1975).

As a system of administration, the encomienda developed a class structure that served colonial interests. By their use of forced labor, the encomienderos reduced the Filipinos, with the exception of village chiefs and their eldest sons, to the status of virtual slaves. A majority of Filipinos lost control of their labor: it was unpaid, involuntary, and appropriated by foreign masters. Such labor, required of male Filipinos between the ages of sixteen and sixty (Constantino 1975, 51), often separated men from their families and communities for a long time, leaving women, children, and old men to take on most of the household and farm work (Eviota 1985, 37). In this way colonialism exploited the productive and reproductive roles of Filipino women. Although women were not themselves subject to forced labor, they were in fact very much integrated into this colonial appropriation of labor power.

Forced labor was most severe when Spain went to war against the Dutch. Spain needed warships and thus required the Filipinos' skill as shipwrights. Shipbuilding took long months, and some laborers had to abandon their fields (Salgado 1985). Thus, colonialism not only took production away from subsistence farming, but it also exploited Filipino labor to support imperialist wars—wars which in turn maintained the foreign power that subjugated those same Filipinos. Women, especially lower-class women, were expected to maintain this war through their productive and reproductive work.

Spanish colonialism not only took control of labor power away from Filipinos, but it also took control of the fruits of their labor. The colonial government imposed a system of expropriating resources called the *bandala* (Constantino 1975, 40, 50). The bandala compelled each province to sell an annual production quota to the government at a low price. The people were paid not in cash but in promissory notes, which the government then failed to pay. This caused great suffering and poverty among the majority of Filipinos, who were forced to buy or borrow rice and other crops to give to the colonial government when there was no surplus production (de la Costa 1965; Constantino 1975). When, in the absence of male labor, the women assumed most of the productive work in the fields, this system of expropriation diverted women's productive and reproductive work from meeting subsistence needs to maintaining instead the state officials and functionaries who perpetuated the colonial oppression of the Filipino people. The economic and household work of poor women thereby gained political significance.

In establishing their colonial rule, the Spaniards coopted native Filipino chiefs and their descendants into the colonial state bureaucracy by extending to them special privileges, such as access to land and other resources, and exemptions from colonial exactions. No longer administrators of precolonial communal lands, this native ruling class—which became known as the principalia—then imposed colonial policies on the communities they governed. This formation of an intermediary class led to divisions among women. For instance, women members of the principalia were usually exempt from working in the fields, while the majority of Filipino women were doing both farm and household work (Eviota 1985, 37). Eventually, this small class of women began to emulate the Spanish women of the colonial ruling class. They began to associate prestige with not doing manual work, and like the Spanish women, they had servants (Eviota 1985). Class formation thus allowed some women to enjoy comfort and wealth produced by the sweat of other Filipino women, who were doing both productive and reproductive work. Gender and class formation hence became a colonial strategy to divide and rule.

Another major change in the Philippine political economy was the development of export agriculture. Export agriculture not only dismantled subsistence agriculture, but it linked Philippine agricultural development to the capitalist world market. As agricultural production was geared to the demands of the foreign market, production for local needs was neglected. Colonialism and capitalism hence intersected in the politics of underdevelopment in the Philippines.

Export agriculture led to the growth of haciendas, large estates primarily producing cash crops—primarily sugar, tobacco, coffee, copra, and abaca. The profitability of export crops led friars, Spanish officials and their families, the principalia, and wealthy Chinese traders to accumulate huge haciendas (IBON Data Bank 1988, 27; Salgado 1985). Many haciendas were enlarged through deforestation, seizure of untitled ancestral lands from certain tribes, and foreclosures of mortgaged lands of small farmers (Salgado 1985).

Export agriculture widened the gap between the few rich and the poor majority. It further enriched the landed class, who now became landlord-capitalists separated from farm work. It developed a small middle class, composed mostly of Chinese traders, who controlled the internal marketing of provincial hacienda products in major urban centers like Manila. It profited the Spanish colonial officials, who placed into government monopoly control of some export crops, such as tobacco. And it benefited the British and American firms that were already in the country as early as 1822 and controlled the export-import business. Even more, it benefited large capitalist firms based in England and the U.S. who were connected to subsidiary companies in the Philippines. British and American capitalists, for example, profited from the supply of cheap Philippine sugar for the processing of such foods as candies, chocolates, and soft drinks (Salgado 1985).

While export agriculture enriched these classes, it impoverished the peasants, who lost their lands; exploited landless agricultural workers, who were paid very low wages; and hurt consumers of the staple food, rice. Rice sometimes had to be imported, for shortages occurred as cash crop production accelerated (Lachica 1963). Peasants suffered because they were no longer producing crops they could eat. In this way the export crop economy became a source of wealth for the landed class, who controlled the use and products of the land, but of poverty among the landless peasants, who labored on the land.

The gearing of agriculture to cash crops brought changes in rice production. Some haciendas, producing such export crops as sugar, introduced agricultural wage work. This practice was eventually incorporated into rice production as more and more peasants became landless. The growth of haciendas also led to the institutionalization of sharecropping (IBON Data Bank 1988, 27). This entailed the leasing of land owned by an absentee landlord-friar to an *inquilino* (lessee), who was charged a fixed rent in the form of a share of the harvest. The inquilinos did not cultivate the land themselves, but instead took a share of the harvests produced by the landless farmers to whom they apportioned the land for cultivation. Most of the inquilinos were Chinese mestizos or members of the principalia.

As sharecropping and wage work became incorporated into rice production, there developed a class of people who accumulated harvests without being tillers of the land. The growing of rice, now removed from subsistence production and consumption, became commercialized as this class gained control of the marketing of the product as well as the milling of *palay* (unmilled rice). For example, Chinese traders, who had a monopoly on the milling process, were able to take control of the retail and wholesale distribution of rice as well (Eviota 1985, 60). The pricing of rice thus intermingled with the dynamics of making profits. The peasant producers had no control over the price of what they produced, and had to buy this staple food from the nonproducers. It is obvious who benefited most from the commercialization and capitalist penetration of rice production.

Export agriculture exacerbated gender and class stratification: women and men from the class of *hacenderos* acquired more wealth and greater access to higher education (Salgado 1985), while the women workers who produced the wealth for the haciendas were doubly exploited as they did both productive and reproductive work. As the hacendero families were able to send their children abroad to study, there emerged a small foreign-educated male elite—the *ilustrados*. These people took economic and political leadership positions in the state bureaucracy, thus partly ensuring the reproduction of development policies that preserved the interests of their class.

In the final analysis, it is clear that colonialism and capitalism together transformed the communal, subsistence political economy of the precolonial Philippines. This process exacerbated gender and class inequality and caused greater poverty among the majority of Filipinos. Poor women, who continued to do both productive and reproductive work, took the brunt of this underdevelopment and exploitation.

American Colonization, 1896–1946

American colonization of the Philippines, although justified with the rhetoric of liberating the Filipinos from Spanish colonial rule and preparing them for self-government, was largely motivated by U.S. economic interests in the Pacific.[3] The success of American colonization in the Philippines required the kind of class structure that Spanish colonial politics had already evolved there. American colonial policy thus reproduced this class structure. It coopted the ilustrados into its ruling apparatus, protecting their haciendas and even giving them opportunities to accumulate more land (Salgado 1985, 25). Since the ilustrados did not cultivate their lands themselves, this policy further increased tenancy and landlessness among the poor peasantry.

It was in the economic interests of the United States to keep intact the structure of land ownership in the Philippines, for private ownership allowed American corporations to acquire land. Sugar production, for example, became concentrated in the hands of corporations, forcing many peasants to work at starvation wages (Pelzer n.d.). Because American corporations owned large tracts of land, they were able to promote export crops that were needed in the U.S. market (such as sugar, coconuts, abaca, timber, rubber, and pineapple), and to ignore crops that would compete with American products (such as tobacco). Indeed, the Philippines, which had in the past exported tobacco, now had to import U.S. tobacco products (Salgado 1985).

Thus, U.S. colonial economic policy promoted the extraction of raw materials for U.S. industries and the control of the Philippine market for U.S. manufactured goods. This capitalist imperialism became imperative for the United States, whose economy needed global sources and markets for its expanding industries. To meet this need, American colonialists established free trade relations between the Philippines and the United States. American factories were then assured of cheap raw materials and a captured market for the processed goods that its local U.S. market could not absorb. Philippine imports from the United States increased from 9 percent in 1899 to 64 percent in 1933, and its exports to the United States escalated from 18 percent to 83 percent in the same period (Hartendorp 1958).

While U.S. colonialism led to greater capitalist penetration of the Philippine political economy, it did not entirely transform the feudal agricultural economy that began during Spanish colonization. Concentration of land among a few landowners continued and in fact increased. Hence, today in the Philippines there coexist different modes of production: feudal, semi-feudal, and capitalist. Feudal elements exist where landless peasants work as tenants and receive a share of the crop they produce on terms dictated by the landlords. Tenants shoulder all production costs, and the share they receive is often inadequate to meet their subsistence needs. Semi-feudal elements exist where landless peasants work as waged agricultural laborers for large, sometimes absentee, landlords. Such elements can also be found where private corporations hire administrators to manage the labor and production on corporate lands so that the corporation itself does not deal directly with the agricultural workers. Most often workers are hired on a seasonal basis. Capitalist elements exist in both industrial and agricultural production where workers earn a wage from the corporate plantation of a local or foreign-owned company, usually an agribusiness corporation. Only a few of the landless agricultural workers, of whom the bulk of the peasantry is composed, have been employed by such corporate farms on a relatively permanent basis.

With the penetration of colonial capitalism into Philippine development, rural women's and men's work became increasingly linked to the exploitative dynamics of the capitalist world system. The entry of more American manufactured goods undermined rural industries controlled by Filipinos. Consequently, labor was displaced, and unemployment and poverty increased. This was the case, for instance, in the native weaving industry, which was the source of income for a good number of women, since they largely dominated the industry. As U.S. textiles flooded the Philippine market, rural women lost their means of income and were pushed into agricultural wage work or tenancy. There was in fact an increase in the number of agricultural female workers, from 90,191 in 1903 to 474,819 in 1939 (U.S. Bureau of Census 1905; Commission of the Census 1941). Male agricultural labor also increased in the same period, from 39 percent in 1903 to 69 percent in 1939 (ibid.).

American capitalists and other landlords could now profit from this increased supply of, and therefore cheap, agricultural labor. Real wages of both men and women during the American colonial period were in fact lower than they had been during the Spanish colonial period (Eviota 1985, 95); women's wages were of course even lower than those of men. An illustrative case is in the export sugar haciendas: male workers received wages only from PO.50 to PO.75 per day, while women and children received only PO.35 to PO.50 per day. In rice production, male workers were paid PO.80 per day, while women workers were paid PO.60 per day (Eviota 1985; PO = centavos). These wage levels were less than half the per capita income considered adequate for minimum subsistence at that time (Kurihara 1945).

It was not in the interests of American capitalist expansionism and accumulation to promote an industrialized Philippine political economy. There was minimal investment in manufacturing, and that was in such extractive industries as canning and mining, which were geared for export. Hence, excess farm labor, displaced from land and undermined native industries, could not be absorbed into the manufacturing economy. American colonial capitalism therefore increased unemployment and exacerbated poverty. Under these conditions, Filipino workers became mobile, and were exploited in the United States as cheap migrant labor. It was mostly Filipino men who worked under harsh conditions in the plantations of Hawaii and California (Takaki 1993). The women who were left behind had to bear more responsibilities. American capitalist growth thus not only extracted raw materials from its colonies, but also imported labor, splitting the labor market to maximize profit. In this way, Filipino peasants became one of the exploited classes that propelled capitalist growth in the United States.

American colonialists promoted public education in the Philippines, but used it as an ideological tool. Education gave American cultural imperialism an institutional medium through which American ideas and a colonial mentality could be propagated among Filipinos (Schirmer and Shalom 1987, 44). This strategy was intended to combat the growing nationalism that had sparked armed revolution against Spanish colonization. The American colonialists were aware that they were subjugating a people who just experienced liberation from a colonial power. An educational system that could "teach Filipinos to accept an image of the United States as a generous benefactor and to forget the nationalist heroes and struggles of their past" (ibid., 45) was a subtle and effective means of control. Although the American colonialists incorporated some Filipino ilustrados in their administrative bureaucracy, they prevented Filipino leadership of the department of education (Constantino 1966); the ideological apparatus of colonial conquest, they realized, must be under the control of the colonialists if it was to be a cultural tool of colonization.

The promotion of public higher education also partly exacerbated class and gender divisions. It contributed to the formation of a small elite class of men and women embracing Western-oriented development. Because of their education and privileged status, they obtained positions in the economy and the government. Even a few women, especially those from the landed class or ilustrados, were able to acquire some professional training (Eviota 1992). This new, American-bred class of petty bourgeoisie, who differed from the working class primarily in their level of education and in the fact that they did not do manual work, eventually occupied positions of economic and political leadership after the American colonialists gave the Philippines pseudo-independence in 1946 (Constantino 1975). The U.S. neocolonial control of Philippine political economy was then ideologically ensured.

The majority of poor men and women were unable to acquire higher education. Women who were not absorbed into agricultural work, migrant work, or the small manufacturing sector turned to either domestic service or prostitution (Eviota 1985). Under deteriorating conditions, poor women—and also men—resorted to domestic work. Female domestic workers increased from 95,016 in 1903 to 230,474 in 1948, while their male counterparts increased from 51,044 to 146,296 in the same years (U.S. Bureau of Census 1905, 1954). By 1939, female domestic servants composed 18 percent (next to female farm laborers, who composed 37 percent) of female gainful workers ten years old and over (Commission of the Census 1941). Poor women worked as servants not only in the homes of wealthy families, but even in the households of the petty bourgeoisie. Women in these latter households, having relatively good incomes, could now afford to hire lower-class women to do housework for them. But live-in domestic workers usually received wages incommensurate to the work they rendered. Thus, the increase in both women and men in domestic service indicated the widening gap between the few rich and the poor majority. Through their low-wage, low-prestige work, domestic servants were actually maintaining the elite and middle classes, who benefited from the same political economy that made many Filipinos poor. Today, domestic work is generally the most common option for poor and undereducated women from peasant families.

Prostitution became an option for poor women when American entrepreneurs began to take control of women's sexuality and turn it into a source for profit. By setting up cabarets (dance halls)—which were considered fronts for prostitution and a source of venereal disease (Brown 1917)—these entrepreneurs made women's sexuality a form of organized business. As cabarets became popular among the better-off classes, poor women experienced greater exploitation. Organized control of sexuality thus became entangled with American capitalist control of the Philippine political economy. Today, a similar commoditization of sexuality takes place as prostitution is promoted along with the tourist industry as a way to bring in more dollars to pay the increasing Philippine foreign debt.

U.S. colonial politics involved not only military suppression but also the shaping of a Philippine armed forces that would be oriented to American ideology (Schirmer and Shalom 1987). The formation of a U.S.-trained Filipino militia was actually a strategy of low-intensity conflict, for these U.S.-trained local units were intended to fight guerrilla forces resisting colonial domination. This was then a strategy of counterinsurgency against nationalist revolutionary forces, as well as one of divide and rule, which could be carried out with few casualties among American soldiers. In fact, the U.S. colonialists saw that "the enlistment of Filipinos was essential because it would send U.S. troops home and quiet protest there" (Schirmer and Shalom 1987, 41). With these economic, political, ideological, and military strategies of colonial control and conquest, the United States was well on its way to making the Philippines its neo-colony, a status persisting to this day.

The Neocolonial Philippine Political Economy

American Neocolonial Control

With the granting of Philippine independence in 1946, the United States government ensured that the structure of U.S.–Philippine relations would remain basically unchanged. The United States sought to continue its control of the Philippine economy so as to protect its established interests. But under a neocolonial relationship, the mechanisms of control had to change so as to make U.S. presence in the Philippines appear legitimate.

The first mechanism of control that the United States was able to establish involved its legislation of full parity rights for citizens of the United States and U.S. corporations and businesses. The Bell Trade Act of 1946, later amended in 1955 as the Laurel-Langley Agreement, legitimized and politically institutionalized a continued U.S. control of the Philippine economy by perpetuating the system of free trade, making the Philippines a supplier of cheap raw materials for U.S. industries and a market for U.S. manufactured goods.

The Philippine Constitution had specifically reserved the right to develop and exploit public utilities and natural resources for Filipinos or corporations that were at least 60 percent Filipino owned. With the U.S. demand for full parity rights, particularly in the Laurel-Langley Agreement, U.S. citizens, business corporations, and investors could have 100 percent ownership in all areas of the economy. Other foreign nationals could have no more than 40 percent ownership (Schirmer and Shalom 1987, 87, 95). This helps to explain why U.S. corporations at present control most foreign investments in the Philippines.

When the terms of the Laurel-Langley Agreement expired in 1974 under the Marcos dictatorship, the United States safeguarded its economic interests by promoting an ideology of export-oriented development through foreign investment. The Marcos government adopted an open-door policy for foreign investment, liberalizing restrictions on the activities of transnational corporations. U.S. economic interventionism was channeled mainly through bilateral and multilateral development aid agencies, such as the World Bank and the International Monetary Fund (IMF), which are largely controlled by the U.S. (Payer 1974; Bello, Kinley, and Elinson 1982; Simbulan 1985).

Through a policy of "tied aid" (Payer 1974), the World Bank and IMF were able to protect transnational capital. This policy included the devaluation of the peso, import liberalization, wage freezes, and the repressive control of labor. The IMF and World Bank required such conditions for the granting of loans, which were largely geared toward infrastructural development. Yet such development projects were mainly designed to provide support services for multinational corporations in the Philippines (Brillantes 1986).

Under the Aquino government, IMF and World Bank policies continued to control the nature of Philippine development and underdevelopment. In March 1989, the Aquino government submitted to the IMF the Letter of Intent (LOI) containing the government's promise to implement the conditions of the IMF for the granting of a $1.3 billion loan. Among the conditions were price decontrol, import liberalization, labor control, promotion of export-oriented development, promotion of foreign investment, and a privatization scheme involving the eventual turning over of government-controlled corporations or institutions to private enterprise.

Under the current administration of Fidel Ramos, which began in June 1992, the IMF continues its stranglehold on the Philippine political economy. At the start of 1994 Ramos added a $650 million loan from the U.S. to the Philippine foreign debt.[4] Likewise, the structural adjustment measures under his Philippines 2000 reflect the IMF policies.[5]

Through the influence of the IMF, poverty, landlessness, and exploitation of cheap labor increased. In free trade zones,[6] the development of which was encouraged and funded by the IMF, there is a "feminization of export-oriented labor" (Santos and Lee 1989), for approximately 85 to 90 percent of the workers are women. Multinational corporations have turned skilled, educated Filipino women into a cheap, expendable labor force concentrated in textile, garment, microelectronic semi-assembly work. With subhuman wages, poor housing, exploitative working conditions, and labor repression, these Filipino women produce consumer goods for foreign, and especially U.S., markets. Thus, while in the American colonial period Filipino women were displaced from the native textile industry where they were predominant, now, in the neo-colonial political economy, they are absorbed into the foreign-dominated textile and garment industry as cheap, repressed labor. In export agribusiness, women and children are drawn into farm work without fair remuneration; some, indeed, are unpaid, especially if they work along with a husband or father who receives wages (Eviota 1986).

IMF policies have also brought the Filipino people into a debt bondage. Foreign debt has consistently escalated, from $599.5 million in 1965 to $28.9 billion in 1988 to $34 billion in 1996; it is projected to increase to $40 billion in 1997.[7] More and more resources are siphoned out of the Philippines to service this debt. Payments increased from $3 billion in 1986 to $6.6 billion in 1990 (IBON 1986), and the Central Bank of the Philippines projected an outflow of $13.451 billion from the economy for interest payments in 1988–92.[8] Indeed, 60 percent of Filipino export earnings does not trickle down but instead goes to debt repayment (Santos and Lee 1989, 12). As of 1991, 37 percent of the Philippine national budget was allocated to debt servicing.[9] Under this debt crisis, the Philippines keeps borrowing in order to pay what it has borrowed.

One impact of this debt bondage is directly felt by the poor: an increase in prices, especially of rice. Peasant women I came in contact with during my fieldwork were very worried about the escalating cost of this staple food. The higher price of rice resulted from a requirement in the IMF Letter of Intent (LOI) that limited the National Food Authority's rice subsidy and allowed the privatization of rice trading.[10] Hence, the IMF is the invisible hand propelling the Philippine free market economy—an economy ensuring wealth for a few but increasing poverty for the majority.

The labor of poor women, especially from rural areas, has now become a commodity for export by the Philippine Overseas Employment Agency, as part of the government's drive to increase dollar reserves for its foreign debt payment. Filipino women are increasingly becoming temporary migrant workers; they are generally employed in the foreign labor market as domestic workers, nurses, entertainers, and service workers. Part of their remittances—earned under exploitative and dehumanizing conditions—are used for payment and servicing of foreign debt (Santos and Lee 1989, 40).

U.S. Military Bases and Counterinsurgency

Economic policies alone would have been inadequate to maintain U.S. control of the Philippine political economy and its imperial position in the Pacific. The formation of a Philippine armed forces oriented to American ideology was a way to ensure a continued American military presence during the neocolonial phase of Philippine-American relations. The present Armed Forces of the Philippines is, in fact, a product of American neocolonial politics, and it is here that the interlocking dynamics of capitalism, imperialism, and militarism can be seen in the politics of Philippine underdevelopment. Within this system, Filipino women have suffered as victims of rape, a form of military torture and repression.

Thus, as a condition for the granting of Philippine independence in 1946, the U.S. government demanded and secured the retention of large tracts of land for U.S. military bases (under the Military Bases Agreement of March 14, 1947) and a direct influence on and control of the Armed Forces of the Philippines (under the Military Assistance Agreement of March 21, 1947). The way was thus paved for the retention of five U.S. military bases: San Miguel Naval Communication Complex, USAF Wallace Air Station, Camp John Hay Leave and Recreation Center, and two major installations, Subic Naval Base and Clark Air Base. Subic Naval Base, which stood on 36,000 acres, and Clark Air Base, on over 117,000 acres, dislocated a self-sufficient farming community. When the United States closed these bases in 1992, it left hazardous and lethal materials that continue to endanger the lives of Filipinos in surrounding villages.

The Military Bases Agreement placed no restrictions on the use of these facilities. It prohibited the Philippine government from granting base rights to any other country, and it allowed the United States to recruit Filipino citizens into the U.S. Armed Forces.[11]

Extensions of the U.S. imperial state, the military bases were used to continue their intervention in Philippine internal politics. For example, U.S. military personnel have consistently been involved in suppressing nationalist organizations working for Philippine self-determination and sovereignty and against the nature of Philippine development. Throughout the 1930s, 1940s, and 1950s, American military bases were used to suppress peasant revolts demanding land and fundamental structural changes in the Philippine political economy (Simbulan 1985, 170). For instance, in the 1950s Air Force Colonel Edward Lansdale directed American support in the suppression of the Hukbalahap and was lauded by the U.S. media as "one of the CIA's great unpublished victories."[12] In the 1970s and 1980s the U.S. government propped up the Marcos dictatorship with massive military arms and financial aid, justifying such aid as "rental" for the U.S. bases. George Bush praised Marcos as the most democratic man in Asia. U.S. military personnel were directly involved in actual combat operations against the New People's Army (NPA, the revolutionary forces of the underground movement) in provinces where it was concentrated (Bello and Rivera 1977).

Under the Aquino government, the United States became even more deeply involved in counterinsurgency. In March of 1987, the U.S. government authorized over $10 million to the CIA in the Philippines for increased covert operations.[13] In 1988, U.S. taxpayers funded 83 percent of all procurement, maintenance, and operation costs of the Philippine military. In 1989 the Bush administration proposed $360 million of military and security-related aid to the Philippines for 1990.[14]

This funneling of U.S. resources to the Philippine military indicates the U.S. government's continued support of counterinsurgency there, today known as low intensity conflict (LIC). LIC is essentially a method of suppressing dissent through the use of paramilitary forces "to fight indigenous people struggling for freedom from U.S. control and domination" (Clark et al. 1987, 39). Under the Aquino government, this has taken the form of integrating vigilantes into counterinsurgency forces. According to a fact-finding mission to the Philippines headed by Ramsey Clark in March 1987, U.S. support in this effort is evident in General John Singlaub's advice to right-wing politicians, businessmen, and military officers to "organize vigilante groups to protect themselves from communism" (ibid., 20). Politicized groups now often refer to LIC as "total war." Since its goal is to defeat the New People's Army by paralyzing all forms of support for it—ideological, political, and economic—it directs its violence toward civilian populations in areas where the military suspects there are NPA guerrillas. Village areas are bombed and their residents forcibly evacuated to cut off support for the New People's Army.

Military operations displaced more than 200,000 Filipinos between January 1988 and March 1989. On the island of Negros in the central Philippines alone, 31,000 people have fled their homes since April 22, 1989, taking refuge in schoolhouses, churches, and cockpits. Approximately 100 people, 55 of whom were children, died from inadequate food and sanitation.[15]

The Aquino government's commitment to militarization as a major part of its development program is indicated by several facts: (1) it allocated 25 billion pesos for defense and only 4.5 billion pesos for agrarian reform (KMP 1989, 10); and (2) it also appropriated 585 million pesos for the organization of Citizens Armed Forces Geographical Units (CAFGU). These CAFGU units—essentially vigilante groups—are being trained, armed, and supervised by the Armed Forces of the Philippines. The Aquino government calls them "reservists" or "citizen soldiers." [16] Civilians thus become combatants through this strategy of counterinsurgency: civilians are made to fight civilians. It is also a strategy of divide and rule at a time when there is a growing organized resistance from below.

The U.S. has used its bases not only for counterinsurgency in the Philippines, but also as springboards for intervention in other countries. For instance, Clark Air Base and Subic Naval Base were used to intervene in Vietnam from 1957 to 1975, to support right-wing rebels in Indonesia and the Koumintang troops at Quemoy-Matsu in 1958, to stage military incursions in Kampuchea in 1975, and to intervene in the Middle East in the 1980s (Simbulan 1985, 195). Furthermore, guaranteed the unrestricted use of its bases, the U.S. stored nuclear weapons, including first-strike weapons, on them in violation of the Philippine Constitution, which states that the Philippines "consistent with the national interest, adopts and pursues a policy of freedom from nuclear weapons in its territory." [17]

Along with the military impact of U.S. bases came the sexual exploitation of poor Filipino women. Legalized prostitution, including child prostitution, became concentrated in the immediate vicinity of the military facilities. Local and foreign businessmen who controlled the recreation establishments around the bases viewed women as objects for making profits: "Instead of endangering our decent and respectable women to the possibility of rape and other forms of sexual abuse, better provide an outlet for the soldiers' sexual urge and at the same time make money out of it" (Moselina 1981).

Consolidation of a Ruling Class

U.S. economic policies in the Philippines could not be implemented without a consolidated ruling class able to preserve that class, its power, and its interests, which are allied to the economic presence of the United States. Through the power of such a ruling class, the United States is able to control the Philippine political economy without directly ruling it. Andre Gunder Frank (1974) refers to such a ruling class as the "lumpen-bourgeoisie," whose position depends on its alliance with international capital and military imperialism. Historically, the U.S. government has been able to intervene in consolidating the power of this class. In the 1960s, there emerged a grassroots awareness of the elitism of traditional politics, which spurred a demand for a more participative coalition government. Marcos planned to declare martial law in order to contain this new political consciousness, and many of the leaders of the emerging grassroot politics were liquidated. Before Marcos declared martial law, he met secretly with U.S. Ambassador Henry Byroade and asked how Washington would react to such stringent measures. Byroade promised Marcos full U.S. support (Kessler 1986). Martial law served not only the class interests of Marcos and his cronies but also the interests of the United States.

After the downfall of Marcos, the U.S. government saw Corazon Aquino as a possible ally in continuing the American economic and military presence in the Philippines. The United States supported Aquino, not because of any feminist considerations, but because she was from the traditional ruling class and was not expected to introduce an agenda of change that would radically transform the political economy or challenge U.S. control. Shortly before her trip to the United States in 1986, the White House urged Aquino to stop seeking peace with the New People's Army (Schirmer and Shalom 1987, 404). In response, the Aquino government refused to consider the legitimate demand of the National Democratic Front that the government pull out its military presence in rural areas during the ceasefire negotiations in 1986. It conceded to the IMF policies, opted to intensify counterinsurgency, and removed the more progressive elements in its administration. Furthermore, it legislated a Comprehensive Agrarian Reform Program (CARP) that exhibits no firm intention to redistribute land to the majority of landless peasants and agricultural workers. Neither did it show genuine concern for protecting workers' rights. All these were political decisions that reflected the alliance of the Philippine ruling elite and American neocolonialists.[18]

Chapter Three
The Dynamics of Exploitation and Repression in the Lives of the Peasant Women of Mindoro

The perspective of poor and oppressed women provides a unique and powerful vantage point from which we can examine the effects of development programmes and strategies. . . . The vantage point of poor women [thus] enables us not only to evaluate the extent to which development strategies benefit or harm the poorest and most oppressed sections of the people, but also to judge their impact on a range of sectors and activities crucial to socioeconomic development and human welfare.
—Gita Sen and Caren Grown (1987)

Mindoro: A Brief History

Mindoro, the seventh largest island in the Philippines,[1] comprises about 1,024,540 hectares, accounting for 21.8 percent of the land area of the southern Tagalog region and 3.4 percent of the whole Philippine land mass. It is located about 45 kilometers from mainland Luzon. In 1950, by virtue of Republic Act No. 505, the government subdivided the island into the provinces of Oriental Mindoro and Occidental Mindoro. The latter, where the peasant women of KAMMI live, comprises 57.4 percent (587,980 hectares) of the island's total land area. It has eleven municipalities: Abra de Ilog, Calintaan, Looc, Lubang, Magsaysay, Mamburao (as the capital), Paluan, Rizal, Sablayan, San Jose, and Santa Cruz.[2]

Although Mindoro is rich in natural resources, it is one of the poorest regions of the Philippines. Its social structure, according to Volker Schult (1991, 11–12), "reflects" that of the whole country: "a small political and economic elite, at the same time a great number of small farmers, poor tenants and land laborers, an agrarian economy . . . and an inadequate infrastructure." While this may be true in general, there are of

Figure 2. Map of Mindoro.

Note: Information for this map was taken from the Mindoro Integrated Development Plan, 1980, by the Mindoro Integrated Rural Development Office.

course regions that have developed quite differently than Mindoro. For example, the growth of metropolitan Manila into a mega-city does not parallel the growth of San Jose, the urban center of Occidental Mindoro. With Ramos's Philippines 2000 we can expect changes in the development of Mindoro and other regions. Nevertheless, at the time of this writing, Schult's observation still appears to be correct.

In pre-Spanish times, and as early as approximately A.D. 872, Mindoro was linked through trade with other countries, and particularly with China because of the island's proximity to the China Sea. Since Mindoro supplied the Chinese merchants with gold, they called the island "Mai," meaning gold.[3] But Mindoro lost its significance as a trading center for Chinese goods when the Spanish colonial government made Manila the center of the galleon trade between Acapulco, Mexico, and China.[4]

Before its Spanish colonial conquest in 1570, Mindoro had its own system of government and a largely subsistence economy. The people knew how to weave, make pottery, and produce weapons with gunpowder acquired from the Chinese. These skills had largely come from the Malay Muslims who settled in the island in the fourteenth century.[5]

Historical developments throughout the Philippines during colonial times partly shaped contemporary Mindoro. The Spanish colonial government made the island a separate province in the beginning of the seventeenth century, with Puerto Galera (then called Minolo) as its capital. It reorganized Mindoro into *pueblos* (main settlements) and *barangays* (barrios or villages), and appointed members of the native ruling class (the principalia) as *cabezas de barangay* (heads of barrios or villages), which was the highest political rank they could attain.[6] This began the formation of a landed, politically powerful Filipino elite.

This elite class in Mindoro was shaped by a combination of factors: (1) the incorporation of a small native upper class, who learned to speak Spanish through colonial education, into lower political positions in the Spanish colonial government; (2) the migration of upper-class families from other parts of the Philippines (such as Batangas, Cavite, and Marindugue), who then became part of the landed upper class (e.g., the Abeleda, Liboros, Morente, and Adriatico families); and (3) the rise of a small number of ilustrados, sons of the elite who studied in Manila (e.g., Mariano Leuterio and Macario Adriatico).[7] One of these names is known to some of the peasant women of KAMMI: they are landlords from whom they have "suffered a lot" and who control huge tracts of land in the municipality of Santa Cruz.[8]

The Muslims strongly resisted Spain's political and commercial domination in the Philippines, and the war they waged lasted until the end of Spanish rule. They used Mindoro as a base because of its strategic location, and so it became the target of "more frequent and longer attacks than other islands" (Schult 1991, 29–30). In addition to causing economic devastation and human casualties in Mindoro, the war pushed people into the hinterlands, to Luzon or other regions, remarkably decreasing its population (ibid.).

Symbolic of their economic interest in the Philippines, the Spanish colonizers named the island "Mina de Oro," meaning "Mine of Gold." The name was later contracted to Mindoro.

Under Spanish colonial rule, the encomienda system (Schult 1991, 26) was introduced in Mindoro in 1572. The common people lost control of their resources, for the colonialists not only exacted tribute but also instituted private ownership of land. The pre-colonial communal structure of land ownership began to disintegrate. Spanish friars also acquired large tracts of land, putting almost the whole of Occidental Mindoro under their control. The biggest of the friar estates was the Recollects', a hacienda of 23,266 hectares (ibid., 33). The encomienderos forced men, with the exception of Filipino officials in the colonial government, to labor in the encomiendas, on such projects as the construction of roads and bridges (ibid., 38).

The small local elite, who gained political positions in the colonial government, benefited most from the privatization of land. In the interest of preserving their status, some members of this class participated in the revolution that broke out in Mindoro on May 22, 1898, bringing to an end the 328 years of Spanish colonial rule on the island on July 1, 1898.[9] This participation ensured the continuance of their economic and political power during the ensuing reorganization of the government. They were able to occupy the highest political and military offices. Indeed, they controlled the electoral process so as to favor their class by making it difficult for lower-class men to be elected to office and denying all women the right to vote. For example, they restricted suffrage to male citizens, aged twenty or older, who were in favor of Philippine independence and were known for their "high character, social position and honorable conduct both in the center of the community and the suburbs."[10]

Under the American colonial government, the local elite remained powerful, collaborating with their new colonial masters in controlling the Philippine polity. Macario Adriatico, for example, a Mindoro ilustrado, served as an undercover informer against the Filipino revolutionaries in Panay during the Filipino-American war.[11]

American colonization perpetuated land privatization and gave American capitalists the right to own land in Mindoro. One entrepreneur, Edward Peale, alone acquired 5,222 hectares of land in San Jose, Occidental Mindoro, and used it to set up the first and largest sugar refining factory in the Far East, exporting mainly to the U.S. market.[12] The Mindoro

Lumber and Logging Company, also American-owned, enjoyed the exclusive right to do commercial logging in Mindoro's forests to supply the U.S. market with timber (Schult 1991, 62).

Under the American colonial administration, the privatization of land in Mindoro was reinforced by the titling of lands. When public lands were made available for homestead, large landlords and the local elite took advantage of their tenants by keeping them ignorant of the law, ensuring that they would fail to apply for homesteads. Some new settlers from outside Mindoro, on the other hand, knew about the law and so were able to acquire titles to public lands or to apply for homesteads.[13]

The process of land titling was expensive for poor people. They simply occupied public lands or cleared forested areas, claiming their ownership not by virtue of a piece of paper but by their actual cultivation of the land (Schult 1991, 68). This indigenous concept of land ownership is the historical root of land occupations in Mindoro engaged in by some members of KAMMI and other organized peasants (see Chapter 4).

Land titling also led to the legal seizure of the ancestral lands of the Mangyans, the original inhabitants of Mindoro. New settlers were encouraged by the government to come to Mindoro in order to enlarge the labor pool needed for an export economy. Some of them simply occupied Mangyan lands and then obtained the titles. The American colonial policy of segregating the Mangyans into reservations—apparently to prevent conflict between them and the new settlers—facilitated seizure of their lands, though of course they resisted this policy.[14]

Privatization of land also led to the existence of tenancy and absentee landlords. Big landlords, who did not cultivate their lands and perhaps even lived outside Mindoro, got tenants to work on their land, or hired managers to recruit others as tenants or agricultural workers.[15] This system, which still exists today, runs counter to the indigenous concept of landownership whereby peasants have a legitimate claim to the land they use and work. This concept is reflected by AMIHAN, which seeks genuine agrarian reform and free land redistribution to landless peasants (see Chapter 5).

Usury, which exists in Mindoro to this day, began there when tenants, without access to banks, depended on loans from landlords to finance their production costs. High interest rates forced many peasants to mortgage their future harvests (Schult 1991, 69), a phenomenon still common among the peasantry.

The American colonial policy on agriculture was oriented to producing, mainly for the U.S. market, nonstaple cash crops such as sugar and copra (the latter remains one of Mindoro's major export crops), to the neglect of the staple rice, which consequently had to be imported (ibid., 64). Paradoxically, however, there were times when Mindoro exported rice to other regions in the Philippines (ibid., 65). While American entrepreneurs and the landed elite amassed wealth from cash crop production, a small class of profiteering merchants, predominantly from the neighboring province of Batangas, hoarded rice, which they bought from Mindoro, and re-exported it there at a much higher price during times of scarcity.[16]

Thus, Mindoro's link to the globalization and transnationalization of the U.S. political economy began with the setting up of an export economy along with the privatization of land.

Power Structures in the Lives of Peasant Women

Several interlocking power structures keep peasant women poor, exploited, and repressed. These are: (a) the feudal and semi-feudal modes of production (including the structure of land ownership and who controls the allocation of farm produce and the terms of production), (b) the system of informal credit (usury), (c) privatization of food production (indicated by the lack of government subsidy for rice production), (d) the commercialization of rice and the monopoly of rice traders, (e) capitalist economic imperialism (seen particularly in the Green Revolution and the IMF), and (f) the militaristic state (militarization). The following sections discuss these structures.

Feudal and Semi-Feudal Modes of Production

One of the legacies of colonialism and neocolonialism in the Philippines is the development of feudal and semi-feudal modes of agricultural production, which coexist with capitalist production. In Mindoro, which is mainly an agricultural province, both means of production can be found in the work of the peasants, who do not own the land they till and therefore do not control the products of their labor. A few, mostly absentee, landlords own huge tracts of land.

Peasant women as producers and consumers.

Contrary to the "integrationist perspective" on women and development, which implicitly assumes that women are not integrated into productive work, the women of KAMMI are in fact very much involved in agricultural production. All the peasant women in this study say they do both farm work and housework. Ate Ara articulates this clearly: "The center of our work is the farm [*bukid*] and the home [*bahay*]." But within these feudal and semi-feudal modes of production they are exploited in their productive and reproductive roles. In their productive role, for example, most of the women work not for subsistence but for those who own the land. Since most do not own the land they till, they have no control over what they produce. Landlords, on the other hand, get a substantial share of the harvest.

Almost all of the peasants engaged in rice production in Mindoro are landless. Most of the women in my study work on the rice lands of a few big landlords and a small number of mid-level landlords. Four of the women in my study own parcels of land, about one hectare apiece, but the output of such a small area cannot meet their families' needs. Two peasant women work on land they have acquired by *kaingin* (clearing a forest area), but their position is very precarious because they have no title to the land. Techay, for example, showed me the small plot of rice she planted on an upland area she cleared herself. The land belongs to someone outside the village, she said. He has title to it, but it has not been cleared for years. The owner told Techay that she could use the land if she cleared it, at least until he has need of it.

The landless peasant women, as well as their husbands or fathers, work for landlords either as tenants (*magsasaka*) or as agricultural workers. The magsasaka have a relatively permanent arrangement with the landlord, although he may arbitrarily decide to terminate it. Under the tenancy system, peasant women give to the landlord an average of twelve to fifteen sacks (*cavans*) of palay per harvest. The women refer to this arrangement as the "*buwisan* system"; the portion of the harvest that goes to the landlord is considered a land tax. At an average price of 175 pesos per sack, the monetary value of twelve to fifteen sacks is equivalent to 1,920 to 2,400 pesos per harvest. For the women, this system of sharecropping is burdensome, since they must shoulder all the costs of production. Because they receive no government subsidy for farm production, the women usually borrow the money they need through an informal credit system controlled by usurers. Sometimes the landlord himself is a usurer. If he is not, the women borrow from rich families, some of whom are small rice traders in the community. For every 1,000 pesos that the usurers lend, the women pay back an average of 14 sacks of palay at harvest time. At 175 pesos per sack, 14 sacks of palay is worth 2,450 pesos, making the interest rate close to 150 percent. What is left after the shares go to the landlord and the usurer is not even enough for the women's and their families' subsistence until the next harvest. If the landlord is also the usurer, which is often the case, then almost all of the harvest goes to the landlord. If nothing of the harvest is left after the landlord and usurer get their shares, the women mortgage their next harvest and borrow money to meet the basic needs of their families.

The women who borrow from rice traders usually receive a loan not in cash but in kind; that is, the usurer lends them sacks of rice. Unfortunately, what they receive is rice that he is not able to sell in the market because of its poor quality. When the women pay him back in kind, their rice or palay must usually be of better quality, because the usurer-trader would reject it if were not. So while the peasant women may produce a good-quality harvest, they do not necessarily fully enjoy it. Not only do they produce wealth for the landlord by their labor, but they also provide a captive market for rice rejected by the rich. Hence, it is because the system makes peasant women and men landless producers and bonds them in debt that wealth and poverty is created in this feudal mode of production. Peasant women are poor because they (and peasant men as well) are the exploited class.

The feudal system rests on exploitation, for the poverty it creates in turn perpetuates it. In other words, exploitation needs the poor to feed the system. Although most of the women in my study feel their work only "makes the rich richer," and that they "only work to feed the rich," they continue working as tenants because usurers usually lend only to those who have land to till. Usurers know that if the borrower has land that she or he tills, even if it is only as a tenant rather than as an owner, he can be assured of eventual repayment. The women usually try to maintain a good credit record by paying their debts immediately after harvest, even if nothing is left for themselves. By doing so they ensure that the usurer will not reject them the next time they come to borrow. There are nevertheless cases of lenders themselves going to the field with empty sacks to make sure they get their share, for they know that the peasants also need the harvest and would certainly keep something for themselves. By all available means the peasants also will secure the needed loans for production on the landlords' lands, because if they are unable to make use of the land, they will be considered in default or negligent, and may not be permitted to continue tilling the land. Hence, contrary to the perceptions of one landlord in Calintaan, who told me that "the peasants are poor because they are lazy," they in fact work very hard. But their hard work exploits them, even as it enriches the landlords and usurers.[17]

In this dynamics of landlessness, debt bonding, and poverty, what is not immediately visible are the gender factors. The first gender factor is that the borrowing of money through the informal credit system is usually relegated to women since it is considered degrading. "I feel so small, degraded when I borrow money," said Ate Liya.[18] "No man has yet come here to talk about borrowing money; usually it is the women who borrow money for the needs of the family," observes Ate Gansa. But there are a few exceptions. Ate Su relegates the task of borrowing to her husband, saying she is ashamed (*nahihiya*) to do it. Hence, contrary to the perception of a male agriculturist in Mindoro, who told me that borrowing is a habit (*nakapagsanayan*) among the peasant women, accounting for why they are always in debt, borrowing has in fact become a survival strategy of these women. They would not borrow if there were a better way. It is an emotional struggle for them: "When I need to borrow, I feel as though I must have strong will (*lakas loob*)," says Ate Liya. They are also aware that usury is exploitative. Ate Liya told me that the usurer from whom she borrows her production costs recently insisted that she pay him back twenty sacks of palay instead of the usual fifteen per 1,000 pesos. She pleaded (*nagpakaawa*) with him, saying that she would not have that much since she did not have even the seedlings for planting. When the usurer continued to insist, Ate Liya told him: "Squeeze, and squeeze me as much as you can, but there is nothing more that you can squeeze out of me. Because we are poor, you treat us as though we are not sisters and brothers (*magkakapatid*) who should help each other (*magtulungan*)." After these words, Ate Liya said, the usurer said no more. But she feels that she no longer has the stomach to go back to him. Ate Liya theorizes from her experience that usurers benefit from the poverty of the poor: "There is no one poor who does not borrow from the rich. The rich get richer." Borrowing from usurers is thus not something that these women like doing. It is a survival strategy—one that is imposed on them by their poverty, their place in the gender hierarchy, the lack of alternative resources for their production expenses, and the exploitative relations generated by the feudal village economy.

The second gender factor is that in government policies, the productive role of peasant women is still unrecognized. Title to the land, for instance, is placed under the husband's name because generally it is he who is considered the farmer or head of the family, even though peasant women do a considerable amount of farm work and take responsibility in meeting the needs of the family. Ate Beni and her husband, for example, received two certificates of transfer (CLTs) from former president Marcos, one for less than a hectare of land and the other for a little over one hectare. But Ate Beni is not named on the certificates; only her husband appears on them.[19] Although their CLTs were signed by President Marcos in 1983, Ate Beni and her husband received them only in 1986. She recalled that the technician who gave them the certificates said that with the CLTs they should now pay their land tax (in the form of harvest) to the Land Bank, because that would serve as their amortization. If they continued paying their *buwis* (rent) to the landlord, it would not count as their amortization. When they showed the CLTs to their landlord, however, he did not believe them and disagreed with the terms of the CLTs. The landlord told them that he had not been informed by Marcos's office or the Department of Agrarian Reform. To make sure he got his *buwis*, he would carry empty sacks to the fields and gather the palay himself. So Ate Beni and her husband now feel that the CLTs are useless (*walang kuwenta*).

Ate Beni's experience is indicative of the failure of land reform in Mindoro, as well as in other parts of the country. The program—which included only rice and corn lands—did not provide adequate support for the peasants to enable them to acquire the lands designated for distribution. Moreover, there was no political support for the empowerment of the peasants as an organized class, since Marcos declared martial law at the same time that he announced his land reform program. On top of this, the program made peasant women's significant contribution to production invisible by omitting their names from the CLTs issued by the government.

Ate Beni is interested in implementing the terms of the CLTs, because a CLT holder has a greater chance of borrowing money for production expenses from rural banks, since they can use the certificates for collateral. But not having her name on the CLTs shuts her out of the formal credit system. That is why it is usually men who deal with the rural banks, while women must deal with the more exploitative informal credit system. But even a man cannot always secure a production loan from the Land Bank in Mindoro. For example, Kuya Tonyo, a husband of one of the peasant women of KAMMI, was rejected by the bank when he sought to borrow the production costs he estimated they would need in the July 1989 planting season. A staff member of the Mindoro Institute for Development told me that most banks in Mindoro no longer make production loans because of the risk involved. In November 1988 a large flood in Mindoro destroyed many crops, especially palay. As a result, many peasants were unable to pay back their loans. So with no access to formal credit systems, poor peasants, like the women of KAMMI, have no choice but to borrow their badly needed production expenses from usurers.

The third gender factor is the sexual division of labor. Women usually do the planting, weeding, and harvesting, all of which require bending and are back-breaking work. Plowing is usually done by men. Two male peasants I talked to at the house of Ate Lory said they would prefer not to do the planting because their "backs ache" when they do it. Weeding is an especially onerous job. Though women sometimes use weed-preventive chemicals, these do not kill all the weeds, particularly the small ones, which must then be tediously removed by hand. Often the agrochemicals used on the farm stimulate weed growth, creating even more work for the women. Household, reproductive work is also still largely relegated to the women. For example, in a group interview of peasant women, all fourteen raised their voices in unison to tell me that they do more work than the men because they take care of both the home (*bahay*) and the farm (*bukid*), while the men take care of the farm only (*bukid lang*).

Not all the women of KAMMI work as tenants under the share-cropping system. Some are employed as agricultural wage workers. This is generally the case in Sablayan, where women receive an average of twenty to thirty pesos a day, well below subsistence level. Such wages are not sufficient to buy even a kilo of fish for the day, which would cost at least 36 pesos. Sometimes the women must spend four to six pesos for transportation to the field, which lessens their real wage.

Agricultural wage workers do not necessarily deal directly with the landlord. Instead there may be a tenant farmer who acts as the adminis-trator of the landlord's land. In some cases this administrator–tenant farmer, who may be a relative of the landlord, also gets a wage for his work.

Agricultural wage workers are in a more precarious position than tenants. The work is generally seasonal rather than permanent, and a worker cannot be sure of being hired every planting and harvesting sea-son. Ate Mely, for example, said that there were at least sixty women who wanted to work in the field where she was employed. At the suggestion of the landlord, the tenant-administrator took only half of them. As sea-sonal workers, peasants become not only a cheap labor force but an ex-pendable one, maintaining the semi-feudal system that exploits them. The existence of this semi-feudal system demonstrates the fact that the penetration of capitalism (wage economy) into agricultural develop-ment did not entirely transform the feudal economy, but instead modi-fied it in such a way that it would serve merchant capital. By paying peasant men and women low wages, instead of a share in the crop they produce, landlords can accumulate more commercial rice for sale in the capitalist market. As wage agricultural workers, women have to purchase all their rice from the market, thus turning them into buyers of the rice that they produce. Because of inadequate wages, however, they are not always able to buy the rice they need. When they cannot secure money to buy their staple food, they usually must eat "*yuro*," a local pastry. Ate Beni cooked some for me, and it was good but quite heavy. She said some children in their village had been poisoned by eating yuro, because its preparation is difficult and must be done correctly. This happened at a time when there was nothing to eat in the village. The crops had been destroyed by the flood, and people could not farm owing to military op-erations. Several women told me that when people in the village begin eating yuro, it means it is *tagkiriwi*, that is, the months of the year when peasants are most poor because they have already used up their share of the harvest, usually three to four months before the next harvest season. Seasonal agricultural wage workers are the most likely to become hungry during tagkiriwi, because usurers usually will not lend to those who have no guaranteed harvest to mortgage in advance. The integration of peasant women into the wage economy thus did not necessarily result in their economic improvement. This contradicts the assumption of the "integrationist perspective" on women and development.

There are also tenant women, such as Ate Glin, who, in an effort to make a subsistence living, not only till their landlords' land under a share-cropping arrangement but also hire themselves out (*nagpapaupahan*) as wage agricultural workers for other landlords after they have worked on their own landlords' land. It is here where the articulation of different modes of production—feudal and semi-feudal—is concretized in the experience of these peasant women. But it is in the articulation of these different modes of production that the peasant women are exploited both as peasants and as women.

Turning tenants into agricultural wage workers, if not sending them off the land, seems to be a way in which large landlords try to circumvent the Comprehensive Agrarian Reform Program of the government. The administrator of a government official's landholdings in Calintaan, for example, mentioned that there had in fact been tenants on his four-hundred-hectare coconut plantation, but he had sent them away. He said the official planned to distribute the land, but there are no tenants to whom it can be distributed. Today, the plantation is generally idle. When there is work to be done, the administrator (who is a relative of the official) hires agricultural workers at twenty pesos per day. He praises the official, saying that he did not grab lands and that his large holdings are a result of his own hard work. He blames peasants for being poor, saying that they do not work hard enough.

Some women, on the other hand, complain about this same official. His farm animals destroy their vegetable gardens because they are allowed to roam loose in the village. Vegetables are very important for peasant families in the village. They are often the only available food to accompany rice at meals, since fish and meat are rarely affordable. When vegetables are not available, families sometimes eat just rice and salt or sugar; then it is the children who suffer most. Hence, these women, unable to feed their own children, produce not only "to let the rich eat" (as I often heard them say) but also to feed the animals of the rich.

Biological reproduction and social reproduction.

The other way in which the peasant women are exploited in the feudal or semi-feudal modes of production is in their social reproductive role. Social reproduction refers to the process by which the system is maintained or reproduced so that it is unchanged over time (see Chapter 1, under "The Emerging Literature"). This could involve the reproduction of the labor force that will work in the system, or the social maintenance of the workers already in the system. Children generally also work in the fields, but their labor has no value. Often the children of peasant women end up as landless peasants who work for a landlord or as agricultural wage workers. Ging and Lou of Calintaan, for instance, are teen-agers who have dropped out of school due to poverty and are now working for a landlord on fields their parents used to till. They aspire to higher education so they will no longer be degraded or exploited by the rich ("para hindi na kami alipustain ng mga mayayaman"). Under the present system, however, they are unlikely to experience upward mobility. For one way to reproduce the feudalist system, which enriches those who own and control the land, is to keep the peasantry where they are. One way to keep them where they are is to keep them poor. And one way to keep them poor is to maintain a system that distributes wealth upward to a few rather than downward to the majority. This is exactly what the feudal and semi-feudal systems do. They keep circulating among a small landed class the wealth produced by the impoverished peasantry.

Under conditions of extreme poverty and where farm work is not available, some daughters of peasant families work as domestic servants with very low pay. For example, Ate Won has a daughter who works as a domestic servant for a family within the same village. She is paid three hundred pesos monthly, which is used for her family's subsistence and to purchase medicines for her sickly father. The family for which she works is not wealthy, but can nonetheless relegate domestic work to a paid servant because they have regular wage work outside the village. Ate Fel's daughter also works as a domestic servant, but at only two hundred pesos a month. Thus, poor peasant families supply the low-paid, low-prestige domestic reproductive work for non-peasants who do wage work outside the home. Through cheap domestic labor, poor peasant families shoulder the social maintenance of those doing wage work outside the home.

Peasant women also are made to reproduce and maintain the system that exploits them through their role in the unsubsidized social maintenance of the active labor force, the reserve labor force, and the elderly who once were active in the labor force. With the absence of adequate government subsidies for social services, welfare programs, support services for the care of children, and social security for the elderly, and with the absence of redistributive economic policies, the maintenance of the labor force is left primarily to the family. Since domestic work still falls mainly to women, the social maintenance of the labor force—which should be a state responsibility—becomes their responsibility, as the following examples illustrate. First, because women will do everything they can to feed their children, they not only perform necessary household work and work on the farm, they also seek other sources of income in order to subsidize the basic needs farm work is unable to meet. Second, because elderly peasants do not get social security benefits from the government or their landlords, their economic and emotional care are undertaken mostly by women. Ate Delita, for example, does all the farm work because she is separated from her husband, and she takes care of her elderly mother, who can no longer work on the farm, as well. Third, because much of a woman's contribution to farm work is done within the household itself, such as preparing meals that provide farm workers with physical energy to work, her labor is not given its true value. Indeed, it is not even considered farm-related work, and is therefore not taken into account in distributing agricultural wages or produce. Ate Lorena and Ate Su, for example, though they prepare the meals for the farm early in the morning and also help with farm work, are not considered when farm produce is allocated. Each family's share is based on the labor of one person, the husband. This situation shapes the women's concept of what she does. For instance, when I asked Ate Su what her work is, she said, "None" ("Wala"), even though she spends the entire day doing domestic chores. She fetches water several times a day and cares for her three young children (the eldest only two years old), in addition to working occasionally on the farm. Although her husband sometimes helps to fetch water, she says, she does it more often. When she works on the farm she brings her children with her; her grandmother, who can still work in the fields, helps her take care of them there. Failure to recognize women's economic contribution to the farm and family serves to maintain both the feudal mode of production and the patriarchal relations that can be exploited to perpetuate that system. While the feudal and semi-feudal modes of production generate inequality and propel the process of class formation that concentrates power and wealth on top of the social pyramid, they also exploit unequal gender relations and ideologies of gender roles. The view that reproductive work is separated from productive work, implicit in these feudal and semi-feudal relations, justifies the way in which peasant women are exploited to reproduce the system. The privatization of reproductive work, which usually takes place in the domestic sphere, also obscures the rationale for more adequate state support for the poor peasants in the village political economy, and for the young and elderly.

Lack of Government Subsidy and Privatization of Food Production

Although the government does not subsidize production of rice—the staple food of the nation—it is expected to subsidize irrigation. Ate Ara says that if the government gave assistance for irrigation, the harvest might increase. Ate Gansa also thinks that if they could get a second crop, their production would improve. But since there is no irrigation during the dry season, women are unable to plant a second crop and instead must simply wait for the rainy season. The National Irrigation Authority (NIA) is supposed to provide irrigation, but peasant women say they have not really benefited from it.

The presence of the NIA in Mindoro has not significantly improved the irrigation system. For example, as of 1988, more than half of the total productive land area of four municipalities (Calintaan, Magsaysay, Rizal, San Jose) was still unirrigated.[20]

The NIA in Mindoro failed to provide genuine aid to poor peasants because it charges irrigation fees, adding to the production costs for both tenants and small owner-tillers of one or two hectares. Ate Ara says that the NIA "charges for the rain"; "even nature is already controlled by the government," she continues, because the NIA levies irrigation fees for water it channels from the river. Furthermore, she says, though some peasants do not use the NIA irrigation water because they can get their own from a river adjacent to their farms, the NIA nevertheless charges them irrigation fees as long as NIA water passes their fields.

The inadequacy of government subsidy for rice production, even in the form of irrigation, indicates that the privatization of food production is part of the policy of development. Such privatization eliminates state subsidies and transfers the state's responsibility for production to peasant women. Staple food production, for which the state should be responsible, is relegated primarily to the landless peasants who are vulnerable to exploitation under the feudal relations of production. Hence, in the wake of natural calamities that destroy food crops and farm animals, peasants get no assistance from the government or from the landlords in paying off their debts. Yet, both the landlords and the state policymakers are part of the complex system that puts rice on their table. The peasant women I spoke to were critical of this burden. The 1988 typhoon caused the biggest flood they had recently experienced in Mindoro and brought great destruction to their crops, they said unhappily. Although it was not the women's fault ("hindi naman namin kasalanan"), the landlords and moneylenders required them to mortgage their next harvest in addition to exacting the usual share of the crop. In this way, the landlords did not suffer loss from the natural calamity, and the usurers put the women deeper into debt. The government provided no relief assistance. After the typhoon, Ate Gansa said, a government social worker came to ask them what they would need to recover from the destruction, but he never came back to deliver the help he promised.

Hence, the feudal relations and privatization of food production, along with the absence of government subsidies, relegate public/state responsibility for growing rice to the peasants. The system creates wealth for the landlords and moneylenders while it leads to impoverishment of the peasants. Women are aware of their role in the creation of this wealth. Ate Lalay, for instance, says, "Without us poor, there will be no rich people" ("Kung wala tayong mahirap, wala namang mayayaman").

The children who do not receive adequate food also bear the miseries of underdevelopment. I observed that the meals of Ate Gansa's four-year-old son often consisted only of rice, water, and sugar, or perhaps salt or dried fish. Sometimes a woman makes *lugaw*, in which rice is cooked for a long time with a lot of water until the grains expand and become soft.[21] Hence, by withholding subsidies on rice production, the state denies the children of peasant women the basic economic right to adequate food, even though these same children contribute to production, when at a certain age their parents ask them to help in farm work.

Commercialization of Rice and the Monopoly on Rice Marketing

The monopoly that rice traders have over the marketing of this commodity has aggravated the poverty of peasant women and their families. Private rice traders have become a power block in both rural and urban areas, enabling them to control the procurement, pricing, and distribution of rice. Often they sell the rice that they procure from local markets not in rural areas but in cities or other producing regions where rice is not grown and its price is consequently higher. Some peasant women in fact sighed about the fact that sometimes they cannot buy rice in the village where they produce it. In a village in Calintaan, for example, women mentioned that a local official—who is landlord, trader, and usurer—would not sell rice locally, although he had a store and people would go to him looking for rice to buy. Some of the women go to urban areas such as San Jose to buy rice. These trips can be both difficult and expensive, however, and what they spend on transportation could instead have been used for other basic needs.

The traders' ability to control the procurement of rice has been enhanced through the Quedan Financing Scheme (QFS).[22] Quedan was established nationally in 1978 as a formal credit institution. It is semigovernmental in that it is not directly controlled by the Philippine government, and its own policy-making body does not have to seek approval from the President. Quedan, with approximately five hundred employees nationally, has financing programs for export crops, including sugar, cocoa, cotton, abaca, ramie fiber, and rice. Its funds are provided by the International Monetary Fund and the World Bank, and its policies reflect this fact. In Mindoro, the purpose of the Quedan Financing Scheme is to provide financing to processors, traders, and market retailers of food. Quedan does not loan money to traders directly; instead, loans are routed through banks such as the Planters Development Bank, the Land Bank of the Philippines, the Rizal Banking Corporations, the United Mindoro Savings Bank, and the Development Bank of the Philippines.

Large rice trader–millers have benefited from the Quedan funds much more than farmers' groups have. In 1989, for example, 25 million pesos were loaned to one individual rice trader–miller; 6.6 million pesos to three traders in San Jose; 5 million dollars to Valiant Corporation (the biggest private family-trading corporation in Occidental Mindoro), in addition to the 7 million pesos it acquired in the previous year; and 1 million pesos to a mayor in Occidental Mindoro. Money loaned to farmers' groups in 1989 amounted to only 180,000 pesos. On top of this, Quedan had already given 5 million pesos to banks to guarantee loans the traders could not pay. The private rice traders' control of the Quedan funds has enabled them to buy rice at a higher price than that set by the National Food Authority (NFA).[23] By buying rice at this higher price, the traders have been able to monopolize its procurement. This has undermined the goal of the NFA, which was to stabilize the price of rice by procuring and distributing it to market retailers at a lower price with the expectation that they would sell it with little markup. Operating within a feudal-capitalist economy, the NFA basically follows a free enterprise ideology, where private investment has the power to control productive and market forces, and the market economy hinges on the law of supply and demand. In fact, because the NFA buys rice at a lower price in harvest season and a higher price at other times, peasants are not able to sell their produce to the NFA at good prices when they have produce to sell.

The peasant women are critical of the NFA. From their perspective, the landlord-traders and usurer-traders benefit most from its policies. Ate Bon observed that the usurer from whom she borrows for production and subsistence has a rice mill and buys rice, which he in turn sells to the NFA. While official policy states that the NFA may not procure rice from traders, employees I interviewed admitted that this practice does occur. In 1983, some NFA employees were discovered accepting bribes from traders, who wanted to be given priority. Though the employees were dismissed, the practice continues. The NFA also discovered that landlord-traders are able to circumvent official policy by using the names of farmers who have no palay to sell. NFA personnel say this is something they cannot control; indeed, the traders, not the NFA, should be blamed since "they are the ones cheating the NFA." But the peasants believe that if the NFA were really serious about its policies, it would have the "will" to implement them. In my view, the NFA does not back up its policies because it is part of the same government bureaucracy that implements development policies that do not truly promote peasants' interests. NFA policies are also circumscribed by free enterprise market relations and feudal and semi-feudal relations of production, wherein landlords or usurers are able to expropriate surplus production from the peasants. Ate Delita pointed out that the NFA does not buy rice from peasants unless they are members of the Samahang Nayon, a government-controlled peasant organization.[24] So when peasants need cash, they cannot sell part of their harvest to the NFA but instead must sell it to small local traders at a price lower than that of the NFA. There is some truth to Ate Delita's criticism. Under its Institutionalized Procurement Program (IPP), the NFA buys primarily from organized peasant groups, and priority is given to Samahang Nayon. In order to sell rice or palay to the NFA, a farmers' group must be licensed by it as well.

Some peasant women have little good to say about the buying practices of the traders to whom they sell their produce. Ate Beni, for example, suspects that she has been cheated by one trader in Calintaan, who she believes has tampered with the scale he uses to weigh what she sells him.

It is, for several reasons, doubtful that the NFA is serious about stabilizing the price of rice through direct procurement from the peasants. First, provisions of the NFA have segregated landless peasants, who form the majority of the peasantry in Mindoro. For instance, from my interviews I discovered that the NFA considers the following as legitimate sources of procurement: (a) landowners, (b) CLT holders, (c) owner-tillers, and (d) leaseholders. People in these categories are only a small part of the peasantry. Second, the NFA has not been able to procure enough rice because the government has not allocated sufficient funds for the purpose. Funds usually last only four to five days, and then the Mindoro NFA has to wait for money from the NFA national office in Manila. In some instances the local NFA bought rice from the peasants but could not pay them immediately. This led peasants to sell their harvest to small private rice traders instead. Prior to my study, traders, especially the large ones, paid less for rice than the NFA, but at the time of my fieldwork they were paying more. For example, Valiant Corporation, the biggest rice trader in San Jose, was buying rice at 4.85 to 5.00 pesos per kilo, while the NFA was paying 3.50.[25] Buying rice at a price higher than that set by the NFA allowed the traders to increase the market price of rice, and thereby increase their profits, since they now controlled almost 90 percent of the procurement of rice. The Valiant trader believes that the price increase reflects the "law of supply and demand," and that by buying rice at a higher price than that set by the NFA, he is "helping the peasants"; he is unaware of the impact of the price increase on the poor peasantry. Third, at the same time that few funds are being funneled to the NFA, money is made available to private traders by the Quedan Financing Scheme. Big rice miller-traders in Mindoro in fact have been given the largest funding from the Mindoro branch of Quedan, entrenching further their economic power in the market. Quedan, because it is funded by the International Monetary Fund, whose development ideology promotes private investment, has become a policy instrument to further capitalist principles in the marketing of agricultural products. Fourth, at the same time that the private traders were gaining greater control of the marketing of rice, the government lifted price controls on agricultural products, beginning August 1, 1989. NFA personnel, whom I interviewed in July 1989, believed that the NFA cannot, and is not supposed to, compete with the private trader's control of commercial rice. Beginning October 1986, the government divested the NFA of its authority to set and enforce controls on the price of rice.

Fluctuations in the price of rice put not only economic but psychological pressures on peasant women. Ate Lorena, with whose family I spent a couple of nights, could not sleep the day she learned that the price of rice had increased from 380 pesos to 400 per bag. At four o'clock in the morning, she woke up sighing about the increase in the price of rice: "You know, I was not able to sleep last night thinking that the price of rice has gone up to 400 pesos."

The Value and Politics of Rice.

Rice, as the staple food in the Philippines, has a special value for Filipinos. But for the village peasant women in Mindoro it also has an exchange value. In the village economy, women use it to barter for fish and other basic needs when they do not have cash. I observed this in a village of Calintaan. One morning a woman carrying a basket on her head came to the house of Ate Beni, where I had slept the night before. She was selling different kinds of fish that her husband had caught early in the morning, and I bought some from her. Later, after she went around the village and sold all the fish, she came back to Ate Beni's place. When I asked her how much money she had gotten, she said that everyone had given her rice, and that I was the only one who had paid her with cash. With the value rice has in the village economy, it is probable that when women do not have either rice or cash, there will be hunger in their homes.

For certain people in the power structure, rice is not a basic human need but a political commodity. A former director of the NFA, and a relative of President Aquino, became a symbol of corruption in the government.[26] During his administration, approximately 45,000 tons of rice were found to be missing from the NFA warehouse in Mindoro. In March 1988, the regional director had ordered it shipped out of Mindoro without an escort, although standard operating procedures required such an escort. Today, no one knows where the sacks of rice went, and their loss has cost the government millions of dollars. It was alleged that the sacks of rice had sunk with the ship they were on, but subsequent investigation failed to find evidence of this. The case was publicized in the papers, and was under investigation by a government agency, the Blue Senate Ribbon, created to look into corruption in the government; this former director was dismissed from his position in September or October 1988.

For the government, rice is a commercial commodity that can boost foreign exchange to pay the Philippine foreign debt. Though peasant women experience scarcity of rice in their village economy, Mindoro has been identified by the NFA as a "surplus area" in its production. This means that Mindoro is one of the sources of rice for export. In 1983–84, Mindoro participated in the export of rice to Malaysia through the NFA. Again in 1989, Mindoro gave its share of rice through the NFA to Malaysia as payment for Philippine loans. The government requires that Mindoro, as a "surplus area," contribute every five years to the stock of export rice in the NFA main office in Manila. The peasant women are made to consume a poor quality of rice; only the best of the Mindoro crop is allocated for export. Women are aware of the relationship between their poverty and the exportation of rice and other products. One of them, Ate Gansa, unequivocally identifies a reason why they are poor: "Because our rice and other products are being sent to other countries" ("Kasi yong bigas at producto natin ay pinapadala sa ibang bansa").[27]

Because it is categorized as a surplus area, Mindoro also supplies other regions of the Philippines, especially those that do not produce rice, such as Manila, Batangas, Coron, Culion Leper Colony, Lucena, Albay, and Romblon.[28] Indeed, more than 60 percent of rice in Occidental Mindoro is sent out of the province.[29] From 1983 to 1988, Occidental Mindoro produced a total of 15,162,502 metric tons of palay (an average of 2,527,084 metric tons per year), but the peasant women did not share in the benefits.[30] Ate Loray, who is a tenant in a crop-sharing arrangement and shoulders all the cost of production, explains why this is so: "Because our land tax to the landlord is very high, only very little harvest is left for us; and we can sell our rice only at a very low price. The ones who get rich are those who own the lands [may-lupa] and the usurers [nagpapautang]."

If most of the peasant women and their husbands shoulder the costs of production in addition to laboring on their landlords' farms, then they are the ones, not the landlords or the usurers, who are significantly contributing to this total production in Mindoro. And in their productive and reproductive roles, women are doubly contributing. Although peasant families have inadequate food, especially during the months of tagkiriwi (usually June through September), they are, in fact, feeding both the nation and the foreign countries to which rice is exported. The women of KAMMI were experiencing *tagkiriwi* during my fieldwork, but ironically, I saw plenty of rice in the warehouse of a big private trader in San Jose, and in that of a small private trader in Calintaan. Hence, *tagkiriwi* is not created by the seasons or the cycle of harvest; it is a social condition created by the complex, though not immediately visible, interaction of various factors, including the landlord system of land ownership, the peasants' lack of control over their produce, the expropriation of rice and other resources, which are then sent out of both Mindoro and the Philippines, and the position of the peasants in the power structures of production and the marketplace.

The scarcity of rice in the village is thus politically and socially constructed; that is, an artificial scarcity results from the politics of rice. The NFA reported that of the total rice production in Mindoro from 1980 to 1987 (22,775,653 metric tons), 61 percent (13,891,291 metric tons) was "surplus."[31] If, indeed, there was a surplus, it was not an indication of abundance in Mindoro. The categorization of the province as a "surplus" region needs to be re-assessed, given the long-standing poverty of the peasants and the frequently inadequate supply of rice they experience throughout the year. During the months of *tagkiriwi* in 1983 and 1984, the NFA had an average stock of 891,684.67 metric tons of rice in Mindoro.[32]

The Philippine market provides an outlet for American rice not viable in the local market. While in Mindoro, I heard on the radio that tons of rice imported from the U.S. were unfit for human consumption. Seen within the context of the global political economy, then, rice acquires a far greater political significance. This brings us to the other power structure in which peasant women's lives are enmeshed: economic imperialism.

Economic Imperialism

Village peasant women's lives, remote they may seem from the rest of the world, are actually tied to the power structure in the world political economy. For economic imperialism has affected the development and underdevelopment of the Philippine political economy. By *economic imperialism* I refer to the process by which the political economy of a developing nation is subjected to external control by an advanced industrial nation or group of nations. The Philippines, whose colonial and neocolonial history continues to influence its present political economy, is a Third World nation whose people feel the brunt of economic imperialism. While the Filipino ruling class and the corporate class of the First World may have benefited from economic imperialism, the poor majority of Filipinos have been exploited by it. The forces of economic imperialism that directly affect the peasant women are the Green Revolution and the International Monetary Fund (IMF).

The Green Revolution.

The Green Revolution brought economic imperialism in Philippine agricultural development closer to the lives of peasant women. A Western-conceived approach to agricultural development in the Third World, the Green Revolution was pioneered in the Philippines by the Rockefeller and Ford foundations. It was officially launched in 1960 with the establishment of the International Rice Research Institute (IRRI) (funded largely by Rockefeller and Ford foundations), whose research has been largely promotive of the interests of transnational corporations.

The ideology of the Green Revolution is based on modernization rather than a redistributive approach to agricultural development. It gave a major role to transnational agribusiness corporations in modernizing agriculture, a process essentially thought of as increasing production through the use of Western technology, such as agrochemicals and farm machinery.

One major change that the Green Revolution brought in rice production was the replacement of the local rice hybrid with foreign high-yielding varieties (HYV). HYV were introduced at various times in different parts of the country. These varieties came to Mindoro in the early 1970s. Ate Morina recalls how the HYV were introduced in her village: "In 1972 or 1973, IRRI gave a seminar here. They told us that the new hybrid [*bagong binhi*] yields more within three months. But we did not know that it would yield more only if you use a lot of fertilizers and pesticides." Some women also mentioned that technicians of the HYV told them that the foreign hybrid was more resistant to typhoons; later the women discovered that the traditional hybrid was in fact better in this regard.

In the 1960s, Ate Morina recalled, there was still some of the traditional local hybrid being grown in Mindoro. But with IRRI's introduction of the HYV, the seed supply for the hybrid slowly disappeared. The peasants then had to use the foreign varieties because "NFA would not buy the traditional rice." Hence, IRRI's replacement of the local hybrid had government legitimation. According to Ate Lorena, "This is what the government did, it ordered that the traditional rice variety should all be removed, and that we use the variety that comes from outside the Philippines ['galing sa labas ng bansa']." Ate Morina asserted that the replacement of the local hybrid was "forced" (*sapilitan*) because the government actually eliminated its seeds from the market.

The peasant women also say that they prefer the traditional variety because it "does not need pesticides and fertilizers." In contrast to the local hybrid, HYV are highly dependent on agrochemicals and, in the experience of the peasants, do not yield a good harvest without them. The introduction of the HYV was part of the Marcos government's Masagana 99 Program, a development package that contained provisions for the introduction of HYV and credit to the peasants along with the adoption of the variety. Ate Lorena explained:

The change in the rice seed, which is dependent [*angkop*] on pesticides and fertilizers, is costly [*magastos*]. What we get is just enough for paying our debts. Sometimes it is even inadequate [*kulang pa*] to pay all our debts. If there are no fertilizer and pesticides, there is no harvest. The credit of the government included pesticides and fertilizers. Even if you did not finish using all of them, you still had to pay. Even now this is the case.

Ate Morina sees the connections between the introduction of the HYV, its agrochemical dependency, and the interests of the transnational corporations: "These pesticides and fertilizers that are needed with the production of HYV, they are there so that foreign transnational corporations ('ang mga dayuhang korporasyon') can market their products ('para makabinta ng kanilang mga produkto')." [33]

According to the peasant women of KAMMI, the cost of rice production has increased since they began using the HYV. Most of them have to shoulder production expenses every planting season, especially if they are tenants under the *buwisan* system. The increase in the cost of production was the beginning of their debt bondage. Ate Lorena rightly considers the high cost of production one of the major problems they have as peasants; every planting season, she says, they have to borrow money at usurious rates.

The use of agrichemicals has also caused ecological damage. The land has become impotent; that is, it would not yield good produce without the use of chemicals. The women have observed that the soil becomes infertile (*inutil*) after they have applied fertilizers for a long time. In times when the peasants are unable to afford fertilizers and pesticides, harvest is poor. And with a poor harvest, very little, if anything, is left for them, though there is always harvest left for the landlords.

The ecological system that provides other food sources for the peasants has also been damaged by the use of agrichemicals. The women claim that edible frogs and fish that thrived in the rice fields would be found dead after they applied pesticides or fertilizers. Now they seldom find those fish at all.

The ecological balance of the land has also been damaged. According to an agriculturist in Mindoro, because the land has been saturated with agrochemicals, the growth of certain weeds that provided natural nutrients for the soil when they dried up is now stunted. Instead of supporting the use of these organic fertilizers, the Green Revolution promoted the use of agrochemicals, since this would be profitable for the multinational corporations that produce and market these products. Peasants have also observed that some pesticides cause the growth of more pests ("mas nakakadami sa mga peste"). This supports what I learned when I worked as a researcher in 1979 at the Farmers Assistance Board, a nongovernmental support institution for peasants: pests develop resistance to pesticides, and when this happens there is usually a widespread outbreak.

Agrochemicals have also affected the peasants' health. Some of the women of KAMMI said that they get dizzy when they smell the pesticides sprayed in the fields. A thirteen-year-old grandson of Ate Morina was hospitalized for almost a month because of overexposure to the pesticide spray he used. Some women complained of skin blemishes and sensitive areas on their hands. They attribute this to exposure to the fertilizers they sow on the fields. Ate Morina has observed the effect of fertilizers: "My hands feel sensitive [*mahapdi*]. My fingertips have become so thin that sometimes they easily bleed and my nails sometimes break [*napupudpod*]. That is why sometimes I cannot do certain things, like holding or touching salt [*asin*]."

Thus, the Green Revolution, as an outgrowth of the penetration of transnational capitalism in rice production, has had a negative impact on the lives of the peasant women of KAMMI. Although it increased rice productivity, it failed to bring the peasant women out of their poverty and debt bondage. It failed not only because it increased the cost of production, but more importantly because it was introduced without addressing the basic structures that make the peasants, and the majority of Filipinos, poor. As a development package based on modernization, it ignored the needs of the landless poor because its formulation did not begin from their perspective and human needs. It is a technocratic, top-down approach to development, which begins from and ends at a foreign, externally determined perspective on agricultural development. It cannot address the politics of underdevelopment in the Philippines because it is controlled by the powerful few who benefit from these same politics of underdevelopment and exploitation.

The IMF and the Philippine Debt Trap.

The International Monetary Fund, through the conditions it imposes on borrowing nations, has been able to control the nature of Philippine economic development. In March 1989, the Aquino government submitted its Letter of Intent (LOI) to the IMF in order to secure a loan of $1.3 billion. With this LOI, the government further strengthened the IMF's control of development policies in the Philippines. Some of the provisions of the LOI required by the IMF are: (1) devaluation of the peso; (2) import liberalization and import-intensive investment (along with subcontracting jobs, a wage regionalization scheme, and labor control); (3) a tax increase; (4) a privatization program (which involves the selling of government-controlled or government-owned corporations to the private business sector); and (5) lessening restrictions on banks' interest rates. Peasant women and their families directly feel the overall effects of these conditions, which include: (a) an increase in the prices of goods and services; (b) a decrease in real wages and income; (c) an increase in the cost of production; and (d) an increase in interest rates. In the larger Philippine political economy, these IMF conditions can increase unemployment, create a cycle of dependency on foreign loans, and lead the country into a debt trap. Just as the Green Revolution has put the peasant women in greater debt bondage, the IMF has plunged the whole Philippine political economy deeper into debt.

Ate Celiza sees the connection between the everyday lives of peasant women and the increasing Philippine foreign debt. During KAMMI's leadership training, when they were discussing the foreign debt issue, she said, "We are paying for this debt indirectly when we buy goods with increased prices." She questions why this must be so, when the government knows that they "do not even have jobs yet." Ate Lorena added that "the price of soap has already increased from 9.50 pesos to 11.50 pesos," and observed that even "the fee for a residence certificate has increased from 3 pesos to 5 pesos, and now to 10 pesos." She also noticed that the cost of special church services has gone up: "Even the fee for baptism has increased." Peasant women are usually the first to notice an increase in prices and feel its impact, since they are the ones who go daily to buy what their families need. Ate Bon came home one morning from the market, sighing about her discovery that rice had already increased in price. She spread her discovery to Ate Lorena, me, and the other women in the neighborhood.

The United States and the IMF.

Because it has the greatest voting power, the United States maintains control of the IMF. Most IMF policies and the conditions it places on borrowing countries are designed to protect the interests of multinational corporations. Far from being neutral, the IMF's ideology of development promotes capitalist development or growth. It veers away from redistributive policies that could slash profits for multinational corporations, empower labor, or radically transform inequities in the capitalist political economy. IMF control of Philippine development is partly facilitated by the creation of a ruling elite aligned with foreign interests. The United States intervened in Philippine political affairs to consolidate this ruling class, which will in turn continue to protect U.S. interests against the growing tide of Filipino nationalism. The connection between the United States and the IMF in the Philippine politics of underdevelopment links the everyday lives of the peasant women to U.S. imperialism.

The Politics of Repression and Peasant Women's Lives

The power structures that I have discussed above, in which peasant women's lives are enmeshed, resulting in their poverty and exploitation, are forcibly and violently tied together by repression. By *repression* I refer to the processes by which the state prevents radical change of the existing power relations that largely benefit those with political and economic power. Poverty and exploitation create the preconditions for resistance and rebellion. To maintain these power structures, it is not enough to rely simply on the logic of capitalist development, or on the existence of a landlord-dominated Congress. The state resorts to repression and militarization to contain resistance against the status quo, especially when there are grassroots organizations that seek to alter these exploitative structures. Even with the ascendancy of Corazon Aquino, which toppled the Marcos dictatorship in 1986, and Fidel Ramos's coming to power in the 1990s, militarization continues to be part of the politics of ruling the Philippines. A discussion of the politics of repression and its impact on peasant women follows.[34]

A View from the Field.

The politics of repression in the Philippines has taken the form of low intensity conflict (LIC), a systematic strategy of counterinsurgency that is fought on different levels: ideological, social-psychological, political, and military. On the first level, the Philippine government has articulated an "anti-communist ideology," which assumes that the security of the nation depends on its defence against communist infiltrations. "Anti-communist ideology" is propagated through the media, which is largely under government control. Media coverage is also selective to prevent the people's awareness of social problems and consequently their resistance to the forces that create them. For example, the two mass demonstrations that I attended in Manila as part of my fieldwork were not reported in the media. The people's demands in these demonstrations included: (1) genuine land reform, as opposed to the government's Comprehensive Agrarian Reform Law, which the peasants criticized as biased toward the interests of landlords; (2) removal of the U.S. bases and an end to U.S. intervention in the Philippines; (3) resistance against the IMF's control of economic policies; (4) demilitarization and democratization; (5) promotion of workers' and church people's rights; and (6) emancipation of Filipino women. One way the government can contain these radical demands is to exclude them from the mainstream media coverage.

On the social-psychological level, low intensity conflict is waged by labeling people's organizations "communist." The government again uses the media to promote its cause, branding these organizations as illegal and warning people not to join them. As a consequence, the ability of organizations to mobilize the masses is undermined, for people who are just beginning to join political groups are generally afraid to associate with anyone the government has labeled communist. Undermining legal and aboveground organizations is a way to repress open mass protest, which can have a wide impact on the populace.

On the political level, low intensity conflict is waged through the consolidation of a ruling class that will use militaristic and exclusionary policies to preclude the radical transformation of Philippine political economy. Although there may have been some divisions among them as they vied for power, members of this ruling class have generally united against redistributive economic policies. They have been united, for example, in maintaining the concentration of land among themselves by legislating loopholes in the land reform laws and creating private armies to protect their control of land. They have also been able to maintain a political economy of elite rule, which is predominantly authoritarian, although at times it may create a legitimate facade through its recourse to electoral-constitutional politics. This authoritarianism has been both blatant, as indicated by the formal declaration of martial law during the Marcos regime, and subtle, as shown by the continuity of repression and militarization in the post-Marcos era despite the formal lifting of martial law. More important it has suppressed the growth of popular democracy and the legitimate voice of the poor majority in development policy-making on the local and national levels.

The ruling class is also united on an ideological level. It does not wish to alter the course of underdevelopment and exploitation in the Philippines, and it lacks a unifying vision that will incorporate progressive grassroots organizations into state politics. It has consistently prevented the left from coming to power, or at least from attaining some significant influence in formulating development policy.

The other political strategy of low intensity conflict intended to contain a radical transformation of the Philippine economy is the creation of a "Third Force" (Bello 1987), that is, moderates who will promote palliatives to Philippine problems while keeping intact the existing power structure. Reforms include civic action projects that are routed through the military in an effort to create a benevolent image despite continuing militarization. Other actions include reforming the military and creating a human rights commission, while keeping military units in rural areas intact.

The military strategy that the doctrine of low intensity conflict uses to repress transformative change in the Philippine political economy is the use of paramilitary troops, or vigilantes, in both rural and urban areas. Created under the Marcos regime and continued under the Aquino and Ramos governments, these vigilantes seek to destroy groups and execute people suspected of being communists or supporters of the New People's Army. According to a report of the Philippine Alliance of Human Rights Advocates, as of February 1988 there were approximately 224 vigilante groups spread throughout the country. Their overall aim is to paralyze all forms of political, economic, and ideological support for the revolutionary movement in the Philippines. Paramilitary troops also use propaganda—a social-psychological and ideological form of counterinsurgency—to discredit such revolutionary forces as the New People's Army. The Aquino administration formalized the paramilitary troops as Citizens Armed Forces Geographical Units (CAFGU). One evening, when I was eating supper in Ate Morina's house, her son-in-law, Kuya Tito, talked about the "CAFGUs," as the villagers often refer to these troops.

The government does big propaganda here. These CAFGUs, they are thieves. They will steal and afterward they will let it come out that it was the NPA who did it. Like the cooperative of KMP, they ransacked it and got everything there. Afterward they said that it was the New People's Army who did it. That is the propaganda of the government. Before it was the MATASADEM [Citizens Loyal To Democracy]. . . . What democracy? . . . Then Alsa Masa . . . "Alsa Bulsa" [here he grinned sarcastically, for *Alsa Bulsa* is synonymous with pickpocketing]. Now we have CAFGUs, but it is the same people.

Members of the CAFGU are recruited from the local population. Some people in Mindoro say the CAFGUs are the same as the former armed vigilantes, like the Alsa Masa, except that at first the members did not wear military uniforms. Although at the time of my fieldwork in 1989, the CAFGUs wore uniforms, by my revisit in 1996 they again no longer did so. According to an AMIHAN officer I interviewed, this is just one of the cosmetic changes brought about by the so-called soft approach to militarization, which aims to "win the hearts and minds of the people."

People who joined the CAFGU did so for various reasons. According to some people in Mindoro, enticements to join include the promise of such economic benefits as a monthly allowance, free uniforms, and paid expenses for the families of members who die in combat or military operations. Local people also fear that if CAFGU seeks to recruit them and they refuse, they will become suspects of the military. Some recruits are very young; most come from poor rural families. There are those who join the CAFGU but later discretely leave when they find that the promised economic benefits are not forthcoming.

CAFGU members are usually given training before deployment. Tonio, a male relative of Ate Beni, was arrested by the military in 1987 because of his political involvement. In an effort to strip him of his political ideologies, he was then made to train CAFGU recruits. In this way he was used against the very movement he supported.

When in military uniforms, CAFGU forces are highly visible. They usually patrol villages in units of ten or more. While in a village in Mindoro, I happened to meet a unit of nine CAFGU combatants, walking in the unpaved street at about 6:45 in the morning, holding their guns as if ready to shoot. I was terribly afraid they would stop me if they suspected I was not from that village. I was carrying a camera and was relieved they did not notice it because I had wrapped it in plastic. I pretended I was a member of the village community by not showing I was afraid of them and by continuing to walk seemingly unperturbed toward my destination. Some of the village people watched them quietly as they paraded in the street with their guns held at the ready. Later in the morning I learned that they had dropped by the house of Ate Beni, where I had spent the night. They had breakfast there and later went to a village community in the interior section of Mindoro because, they said, they "had a mission." Ate Beni mentioned to me that sometimes she runs short of food because she has to feed soldiers in addition to the many people and relatives who come to her house. She has ten children to feed. Like Ate Beni, other peasant women are made to contribute to the social maintenance of the military force that represses them. Their hard-earned meager resources are diverted from the subsistence of their families to support of the military, which in no way benefits them. The story of Ate Bering, an evacuee from a village in the interior of Mindoro, further illustrates this:

It was about four o'clock in the morning, just when I was falling into a sound sleep because I was very tired that day, that the CAFGUs came. They made noises at my door. They entered my house. They made noise with my casserole. I asked them what they wanted. They said they had not yet eaten and that they wanted to eat. I told them then, oh, then I will cook, that only. They were many. After they ate, when they were about to leave, they took my chickens [*manok*], milk, and sugar. They even took the belt I use to tie around my carabao's neck ["yong pangtali ko sa leeg ng kalabaw"] because they said they could use it to carry bullets around their waists.

While peasant women are made to contribute to the social maintenance of the CAFGUs, big landlords in Mindoro have used these paramilitary units to protect their control of land and its resources. Ate Bering further recounts:

> G—— says that he does not use the CAFGUs. But he did. Before the military operation was conducted in our place, according to a tenant who was working on his land, he told the CAFGUs that if they entered his land he would give them lands to till. When military operations were conducted the people began evacuating from the village and some of his tenants could no longer work on his land. Now, it is CAFGUs who are working on those lands.

Some people in Mindoro also talked about a certain big landlord whose landholdings are protected by CAFGUs. They said that the CAFGUs protecting his lands have killed peasants who happened to step onto his property. And in San Jose, another big landlord had a headquarters for the CAFGUs where they could rest, sleep, and eat. I saw this place myself.

There are cases in which the CAFGUs intervene in local village elections to undermine officials they suspect are supportive of the revolutionary forces. Ate Beni said that in her village, support for the predecessor of the present barrio captain (at the time of my fieldwork) was subverted by the CAFGUs, who suspected that she supported the New People's Army. Ate Beni recalled, "Although the village people liked her, the CAFGUs told us that if we voted for her and she won the election, our houses would be reduced to makeshifts [kubo-kubo]. Of course the people became afraid, so the former captain was not re-elected."

In its anticommunist crusade, and with its goal to wipe out all forms of support to the revolutionary forces in rural areas, the military stereotypes its enemy in order to identify suspects that can be arrested, interrogated with torture, harassed, or "salvaged" (a colloquial term for an extrajudicial execution). In Mindoro the stereotypes for a suspect are: she or he (1) is a new face in the village, whom nobody in the community knows; (2) uses Ka (a term showing respect to elders) to address people in the village; (3) uses the word "feudalism"; (4) often carries a knapsack and wears jeans; (4) speaks pure Tagalog; (5) refuses to give food or animals to soldiers; (6) is a member of the KMP (Kilusang Magbubukid ng Pilipinas, or Peasant Movement of the Philippines); (7) refuses to join the CAFGU; (8) refuses to appear when summoned by the military for interrogation; and (8) is a leader of a nongovernmental organization.

Ate Gansa recalls an incident where this stereotyping resulted in the salvaging of a suspect by a CAFGU member:

There was one person who came to this place. He did not know anybody here. He happened to go into the house of the CAFGU member who is in this community. He helped them in farming. But after they made use of him, the CAFGU killed him because he said no one in the community knew him. It was in the middle of the night, we heard him shout, "Have pity on me! Do not kill me, have pity on me, I have not committed any offense!" His pleading remained unheeded, and we heard the shooting of a gun. In the morning we saw his dead body near the stream there. That is why do not go to that area there. There is an informer there.

Using stereotypes to identify suspects has resulted in many human rights violations, indiscriminate counterinsurgency killings, and massacres. That is why politicized people now call low intensity conflict "total war."

Militarization has made the lives of peasant women more difficult. It has badly affected their families and their economic, political, and community lives.

The Impact of Militarization on Peasant Families.

Militarization has an impact on the family life of the peasant women of KAMMI. It has, for example, separated family members. Some husbands have fled their villages to escape military harassment and cannot return. The military raided their homes as part of a systematic campaign conducted in 1987 against nongovernmental peasant organizations in Occidental Mindoro. The following story of Ate Gansa is typical.

In the early part of 1988, several soldiers entered the house of Gansa's family. Only their son Mario (twelve years old at that time), daughter Josie (eight years old), son Jojo (three years old), and relative Teka were in the house. The soldiers, who all had guns, asked the children where their father was. One soldier poked Mario's chest with his gun to pressure him to take them to his father. Teka was horrified: "When I saw them poke him [*binugbog nila siya*], I felt as if my chest would open up. Because of fear I was able to climb up on the roof, and the soldiers pointed their guns at me, asking where Gregorio was." The soldiers wanted to take small Jojo with them. Josie cried and begged the soldiers not to do so: "Please don't take him because I will have no companion here anymore." A relative of the family who knew what was happening immediately told Ate Gansa and her husband not to go home, since their house was surrounded by soldiers. Ate Gansa and her husband had to go elsewhere, leaving their children in the care of relatives. After some months, Ate Gansa risked coming home because she missed her children so much. It was still too risky for her husband, however, so Ate Gansa had to support the family by herself. She felt this situation had made her life very difficult: "You know, Gaya, I want my husband to be able to come back here because I am already finding it so difficult. He cannot work, . . . my daughter who is with him is sick and has no work. I send both of them money for their support."

Ate Gansa's experience of military repression had such an emotional impact on her that she cried every time she told her story. It hurts her to know that Mario continues to feel pain in his chest where the soldier poked his gun. Also young Jojo often cried, and sometimes woke up at night crying, since her husband left the village. She said, "Every time he sees a soldier he would say, 'Mommy, there are the soldiers, they are searching for Daddy' ('Nanay, ayan ang mga sundalo, hinahanap nila si Tatay')." Military atrocities affect not only adults but also children, who are deprived of normal family life and who experience violence very early in their lives. The emotional and psychological impact of such experiences on children can have social repercussions in the future.[35]

Ate Morina told me of a similar experience. The first time I visited her, she immediately showed me a picture of her husband, who was a well-known and active leader of the Mindoro chapter of the KMP. In 1987 a group of soldiers raided their house looking for him. He escaped from the village to save his life. The military placed a price on his head, making it too dangerous for him to return. Ate Morina's married daughter also has a price on her head, so she cannot go out of the house alone. Every day at sunset she closes all the windows and doors, which gives them some sense of security. She told me, "You know, I have developed a phobia; closing doors and windows early . . . it is better to take precautions."

In another village, Ate Yanita talked about a gang of soldiers who surrounded her house in July 1989. Her house was under surveillance night and day because the soldiers suspected that a member of the NPA often visited there. She was concerned that the children in the neighborhood would be frightened of the soldiers, who positioned their guns as if ready to shoot. Ate Yanita had an encounter with the military in 1987 as well. She and other families had left their village because of military operations there. The military had announced her name over the radio, saying she was a commander of the New People's Army and that she had surrendered. Ate Yanita laughed at this. She recalled the occasion when she and about thirty of her neighbors were evacuated from the village and brought to the military detachment in a truck. They were told to sign a confession that they were guerrilla surrenderees. None of them signed.

They refused to be labeled in this way and denied that they were what the military claimed they were.

Another peasant woman, Ate Lorena, spoke about her forty-nine-year-old brother, who was arrested, jailed, and tortured by the military on September 5, 1988:

For sixteen days the soldiers blindfolded him, then covered his head with a helmet, and when they removed the blindfold, he could not see and his eyes became extremely sensitive to light for some time. They tied him and kicked him. The soldiers struck him on his chest and broke two of his ribs. Today he still feels the pain, cannot breathe well when working in the fields, and cannot do certain tasks because of it. The doctor said that he cannot do heavy work anymore.

Ate Lorena told the soldiers that her family knew they were keeping her brother in jail. At first the soldiers denied knowledge of his whereabouts, but Ate Lorena did not give up, insisting that she knew they were detaining him. Finally, the soldiers agreed to release him if she would put up a certain amount of money. Ate Lorena and her family raised thousands of pesos by borrowing here and there:

We spent more than nine thousand pesos in all, doing everything to take our brother out of jail, like expenses for transportation to get information about our brother. We gave the military four thousand pesos cash so they would return our brother to us. He was the first one in our village to be picked up by the MATASADEM [paramilitary troops]. They planned to kill my brother after three days in order to make him an example to the people of what could happen to them if they were suspected. We just paid for his life.

This experience put her and her sisters in debt. Ate Lorena said the soldiers "had an all-night drinking spree" after her family gave them the money.

Another human rights violation that has occurred under militarization is military rape. Girls and women are the most vulnerable. During my second visit to Mindoro in 1996, some of the women I talked to told me that one member of KAMMI had a thirteen-year-old daughter who was raped by two CAFGUs in 1994. The girl was hospitalized for bleeding and infection of the vagina. She was also affected psychologically, as indicated by her absent-mindedness (*tulala*). When her case was made public, she had to live incognita, away from her family, to shield her from reprisals by her victimisers. Military rape cannot be viewed simply as an uncontrollable sexual outlet; it is a tool of repression to make women and their families submit to the power structure that militarization preserves (Bunster-Burroto 1985).

Militarization has also disturbed the conditions necessary for normal family life. Bombings and military operations have led peasant families to evacuate villages in the interior of Mindoro. Ate Gansa and Teka talked about a mass evacuation of people from the village of Malpalon in 1988. Young children, old people, and even pregnant women had to walk many miles with whatever household belongings and farm animals they could possibly save. Living like refugees in their own community, they stayed for several weeks in an overcrowded school building, under unhealthy living conditions and with inadequate food. For the village people, then, evacuation and bombings mean not only extreme inconvenience but also loss of their meager property and exposure to disease and hunger; for the government, however, these are the normal consequences of counterinsurgency. Evacuees are not compensated for the inconvenience they suffer, or for their loss of property. So while counterinsurgency preserves the system that benefits the ruling class, the peasant families who are directly affected by it pay the price of maintaining that system.

The Economic Impact of Militarization on Peasant Women's Lives.

Militarization takes a financial toll on peasant families. Evacuations prevent them from working on their farms. Since rice production is seasonal, military operations and evacuations can keep peasants from putting in their crops when it is planting season. Once the rice simply dried up because the farmers could not harvest it. Some women who evacuated their homes because of military operations found their vegetable gardens gone when they returned. Others lost their farm animals and belongings. For peasants, water buffalo (*kalabaw*) are indispensable as draft animals. When they lose them, it is not just a significant economic loss. They may not be able to farm at all.

During military operations, paramilitary troops also seize property of peasant families. Ate Loray, for example, talked about the soldiers taking their chicken, which they could have used for a meal. Ate Beni talked about her cousin, who complained that soldiers kicked the door of her house and acted arrogantly when they entered, throwing some plates and cups on the floor; they then took canned goods, sugar, coffee, soap, and other household items. Ate Lorena talked about a village woman who out of fear gave her last pound of rice to some soldiers. They had shot bullets into the air as they approached her house. Her children cried that day because they were so hungry.[36]

Militarization has also removed peasant families from the convenience and benefits of living close to their farms. Some of the peasant women who were evacuated from a village in the interior because of military operations and bombings settled in the town of Magsaysay; they now must spend money on transportation to reach their farms. When they were living at home, they could plant vegetables for domestic consumption. They cannot do so while living in town. Thus, militarization not only has separated members of peasant families but also has exacerbated their poverty.

The Impact of Militarization on Peasant Organizations.

Militarization has made all types of organization difficult. The military is suspicious of any group gathering in the village, if it is not government related.[37] When the women of KAMMI plan to gather for group sessions for some days or at night, they have to get a permit at the mayor's office. At least two women I talked to had been part of the peasant women's organization but had ceased to be actively involved because of fear of reprisal or because they were advised by relatives connected to the military that they should withdraw from political activities. There are informers in every village who, without intelligent verification, report to the military new faces or gatherings of people they suspect to be subversives or members of the New People's Army. For example, an unknown informer reported that a leadership training meeting of the peasant women in one village chapter of KAMMI was a meeting of the NPA. Soldiers came after the meeting was over. They learned from the leader of the organization that the group had a permit from the mayor to meet.

The women experienced setbacks when the military conducted operations against peasant organizations in Mindoro in 1987. Ate Bering talked with regret about how military harassment in 1987 aborted a project their village women's organization of approximately twenty members had begun to put into effect: "Our plan was good. We already had some capital to start with. Each member was able to save one hundred pesos. Our plan was to put up a cooperative. Each member would contribute to the cooperative one can of rice and would help in running the cooperative. But there were military operations in the village. We were separated from each other, and some members evacuated to other places. We could not continue with our project then."

Consumer and credit cooperatives on the village and community levels enable peasants to learn about and try out collective modes of producing, storing, and marketing agricultural products. They are small, alternative ways through which peasants learn cooperative values in economic organizations. These cooperative values are important in sustaining economic organizations that can empower them. Through credit cooperatives, for example, peasants can subvert the monopoly of usurers over informal credit systems. Consumer cooperatives are viable economic organizations that allow peasants to control the marketing of their produce. But the instability created by militarization deprives peasants of the social environment necessary to sustaining such organizations.

Sometimes cooperatives are directly sabotaged by the military when they are suspected to be a "store of the New People's Army." This can be costly for poor peasants. For example, the KMP-Mindoro, with which KAMMI was originally linked, lost 25,000 pesos worth of goods when their cooperative was, they believe, sabotaged by the military. Ate Delita, who was then an officer of the cooperative, said that this once successful venture is now inoperative.

The KMP was also in the process of setting up a warehouse and rice mill in 1988 in a village in Mindoro. The military threatened to destroy the building if they continued with the project. I saw the part of this building that the peasants had already built and spent money on; it stands unused today. The members of the organization are afraid they would again lose thousands of pesos if they began construction, only to have everything destroyed by the military. In fact, although they had already secured approval for a loan to put into the project, the sabotage of their consumer cooperative made them decide to sit on the project instead. Thus, militarization has not only caused setbacks in the growth of peasant organizations but has also wasted their meager resources.

In 1987, when the military systematically harassed the KMP by arresting, torturing, and detaining its leaders and members, the Peasant Women of Mindoro (KAMMI) also experienced an organizational setback. Through psychological warfare, the military succeeded in breaking the leadership of the organization. The women heard on the radio that peasant women's organizations were "communist organizations," that they must not be allowed to exist, and that they would be raided and searched. The women burned or buried all their organizational documents, some leaders left their villages, and meetings ceased for some time. The military also called some of the peasant women in for interrogation and warned them not to join organizations unless they were sponsored by the government.

While before the systematic harassment in 1987, the KMP and KAMMI freely conducted mass demonstrations, at the time of my fieldwork, they no longer did so. The peasant women concluded that mass demonstrations under conditions of heightened militarization in the villages and rural areas would not be strategically effective because their leaders could be easily identified.

The experience of the peasant women of KAMMI with the politics of repression is not an isolated case in the Philippines. In July 1989, twenty-two members of the National Council of AMIHAN, representing local chapters across the country, met in Manila for three days. I observed their meetings and found that their collective experience indicates that a national policy of militarization has been systematically implemented throughout the Philippines.[38] Each woman believed that militarization was one of the major difficulties she encountered in her family, work, and political lives. The father of Selly, a young peasant woman from the Visayas region in the central Philippines, was killed by the military. Rosa, from the same region, told how the military accused a whole village of supporting the New People's Army and called on the villagers to declare themselves NPA surrenderees. Anita, another representative from Mindanao in the southern Philippines, described the massacre of the family of an AMIHAN member. Others spoke of the dislocation their families experienced when their husbands were harassed or imprisoned by the military because of their political activities.

These experiences of repression, similar to those in Mindoro, contradict President Corazon Aquino's claim during her visit to Europe that human rights violations from militarization were "isolated cases." Ate Isabel, for example, says, "The position of Cory Aquino in Europe was that she was innocent about the human rights violations, that if there were human rights violations, they were isolated cases and they have acted on them. But within a span of three years there has been an intensification of militarization and human rights violations have gotten worse."

The lives of two national leaders of AMIHAN at the time of my fieldwork, Ate Loy and Ate Deding, have suffered from the politics of repression. Ate Loy misses her family very much, but she cannot go back to the province in which they live because the military raided her house searching for her. In spite of the price she has had to pay, Ate Loy continues her commitment to the movement for change in the Philippines.

Ate Deding comes from another region of the country. Her husband was publicly and slowly tortured to death by the military to show the village people what could happen to them if they joined political organizations. Ate Deding recalled, "The military slashed his face several times, and while blood was oozing down his whole body, they hit him on his stomach. Then, finally, they shot him in the head. If they knew that they were going to kill him anyway, why did they not do it at once? Why did they still have to let him suffer slowly?" According to Ate Deding, her husband was well loved by the village people, and they were angered, not frightened, by what the military did to him. At twenty-three, Ate Deding became a widow with five children. She had to support her family by herself, working not only as a peasant but also as a laundry woman and a market vendor. Her experience has not broken her spirit, however. Instead it has strengthened her commitment to the movement for change in the Philippines: "As long as the people whom my husband has awakened are still in the movement, I will not stop being in the forefront for change."

National and Global Connections.

While the politics of repression is rooted in the national structures of the Philippines, it also has global connections. The politics of repression in the Philippines has been supported by the United States through military aid.[39] The maintenance of the present power relations in the Philippines serves the U.S. multinational corporations that control most foreign investment in the country, including the agribusinesses that have taken lands away from peasants.[40] At the same time, these power relations serve the interests of the ruling elite in the Philippines, composed mostly of the landed class. This class also largely benefits from the capitalism that has become interlocked with the Philippine feudal relations of production, in which landless peasant women and men are an exploited class. Peasant women experience double oppression as gender hierarchies intersect with these coexisting modes of production. The connection between gendered capital transnationalization and the Philippine ruling elite cannot depend simply on the logic of capital accumulation to entrench itself over time. State repression then becomes part of the politics of development and underdevelopment in the Philippines. In the politics of repression, peasant women and their families become not only victims, but also invisible participants in the maintenance of the system. This invisibility prevents public awareness of their plight and is a subtle way to obtain the consent of the women to the very system that exploits them. This is how the Philippine state, which is linked to the U.S. imperial state, doubly oppresses the peasant women of Mindoro. But repression—as part of the politics of ruling, and the power structures and dynamics of exploitation that it maintains—engenders resistance, as I will illustrate in the following chapters.

Chapter Four
KAMMI's Local Politics of Resistance

KAMMI's goal is to raise the status and struggle for the rights of peasant women, to improve and raise the livelihood of peasant women, and to work for genuine agrarian reform. The first and second objectives are channels to the third, which is the ultimate objective. Through a gradual process we can reach the third: how we can gain the right to own land.
—Provincial leader of KAMMI

KAMMI's politics and strategies for change confront the power structures discussed in Chapter 3, which affect peasant women's everyday lives. The existence of KAMMI demonstrates that peasant women are not simply passive victims of underdevelopment. They have alternative views, ideologies, and strategies of development that are worthy of consideration in national and international policy-making, but are currently ignored.

Resistance Against Repression: Collective Empowerment Through Organization

Since one tactic of state repression is "divide and rule," an important weapon that peasant women can use to empower themselves is organization. Ate Nor says that organization is important because it serves as a "defense of the people" ("depensa ng bayan"). To resist in a repressive society, then, organization is essential.

Peasant women feel a sense of empowerment when they come together and collectivize themselves: "If we have no organization, we cannot do collective action. We can make ourselves strong if we are organized," says Ate Lorena. It is in coming together that the peasant women realize their capacity to take action: "Now I realize that peasant women can also act [puedeng kumilos]," says Ate Laya. These women believe that only with a collective voice can they make the government respond to their needs and rights: "If you deal with the government as an individual they will not listen to you," says Ate Sarisa.

To act together to solve their problems, however, the peasant women know that they need a collective understanding of their situation. This can come about only if they are organized. One peasant woman succinctly articulates this: "The organization also facilitates exchange of ideas ['nagpapalitan ng kuro-kuro']. Because if we have no common understanding of our problems, and take no common actions, we will not solve our problems."

The peasant women's views and theories of organization come from their active involvement in an organizational politics of their own creation. While repression creates the preconditions for organized resistance, it is the peasant women themselves who choose to form such resistance. This is clearly illustrated in the history of KAMMI, which is characterized by persistence and creativity despite militarization.

KAMMI was formally launched in a provincial congress held in San Jose, Mindoro, on February 23–25, 1987, attended by approximately a hundred peasant women from seven preorganized local village chapters. Most of the initial organizers of KAMMI were wives of members of KMP-Mindoro. This influenced the original structure of KAMMI, for it began as a joint organization with KMP–Occidental Mindoro. The KMP (Kilusang Magbubukid ng Pilipinas, translated as Peasant Movement of the Philippines) is a militant national federation of peasant organizations in the Philippines comprising both men and women.

Only a few months after KAMMI was formally launched, the military harassed, arrested, tortured, and killed many KMP members. This caused disorganization within KAMMI, as many of its local leaders and members dispersed. Although for several months KAMMI could not hold formal meetings, the situation did not entirely paralyze the organization. Some members continued to be involved, and some leaders, in exile from their villages, found ways to return from time to time, or otherwise to stay in tune with local events. Despite harassment, a few local chapters persisted, such as that in Magsaysay.

On March 8, 1988, on Women's International Day, peasant women leaders, who had found ways to mobilize dispersed members, formally revived KAMMI. In San Jose they held an ad hoc consultation of local leaders and members of the previous chapters that could still be contacted. They held a community Mass (*Misang Bayan*), using rice as an offering for their prayers. Usually, the host is made of imported wheat, but in this ritual, the women chose to use rice because it symbolizes their work, their needs, their everyday lives. The women and the priest said a thanksgiving prayer for the rebirth of the women ("pasalamat dahil nabuhay uli and kababaihan").

During the consultation, those present discussed how to revive and reorganize KAMMI. They decided it should be a peasant women's organization, independent from the KMP, mainly because after the 1987 military harassment, which was mainly directed at the KMP men who had assumed more visible leadership in the peasant movement, the KMP could not continue its public presence in Mindoro. The women of KAMMI saw that it was now their turn to take the lead and assume more public responsibility. This role was more assertive than the supportive and less visible place assigned to KAMMI when it was a joint organization with the KMP. Thus, the decision to be independent from the KMP was a strategic response to the political situation during which they were reorganizing and reviving KAMMI.[1]

The peasant women also decided to change their tactics. Now membership could be extended to all peasant women, not just to KMP members or their wives. Socio-economic cooperative projects would be made the focus of the organization, rather than public demonstrations, which openly and directly attack the government. Some leaders would be replaced, and new members recruited.

To set up a structure for the reorganization of KAMMI, the peasant women put together an ad hoc committee to lay the groundwork for a formal conference of former chapters in April 1988. This involved reviving the local chapters, first by personally visiting them. At the formal conference KAMMI elected its provincial leaders. Since then, the provincial leaders have visited the local chapters, organized a seminar on the provincial level, trained thirty-two provincial instructors, reorganized five village chapters, and set up two new chapters. They have also held monthly provincial meetings and consultations for the purpose of coordination, planning, and discussion of problems. At the time of my fieldwork, KAMMI had 201 active members on the provincial level.

Several factors enabled KAMMI to achieve a revival. One is the persistence of its leaders and their courage in continuing their work of organizing in the midst of militarization. Ate Ara, a brave and committed provincial leader, succinctly articulates this: "Inner strength, courage, even if there is militarization we persist in organizing. Like me, even if I was harassed, I did not give in to fear. Instead I faced up to them." Another factor is the political consciousness and social awareness of the peasant women. Their words often revealed their political consciousness and social concern: "matatag na prinsipyo" (strong principles) and "hindi makasarili" (not to be self-centered). This consciousness does not grow in a vacuum; it is fertilized and nourished in the process of organized resistance. Political consciousness dawns as one becomes more aware of why one is oppressed or poor. Once consciousness is attained, it fuels action, leading to deeper consciousness, which stimulates further action. The expression of this consciousness may be uneven but is none-theless always articulated. In fact, most of the leaders of KAMMI were politically involved even before they took part in organizing KAMMI. For example, Ate Delita was a member of the Federation of Free Farmers that emerged during the Marcos regime. Ate Morina, along with her husband, had been politically involved in the 1950s in the HUK movement, which was crushed by the counterinsurgency strategy of the U.S. CIA's Edward Lansdale under President Ramon Magsaysay.

KAMMI's strategy of organizing involved: (a) tapping kinship relations and existing community and church networks, (b) identifying the political affiliation of potential recruits, (c) identifying the leadership capacities and abilities of new recruits, (d) starting with a concrete project responding to women's needs to initially bring women together, and (e) organizing from both "bottom to top" and "top to bottom."

In Philippine villages, kinship—by blood or by marriage—is one of the most common ways in which people are connected to one another. In most cases, the beginning point of formal organizational relationships in KAMMI is kinship. Sometimes political organization begins with pre-existing friendships. At other times, it begins with peasant women's contacts through church work. Tapping kinship, friendships, and church networks allows KAMMI organizers to apply the strategy of what I call *chain mobilization,* wherein leaders encourage the people they invite to come to KAMMI's meeting to bring other women they already know and trust.

Since KAMMI is a mass organization, however, it must go beyond kinship. And because of the presence of informers in the village, it must also look into the political affiliation or views of potential members. One of the criteria they have for recruiting a member is trustworthiness (*pagka-katiwalaan*). They also assess her "convictions" (*may paninindigan*), and, whether she has the willingness to participate in collective action to change existing situations.

Some of the organizers find it useful to recruit new members who they believe have potential for leadership, since such women are more willing to initiate action. Others find it easier to begin organizing local chapters when their initial members have had previous experience in being part of an organization.

To bring peasant women together and sustain their interest, KAMMI organizers find it helpful to start with a concrete project that may respond to the local needs of the members. They have learned from past experience that people get tired of simply demonstrating in the streets.[2]

Organizing from "bottom to top" and "top to bottom" means that KAMMI's beginning point is the village. Local village chapters of at least fifteen to twenty members must first be organized before they can be federated on the provincial level. Provincial leaders facilitate the organization of local chapters in their respective areas by setting up ad hoc steering committees. These committees are composed of village women who are willing to take on the responsibility of organizing their own chapters. Peasant women with leadership positions on the provincial level cannot be elected as leaders of local village chapters. This policy promotes village leadership, an important factor in sustaining the life of the local chapters.

KAMMI's overall strategic goal is to empower peasant women in relation to their work (as peasants), to men (as women), and to the state (as citizens). With regard to work, KAMMI supports the struggle for peasant women's economic right to: (a) a decent and dignified livelihood, (b) ownership of the land they till, and (c) full benefits from and recognition of their significant role in production. With regard to men, KAMMI supports peasant women's struggle against patriarchal relations and promotes equality between men and women. With regard to the state, KAMMI supports peasant women's active participation in national politics and the struggle for demilitarization and democratization. The road to reach these goals is organization. Thus these peasant women say:

I thought that it is necessary for us peasant women to have an organization, because it is of much help. You are made aware of the situation of women, that it is not just the men who must decide, that women also have rights. That we are not just for the home, that we also have rights. It is hard when you are just limited to the home. In land reform, women also have a right to the title to the land. They also have a right to have their name on the title to the land. (Ate Jo, local village organizer)

It is the goal of the organization to have unity for the progress of the people, and to improve the situation of the women. (Ate Sarisa, new organizer)

Put women's rights equal to that of men. It is our aspiration to have our own lands we can till. This is the essence. If there is organization we will have a voice and strength. (Ate Lorena, provincial leader and organizer)

Resistance Against Landlessness

Everyday Discourse on the Structure of Land Ownership in Mindoro

Terence Ranger (1989) says that discourse is also a medium by which peasant consciousness expresses itself. It is therefore an important aspect of their politics. Peasant women and men use terms in their everyday language that refer to hierarchy and class position in relation to land ownership in Mindoro. These terms include *panginoong may-lupa, panggitnang magsasaka, mahirap na magsasaka, magsasakang walang lupa, manggagawang bukid, katulong, nagpapaupahan,* and *nagkakaigin.*

The *panginoong may-lupa* is on top of the class pyramid because of the structure of land ownership. He owns large tracts but does not till the land himself. He hires other people to manage his land, and these administrators in turn hire agricultural workers or supervise tenants. He may also have other sources of income and wealth, such as business investments. In addition to economic power, he has political power, which is sometimes wielded—through the use of the military—to suppress peasant demands or initiatives for reform. Sometimes he may hold political office. Intrigued by the term *panginoon*, which means "god," I asked Ate Ara why it was often used to refer to big landlords, since they are not gods, and such a term should be used only for God (*Diyos*). She replied, "It does not mean we consider them our God, it means they are powerful." The peasant women often referred to the governor of Mindoro as a panginoong may-lupa. Some panginoong may-lupa are absentee landlords, which means they do not live in Mindoro. Ate Norita speaks of an absentee panginoong may-lupa who uses the military to protect his family and their lands: "A businessman in Manila, he has huge rice lands. He is now abroad, visits here only occasionally. It is the Philippine Constabulary [PC] who visit and guard the work of the tenants. They are the ones who carry out the orders of the panginoong may-lupa. The guards at his home are PC, they are paid by him."

The term *panggitnang magsasaka* refers to middle-level landowners who are better off than average landowners. They own more than the usual amount of land, which they may not necessarily till. If the land is used, it is made productive by tenants or agricultural wage workers. The panggitnang magsasaka may have some capital for production costs, and may have access to formal credit, such as bank loans, because they can use their land as collateral. Sometimes they hire seasonal agricultural workers or have tenants work on their lands. They do not necessarily hold political office, but if they do, it is usually a local government position. Because they do not work on the land, they may engage in other forms of economic activity, such as trading or marketing rice, lending money in the local informal credit system, or even managing a grocery store. Some of the peasant women refer to their landlords as panggitnang magsasaka.

Next to the panggitnang magsasaka in the feudal hierarchy is the *mahirap na magsasaka*. The peasant women use this term to refer to the poor, small owner-tiller who usually owns only a small piece of land, less than one or two hectares. Although this group may not have landlords with whom they must share their produce, the returns from their harvest are for several reasons usually inadequate to meet their basic needs: (a) the amount of land they farm cannot yield enough produce, (b) the costs of production are too high because they must borrow at usurious interest rates, (c) they cannot produce a second crop due to lack of irrigation, and (d) there is no government subsidy for small producers.

The largest class of peasants are the landless, who are at the bottom of the feudal pyramid. This class comprises the *magsasakang walang lupa*, the *manggagawang bukid*, and the *katulong*, who are all poor. The *magsasakang walang lupa* work as tenants on the land of big landlords (panginoong may-lupa) and middle-level landlords (pangitnang magsasaka). Although they can generally expect regular farm work because they have land to till, even if they do not own it, they are mainly responsible for making the land productive. Under the existing landlord-tenant system of sharecropping, they are at a disadvantage since they give large portions of their harvest to the landlords, even if they shoulder all the costs of production and provide the labor. The peasant women categorized the sharecropping system in Mindoro as either *buwisan* or *partihan*. In the *buwisan* system, the tenants shoulder all the costs of production and give the landlord twelve to fifteen cavans of palay per hectare of land they farm, even if they lose the harvest due to natural calamities. In the *partihan* system, the arrangement varies. Most commonly, the tenants are expected to shoulder all the production expenses and give 25 to 30 percent of their harvest to the landlords. Less frequently, the landlord and the tenant share equally the costs of production and the harvests, with the tenants providing all the labor. According to Ate Lorena, neither the buwisan system nor the partihan system is strictly legal: "According to the law, if the farm is irrigated, only 15 percent of the harvest should go to the landlord; if it is not irrigated, just 10 percent, and if the harvest is not good, 5 percent."

The *manggagawang bukid* are landless agricultural workers who work on landlords' land and are paid daily wages or, in the "*pakyaw* system," a fixed amount for a particular task regardless of the number of days required to complete it. The manggagawang bukid—probably the most numerous of the landless groups—are worse off than tenants because they usually experience both job insecurity and a substandard wage. The *katulong* seems to be at the bottom of the feudal class hierarchy, and are perhaps even worse off than the manggagawang bukid. Katulongs usually offer to help a tenant working for a landlord; they do not receive a daily wage, but instead are offered a portion of the tenant's share of the harvest. While the landlord benefits from the labor of the katulong, he does not remunerate him in any way.

The peasant women refer to themselves as *nagpapapaupahan* when they work for a wage on other landlord's lands, after they work on their landlords' farm or their own tiny piece of land. They perform such labor in order to earn additional income or immediate cash for their daily needs.

There is also a small group of landless peasants who, in their desperate need for land to till, resort to clearing a tiny portion of woods, to which they have no title; they are the nagkakaingin. Their harvest is inadequate for subsistence, since their holdings, usually in the upland, are small and unirrigated.

That the peasant women have developed a language for the structure of land ownership in Mindoro and its consequent classes shows that political perspective and people's lives are joined (Scott 1985). It also shows that native people have their own discourse about hierarchy and class relations.[3] Their views and conceptualizations indicate that ordinary people can theorize. Their discourse influences the articulation of their organizational goals and their actions to correct inequality.

Land Occupation: A Grassroots-Initiated Land Reform

Peasant women and men resist landlessness not only in their discourse but also in their actions. Owing to the government's failure to implement true and effective agrarian reform, the KMP and KAMMI have promoted a radical and indigenous alternative in order to implement land redistribution to peasants in Mindoro: land occupation, which is the process of collectively occupying idle lands (*lupang tiwangwang*) and making them productive. These idle lands are usually owned by absentee landlords or corporations. After land occupation was first tried in Mindoro in 1984, the strategy has been tried in other regions of the Philippines, such as Laguna and Negros.[4]

The land occupation in Mindoro, originally led by the KMP and now being initiated by KAMMI, is actually a radical attempt to make land immediately accessible to landless tillers.[5] An indigenous way of implementing land redistribution, it has been met with violent resistance from those in power.

The History of Land Occupation in Mindoro

Sablayan.

The first land occupation in Mindoro took place in Sablayan in 1984, when a KMP chapter was organized there. Philippine Long Distance Company (PLDT) has large tracts of land, a huge portion of which were idle. The Sablayan chapter of the KMP occupied about 150 hectares of this land, which they entered collectively and simultaneously. This is the peasants' usual modus operandi, apparently because it is a way to build organized power.

The peasants made the land productive and were able to benefit from the first harvest. This benefit did not last long, however, since the military harassed the occupiers. Some of them surrendered, some sold their land, and still others went back to forest land (*gubat*). There were peasants who persisted in remaining in the occupied area, however. Ate Ara attributes their perseverance to their having strong principles (*matatag na prinsipyo*). The example of those who remained in this first land occupation apparently paved the way for the land occupations that followed.

AQUAFIL.

Aqua Culture Filipinas (AQUAFIL) is a 1,822-hectare corporate farm in San Jose, Mindoro, devoted to the production of salt and the raising of prawns for export to Japan. It is owned by a crony of former president Ferdinand Marcos. An absentee landlord, he is from another province, Cagayan, in the northern Philippines. He has a business partner in San Jose, from the Ortigas family.

For more than fifteen years, AQUAFIL used less than twenty hectares of its land for prawn and salt production, leaving a good portion of it idle. The original members of the KMP thought of making the land productive, and so sent a petition to President Corazon Aquino, asking her to grant them the land. At that time Aquino had called for lands acquired through deception during the Marcos administration to be given to the peasants. When the KMP received no response from Aquino, they decided to proceed with land occupation.

On May 21, 1986, at two in the afternoon, five hundred peasants together marched to and entered AQUAFIL. They were blocked by security guards, along with some reinforcements from the Philippine Constabulary. The guards directed one gunshot upward, but the peasants did not retreat. Instead, they all ran into the farm. When they were inside, the manager of AQUAFIL came, and the peasants negotiated with him to be allowed to make the land productive.

Fearlessly, five hundred peasant families occupied the land. At first it was only the men who settled the area, building *kubo-kubo* (makeshift huts) for shelter. After about a month their families came, bringing with them their farm animals.

The peasants worked hard to plow the land, which had hardened after many years of disuse. It was not enough simply to use the carabao to prepare the land for planting, so they tried using tractors. By September, they were able to plant rice.

Various nonpeasant sectors supported the land occupation. Nuns, professionals (mostly teachers), and employees of such some government agencies as the Department of Social Welfare contributed funds to the peasants. After five months the land yielded its first harvest.

But there was a counterattack from the military. Jeepney drivers and operators were told that they must not give rides to the members of the KMP or to the *petisyoneros* (petitioners), the five hundred peasant families who petitioned President Aquino for the AQUAFIL land. In the evening they and the security guards strafed the land. The company paid the commanding military officer to harass the farmers, and its management filed a case in court accusing the peasants of trespassing and "malicious mischief." Some occupiers were imprisoned. One of these was very old, and another was a deaf mute.

But the peasants persisted in producing on the land. They were able to make use of a local farm fish, called *hito*, that they could catch around AQUAFIL. If they caught small *hito*, they would raise them until they were big enough to sell. If they caught big ones, they would immediately sell them in the market, walking fifteen kilometers just to do so. When they were able to sell their fish, they would go back to the occupied land, already bringing home food for their families.

During the next season, the peasants again planted rice. But the AQUAFIL management sabotaged the farms by constructing a canal and pumping salt water into the rice fields, which killed the sprouts. Those fields that were not ruined by salt water, were burned. The military extrajudicially executed one KMP leader and some *petisyoneros*. They also forcibly dismantled peasants' huts, cut their posts to the ground, and threw away their household belongings. One peasant woman had a miscarriage.

This harassment and counterattack began to take its toll and eventually became too difficult to bear. The *petisyoneros* were forced to surrender. Gradually, one by one, they left the once-idle land that they had so earnestly made productive. Once again it was the military that was the major factor in aborting the life that the peasants had begun to nurture in the occupied land. While AQUAFIL had access to the repressive military, the peasants had neither arms nor legal support from the government in their radical attempt both to transform the structure of land ownership in Mindoro and to alleviate poverty and hunger among the landless peasants.

Rizal.

In 1987, the local chapter of the KMP in Rizal occupied idle rice lands owned by a landlord who maintained headquarters for CAFGUs. About fifty tenants simultaneously entered his land. When they asked the landlord if they could farm it since it had been idle (*katiwangwang*), he insisted that the peasants pay tax by remitting to him 30 percent of their harvest. The peasants accepted these terms. The following year they asked that the tax be decreased to 25 percent. This time the landlord refused and began to harass the peasants using the CAFGUs at his disposal. The CAFGUs extralegally arrested some of the peasants and seized their belongings, their pigs and chickens. Now, having driven the peasants away, the CAFGUs are farming this land. They took and benefited from the harvest that the peasants planted. They also took the peasants' carabaos, claiming that it was the NPA who stole them. The triumph of the landlord in this case failed to end land occupation in Mindoro, however.

Magsaysay.

In 1987 in Magsaysay, the twenty-some members of a local KMP chapter occupied about eight hectares of unproductive land owned by an absentee landlord, cleaned it, and made it productive by planting rice. About four peasant families worked on an area that has a fishpond. The landowner sought to remove the occupiers by filing a case in court, but after two years the peasants won, and the Land Bank took custody of the land. This meant the peasants could stay and, beginning in 1989, pay the bank amortization for the land. The peasants' position is precarious, however. If they fail to pay the amortization, the land can be taken away from them, as stated in the Comprehensive Agrarian Reform Law (CARL). That is why the development ideology of the national KMP is "free land to the tiller," since in this way the burden of land reform can be taken from the poor landless peasants, who may not have enough income to pay amortization. By "free land to the tiller," the KMP means that the government must subsidize land reform and not burden the peasants, who have long been exploited. In other words, tilling the land is deemed sufficient payment for it. This perspective is based on the peasants' experience with past land reforms, which failed because poor peasants could not afford the amortization of their land.

Mamburao.

The land occupation in Mamburao, which also took place in 1987, is an indication that this form of action initiated by the KMP was gaining acceptance among landless tenants who were not members of that organization. An absentee landlord, perceived as despotic by KMP members, owned some thirty-four hectares of land. Originally there had been tenants, but he sent some of them away. An administrator managed the land for him, while he lived outside Mindoro and visited the area only occasionally. The tenants who had been sent away considered occupying the land but thought they did not have enough force to be successful. They thus approached the KMP for help, asking members to join them in their occupation, although they did not want the KMP's name to figure prominently in the campaign. Eventually these tenants became members of the KMP. That the peasants wanted their action to be perceived as a tenant occupation was a legal strategy, since under the law tenants have the right to eventual ownership of the land.

As a form of counterresistance, the landlord used his private army to imprison ten peasants and to burn their houses. He also brought the case to court. But the peasants found ways to assert their rights legally. Using as justification the provisions of the Comprehensive Agrarian Reform Law, they negotiated with the landlord for almost a year regarding their rights to the land. At the time of my fieldwork, the landlord had agreed to transfer ownership to the peasants. Some of the land had been measured, and there were apparently no further instances of counterresistance.

Calintaan: Confronting the Power of the Governor.

A former government official of Mindoro is a panginoong may-lupa who owns large tracts of rice land in Calintaan and elsewhere. Ate Feliza calls him a "despotic landlord." In asserting their right to land ownership, the official's tenants used the strategy of "persistent negotiation" (*panay na pakikipagnegosasyon*). The peasants held a meeting (*talakayan*) with him just before the election, since this is usually a time when political candidates are generous. In this meeting the official promised the tenants eventual ownership of the land they till (which is in fact required by CARL). After the election, however, the tenants claimed that upon knowing that he lost in that particular area, the official drove them away from his land. His private army, composed of CAFGUs and ordinary civilians, harassed the peasants. So to this day, the official has not yet transferred ownership to the tenants. In fact, by sending them away, he has circumvented CARL. The CAFGUs, whom he told to harass his tenants, are now allowed to farm his lands. According to Ate Feliza, more than fifty peasants would benefit if the official carried out his promises to them, but the prospects of his doing so are dim. Having both political and economic power, the official was able to control not only the critical resource of land but also the military machinery to resist change in the structure of land ownership in Mindoro, from which he benefits. Having political power, he was also able to circumvent the land reform law, which is already biased in favor of the landed classes with its provision of making implementation voluntary on the part of the landlords.

In the midst of the stringent power relations in which the peasants live, land occupation becomes a radical, although risky, alternative to landlessness and the poverty that results from it. Organized land occupation becomes the peasants' weapon against the use of military force by land-lords, who themselves are resisting the demands of peasants for land reform. Such occupation, in the last analysis, is a form of political class struggle between the landless peasants and the wealthy landlords. It is an organized articulation of the slogans "land to the tiller" and "uphold genuine land reform" ("Itaguyod ang tunay na reforma sa lupa"). Although illegal under the government's Comprehensive Agrarian Reform Law (CARL), land occupation is a strategy of agrarian reform that originates from below. It is an assertion of the poor peasants' demand to have a voice in development policies affecting them. And it indicates that ordinary people have the political will to change the power relations that subordinate them, independent from the official and legal routes through which change can be sought. This supports the findings of Benedict Kerkvliet (1990) and James Scott (1985) that subordinated people do not always accept the dominant classes' claims and definition of social reality, even in the absence of open violent resistance.

KAMMI's Initiative on Land Occupation

Despite the harassment the KMP experienced in 1987, KAMMI recently took the initiative on land occupation as a step toward achieving true agrarian reform in Mindoro. At the time of my fieldwork in Mindoro (summer 1989), Ate Ara, Ate Lorena, and Cristina had mentioned to me a plan for land occupation in Mamburao. Later that year two land occupations did take place in that area, and KAMMI played a significant role in them. They occurred at Odlen Country Farms, Inc. (OCFI) in September 1989, and on a large piece of idle land in Mamburao on October 20, 1989.[6]

OCFI.

The OCFI land occupation was a grassroots attempt to redistribute wealth amassed through government corruption during the Marcos regime. Illegally acquired from the original owner, a brother of former first lady Imelda Marcos, the approximately five hundred hectares of OCFI are used to produce rice, mangos, poultry, and fish. When Corazon Aquino was elected president, the Presidential Commission on Good Government confiscated the land as "ill-gotten wealth." Despite the Comprehensive Agrarian Reform Law, however, the government planned to sell the land to private individuals instead of redistributing it to landless peasants. Charging the Aquino government with inconsistency, KAMMI, working with KAMIPCI (Kanlurang Mindoro Peasants' Cooperative, Inc.), occupied OCFI. They mobilized a group of 103 peasants, 15 of whom were KAMMI members, to occupy the rice lands (*palayan*), mango plantation (*manggahan*), and poultry farm (*manukan*). Making the *manggahan* communal, they parceled out the rest to the members. Some 20 peasants have been able to work on the *manggahan*, 15 of whom are women. They have let the mango trees bear fruit and have earned 11,600 pesos from their first harvest. They decided not to continue raising poultry, since there were no more chicks, but instead cultivated the land. They also cleaned the fishery (*palaisdaan*), which had been unproductive for many years. Not all the land of OCFI was occupied by KAMIPCI and KAMMI; some of the area, which was rice land, had already been occupied by the FFF (Federation of Free Farmers) since 1986. The FFF is a nongovernmental organization of peasants, which, like the KMP, demands genuine agrarian reform and the redistribution of land to the tillers. The OCFI land occupation thus brought together different peasant organizations in Mindoro. Implicit in this action is the belief that peasants who are tillers, regardless of their organizational affiliation, have a basic right to have access to land. This is in fact a resistance against the concentration of land and its wealth among nontillers.

The presence of the military in the area limited the peasants' claim to the land, however. Some soldiers grabbed from the peasants about 9 hectares of the mango plantation, containing approximately 400 mango trees of the 1,800 trees that KAMIPCI and KAMMI had been able to control. They came to the area twice and tried to force the occupiers to leave, destroying at least one peasant's hut. But the peasants, particularly the women, resisted by not leaving the land.

The OCFI occupation has apparently been successful. The Presidential Agrarian Reform Commission (PARCOM) issued an order to OCFI, giving protection to the peasants who have occupied the land beginning in September 1989. Although this makes the presence of the military in OCFI illegal, the soldiers have retained the land they seized. Their continued presence in the occupied area makes the position of the peasants precarious. This illustrates the point that economic agrarian reforms through legislation cannot be isolated from demilitarization of the countryside. Economic and political democratization are inseparable.

Mamburao.

In one village in Mamburao, there are many large tracts of land that are idle and unproductive. For example, five families claim to own about a thousand hectares of unproductive land. The members of KAMMI who occupied this land believed that the families' ownership of the land had no legal basis, since their claim had no written documentation. It came out that these areas were forest land and government-owned.

Twenty-five women from the local chapter of KAMMI in Sablayan and twelve from that in Mamburao took the initiative and joined forces to occupy 110 hectares of this land. They also allowed eighteen members of the youth sector of the peasant movement (*kabataan*) to join them. In a short time they were able to clear six hectares, three of which they have made into a communal farm. On less than half of the communal farm they have been able to plant corn. The petisyoneros (as those who occupy the land call themselves) drew up bylaws in which they stated that each of the fifty-five members was entitled to two hectares of the occupied land. This indicates their sense of equity in the access to land; it is a concretization of their concept of true agrarian reform.

The Mamburao occupation, although not met with harassment from the military, was not entirely spared from problems. The petisyoneros lacked sufficient production capital to fully utilize the land, which meant they had to stop farm work in order to look for other sources of income. They did, however, plan to recommence their collective work on the occupied land on February 25, 1990. This problem provides a rationale for AMIHAN's concept that genuine agrarian reforms must consist not simply of land redistribution but also of such issues as government subsidy for food production and peasant women's organization for self-reliance.

KAMMI initiated its own land occupation not only because it had become distinct and separate from the KMP, but also because it saw land occupation as relevant to its ultimate goal of "equality of women in genuine land reform" ("pantay na karapatan ng kababaihan sa tunay na reforma sa lupa"). KAMMI's occupation was a rational act, arising from its own definition of who has the basic right to ownership and control of land as a critical means of agricultural production. That the members are women does not prevent them from initiating a type of action that previously was largely led by the KMP. From their perspective, they too have a claim to leadership in the peasant movement; they cannot be simply dependent on men. Ate Ara eloquently articulates this: "Now that the men are not able to lead in land occupation because of harassment, we, the women, will now be the ones at the forefront of the struggle."

In its provincial convention on March 6–8, 1990, KAMMI collectively resolved to intensify the land occupation in Mamburao as a peasant women's initiative toward achieving agrarian reform.[7]

Santa Cruz.

The land occupation in Santa Cruz, which a local chapter of KAMMI began in November 1993, shows the persistence of the peasant women in exercising their right to have land to till.[8] When I revisited Mindoro in 1996, I was impressed by the determination and courage of the women I talked to, who are engaged in this effort. One of them, Ate Tapang, who was about eighty years old, said,

I will never leave this land! It will be on this land where I will die! We have already suffered a lot from this landlord! Where will we go? We have no place to go! We have worked and lived on this land for sixteen years. This landlord had driven us and made us move many times. He even lets his cows loose, and they eat our crops. I would have harvested corn and vegetables if his cows had not eaten them. He had this whole land fenced with wire. How could we go out? Naturally we had to create an entrance so we could come and go into our houses.

The landlord that Ate Tapang refers to is a local politician who owns almost the whole of the municipality of Santa Cruz. In November 1993, when he started to drive individual tenants away, the women mobilized others to occupy some of his land. They were able to get good support from three chapters of KAMMI. In response, the panginoong may-lupa called on the military. He got people to ravage the crops (mango and corn) with tractors. The women assembled a huge crowd and frightened away the men driving the tractors. But the landlord had the land planted with grass and used it to graze cattle. The women made arrangements to negotiate with the landlord, and they agreed that neither the landlord nor the peasants would work the land. The landlord then went to the Department of Agrarian Reform (DAR) and demanded that those who had occupied his land be removed. The women objected to leaving without a guaranteed place for them to move to. The Department of Agrarian Reform took the side of the peasant women. Dissatisfied with the decision, the landlord brought the case to court in an effort to criminalize the women's political struggle for land, accusing them of illegal entry, stealing, and destruction of wire fences.

On March 22, 1995, the women organized a rally, supported by the men and other people in the community. They met with local government officials and submitted a petition protesting the landlord's cows grazing on their crops. They also demanded that the land, consisting of 307 hectares, be covered by the Comprehensive Agrarian Reform Program (CARP) and that the peasant women be made the beneficiaries. The women gave copies of their demand to the President, the secretary of the DAR, and other relevant government agencies and local officials.

The DAR secretary responded positively to the demands of the women and placed the land under the coverage of CARP. Evidently he failed to inform the director of the DAR, however, so in the end, the DAR decided against the peasant women by approving the landlord's application to convert the land for pasture lease. The women submitted an appeal to the DAR's director to invalidate (*ipawalang bisa*) the approval. Apparently the landlord is converting the land for raising cattle, which is considered a high-value export product under Philippines 2000. Here we see how land-use conversion, rapidly effected by Philippines 2000, undermines peasant women's struggle for land.

The women plan to continue working to have the 307 hectares placed under CARP. They found a loophole that they think might work to their advantage: the land is titled to someone who is deceased.

As landlords continue to defy or circumvent agrarian reform laws, the peasants' need for land becomes more critical. Land occupation, legal or not, becomes the only way for landless peasant women and their families to gain access to land. Given the number of hungry people in the Philippines, their action to make idle lands productive is an expression of social responsibility. Yet the exercise of such political virtue is penalized when government agencies take the side of the landlord. Their struggle becomes more arduous when military and paramilitary forces protect the landlords' interests.

Resistance Against the Exploitation of Farm Labor

Indigenous Collective Forms of Work

In Mindoro, there exists a local practice in which some farm work is done collectively. One form is called *suyuan*. Suyuan is the practice among peasants of pooling their labor for efficiency. It is done this way: Peasants who have lands to till, usually as tenants, work together on one plot, which is under the care of one member of the suyuan. Since many do the work, they finish whatever they need to do in a shorter time. Then they work on the plot of another member in the suyuan. They follow this pattern until every member has his or her work finished.

Unfortunately, concentration of land and the dynamics of inequality shift the impact of older forms of labor and gives an advantage to the wealthy. Ate Ara's stance on suyuan makes this clear: "Suyuan appears to be good, but it is possible for it to be exploited by others. Some join the organization because of the suyuan. Others have bigger plots to work on, some have one hectare, others may have three to five hectares. The one with only one hectare to work on is shortchanged [*lugi*]."

The capitalist exploitative norms of labor, which interlock into existing feudal relations of production, also provide a context for some landlords to exploit suyuan to their advantage by not hiring agricultural wage workers, even if the labor being performed requires more workers. The experience of Mely, a twenty-year-old peasant woman who is involved in suyuan in Calintaan, is one example. She said that the landlord of the land that they were working on that day refused to hire many of the sixty agricultural workers who asked for work (*gusto magpaupahan*) because he preferred to make use of the suyuan. While tenants generally find suyuan to be efficient, landlords can exploit this system if they have a bigger plot than most and refuse to hire wage agricultural workers, instead depending on the suyuan to provide the needed extra labor.

To avoid the exploitation of the *suyuan* for the advantage of a few, since the system is intended to benefit equally the tenants who are involved in it, the local chapter of KAMMI in Sablayan collectively discussed the problem and resolved to regulate their organization of suyuan in such a way that it will protect the interests of the peasants. The members set up rules for their suyuan and incorporated them in the constitution of their local chapter. Ate Ara explains: "We controlled suyuan. We have set up that only one hectare should be included in the suyuan. What is beyond one hectare should be done by hired labor [*paupahan*]. This way we do not take away jobs for the landless agricultural workers [*mga walang lupang masakahan*]. That is why we put this in our constitution."

While Ate Ara, who is a provincial leader, has a critical stance on the suyuan, which has resulted in the Sablayan local chapter safeguarding the system against possible exploitation by landlords, Mely, being a very new member in the local chapter of Calintaan, has not developed a critical view of suyuan. In fact, the other peasants with whom she works in the suyuan are not yet members of the Calintaan local chapter. This is a problem that KAMMI has yet to address. How can a local chapter, as well as the provincial and national federations encourage new members to articulate their experience with agrarian relations and make it a context of collective consciousness-raising and organized resistance? At the National Council Meeting of AMIHAN in July 1989, it was pointed out that the focus and ultimate goal of the peasant women's organization is agrarian reform. We must then ask, what details in the experience of peasant women must be articulated and brought to awareness in concretizing this goal?

The stance of KAMMI's Sablayan chapter on suyuan indicates that as peasant women become more politically organized, their critical consciousness and their capacity to safeguard collectively their class interests increase. This is their weapon against those who benefit from the existing relations of production. The landlords' exploitation of existing indigenous forms of collective work fragments the peasants' potential power as a class. The members of KAMMI's local chapter in Sablayan saw the subtle politics of this exploitation and fragmentation, and they responded collectively. Other local chapters, on the other hand, still need to be made politically aware of this problem in order to be able to confront it directly and collectively.

The practice of suyuan and the peasants' attempt to protect it from exploitation also indicate resistance to capitalist penetration of indigenous forms of collective work that serve as the basis of collective class consciousness. Hence it is clear that there is a local native articulation of work relations that resists capitalist hegemony. This limits the explanatory power of the Eurocentric classical Marxist tradition, which says that to move to socialism, capitalism in the Third World must first reach its highest stage, in which extreme contradictions will create a context that is ripe for socialist transformation. Colonialism, the harbinger of capitalism, is considered a "necessary evil" (Blomstrom and Hettne 1984, 10). This idea, based on a linear concept of development, fails to account for the complex matrix of peasant experience in the Philippines, and particularly that of peasant women. It fails to recognize local forms of communalism that withstood the penetration of colonialism and capitalism, which can be harnessed more fully in the struggle for communal social justice in the neocolonial period. The existence of suyuan indicates that there are indigenous forms of work relations in the peasant political economy that can become the basis for class struggle, a definition of resistance to underdevelopment, and the reconceptualization of women in development from the perspective of Third World peasant women.

Initiative to Participate in Determining Agricultural Wages

Agricultural workers receive very low wages, insufficient to meet even basic daily needs, such as adequate food. Ate Glin of Magsaysay, who gets paid thirty pesos a day for doing agricultural work, says, "What I earn is not even enough for one kilo of food (*ulam*). One kilo of milk fish [*bangus*] is 35 pesos, *sap-sap* is fifteen pesos a kilo, *galunggong* is twenty pesos a kilo. Meat is forty-five pesos a kilo." I observed when I returned to Mindoro in 1996 that the prices of these goods had gone up even further. So one can imagine the gap between poor people's income and what is needed to put food on the table.

Agricultural wages are low because peasants generally do not have a say in determining the price of their labor. Especially when they are unorganized, they have no bargaining power. And in the context of a large pool of landless peasants looking for work, they do not have much power in the wage market. Rural unemployment means that peasants will accept low wages if the alternative is no income at all, especially when they are seasonal workers, as most of them are.

Keeping agricultural wages low is also a way to maintain the existing concentration of land among a few landlords. While the large number of landless agricultural workers is a result of the existing structure of land ownership, keeping this mass of low-paid agricultural workers is a way to maintain such a structure. And this is how the dual mode of feudal-capitalist relations of production in the Philippine political economy is reproduced at the village level.

Another form of collective action that KAMMI attempts to organize when the members are ready for it is demanding an increase in the agricultural wage. For example, one local chapter in Sablayan, comprising mostly peasant women who are agricultural workers, began a campaign (*campanya*) to increase the agricultural wage rate in Sablayan. Ate Ara explained: "We did a campaign to increase the wages of peasants. In the *barangay* formal meeting we presented a demand that the wage for peasant women and men should be raised from 25 pesos to 30 pesos a day. In the case of *pakyawan*, where twenty people work together, we asked that it be raised from 650 pesos for the entire contracted work to 35 pesos a day [per worker]. We based our negotiation on the fact that the price of one *ganta* [a dry measure equivalent to about 3 liters] of rice is already 18 pesos."

When a local chapter of KAMMI initiates a demand for an increase in agricultural wages and succeeds, there is what I call a trickle effect: the benefit trickles down even to those who are not members of the organization. This was the experience of a local chapter in Mamburao. Most of the members work as agricultural wage workers (*nagpapaupahan*) when they are not working on their landlords' land as tenants. They were paid only twenty pesos a day. Ate Norita, a local leader of this chapter, explains:

In July 1989 about 20 members of the local chapter met and arrived at a collective decision to demand an increase in agricultural wages. They decided that each of them should charge thirty pesos a day with meals to those rich landlords who do not till the land [*hindi nagbubunkal ng bukid*]. The meals should include lunch [*tanghalian*], and snacks [*merienda*] at ten o'clock and three o'clock. When landlords who hire them for the work asked how much they would charge, they all said the same thing. Other women who are not members of the organization began charging thirty pesos when they learned that the wage rate [*ang upa*] is already thirty pesos. The women were happy.

The benefit also trickles down to the men. Ate Norita provides an example: "I suggested also to the men that they should increase their charge from fifty pesos a day to sixty pesos a day. They get paid fifty pesos a day for plowing and tilling the soil with all the implements being provided by them, like the carabao."

While demanding an increase in wages may not be as radical as occupying land, it is in fact a form of struggle toward having a say in determining the price of labor. While it does not directly confront the structure of land ownership in Mindoro, the demand for a wage increase does resist the exploitation of peasant labor by those who do not till the land. And while land occupation directly confronts the feudal economy, the demand for increased wages resists the capitalist penetration of Philippine agriculture. When seen in conjunction with the radical concept behind land occupation—"land to the tiller"—the demand for wage reform is a step toward transforming the feudal-capitalist economy from the bottom, and from the experience and perspective of the peasantry. When peasants demand a share in determining the price of their labor, they are in fact resisting the tendency of capitalist agriculture to make that labor a commodity. What is implied here is that a transformation of the Philippine political economy would involve changing both the feudal relations of production and the capitalist relations that exploit human labor. To share in the fruits of such a transformation, however, peasant women must take an active role in the process of change. This is what KAMMI is attempting to do.

Resistance Against the Green Revolution

Experiments with the Traditional Rice Hybrid

As discussed earlier, the Green Revolution brought capitalist imperialism close to the farming village and had an impact on the peasants' work. It increased the costs of rice production by replacing a traditional variety of rice with one dependent on expensive agrochemicals and less resistant to local pests and typhoons. Some of the women of KAMMI have sought alternatives to the Green Revolution in order to lessen its impact. For example, a few of the women I talked to, eight from the local chapter of Magsaysay and three from that in Calintaan, were experimenting with planting a rice variety that they say does not need a lot of fertilizers and pesticides to produce a good yield. This is in contrast to the foreign high yielding variety (HYV), which is also known as miracle rice. The women refer to this experimental variety as the *bagong binhi* (new seed) or the *traditional*; sometimes they call it *mataas na butil* (tall grain). According to a technician in the Mindoro Institute for Development, this variety was a result of an agricultural experiment at the University of the Philippines, Los Banos, to recover the displaced traditional rice variety. Since this variety had almost disappeared and very little of it could be found, they combined the local traditional variety with the foreign high yielding variety (HYV). It seems appropriate that some of the women call this variety "*traditional*" or "tall grain," since it looks like the pure traditional variety with which I am familiar. I have visited some of the women's fields sown with this variety; it does indeed look taller than the foreign miracle rice.

The women are interested in experimenting with this variety because, they say, they do not have to spend money on fertilizers. Thus they do not have to borrow as much from usurers, which lessens the debts they have to pay at harvest time.

The women acquired this experimental variety from the Mindoro Institute for Development, which in turn acquired it from the University of the Philippines in 1988. Since the supply of seeds was limited, the women who were interested in trying it used first one to three kilos for sowing in the fields. At harvest time they set aside twice that amount so that they could increase the number of seedlings in the next planting season, and more peasants could try the variety. They hope to repeat this pattern in every planting and harvesting season to give those who have been unable to try the variety an opportunity to do so.

The peasant women who were the first to use this variety gained technical expertise from their experience, which they shared with others. For example, Ate Lorena suggested to other women, especially those who were trying the variety for the first time, that they plant the grains with some distance in between so that the rice shoots could grow more freely. It would be wasteful to sow the grain randomly as they do with the miracle rice (HYV).

The peasant women's willingness to experiment is both a form of resistance against the impact of the Green Revolution and a constructive response to the search for ways in which to make agricultural development in the Philippines more suited to local conditions.

Harnessing Local Resources for Sustainable Agriculture

Most peasant women, as well as men, are unhappy about using pesticides and fertilizers in rice farming. Some call fertilizers "pests"; others say, "When a fertilizer is not suitable to the soil, it will destroy it."

Ate Lalay, one of the provincial leaders of KAMMI, does not use fertilizer or pesticides. To drive away farm pests, she uses a local resource. She extracts the sap from the leaves of a local shrub called *kakawati* and spreads it over the fields she acquired through kaingin. Sometimes she plants the shrub around her fields. She says the pests do not like the smell of the sap, so they keep away from her farm.[9]

Ate Lalay, like other members of KAMMI, also refrains from using fertilizers. I learned during my second visit to Mindoro that some chapters of KAMMI—such as the one in San Jose—have undergone training with the Mindoro Institute for Development on how to prepare organic fertilizers (*organikong pangpataba*). Now the women know how to make compost, and they use it in place of chemical fertilizers.

The peasant women's indigenous attempt to use local resources in lieu of chemicals is significant when seen within the context of not only the massive promotion of agrochemicals by transnational corporations but also the government's neglect to explore sustainable methods of food production. The women's alternatives show that there are local methods of food production that can be promoted, and local resources that can be harnessed, to revert dependency on health-threatening and ecologically damaging agrochemicals.

Resistance Against the Monopoly on Rice Marketing

In the previous chapter, I talked about the control of rice marketing in Mindoro, which is becoming increasingly concentrated among private traders, and its impact on peasant women's everyday lives. Local trader-usurers, from whom poor peasants borrow rice for daily consumption, usually lend rice of poor quality, which would not readily find a market among rich or better-off consumers. According to Ate Fel, "The ugly rice is what the traders lend out. That is why even if we also like to eat rice that is more delicious, we cannot. When we complain that the rice is reddish [poor quality], the rich will tell you, 'We are already lending rice to you, and still you complain.'"

To resist these power relations in the marketplace, KAMMI's local chapter in Calintaan attempted to claim some control over the sale of rice in the village. The women decided to set up a cooperative as their first collective project during the revival and reorganization phase of KAMMI. On June 27, 1989, after a three-day leadership training organized by this chapter, the women conferred with each other and decided to meet again on June 29 to discuss what project they would like to implement. Their newly elected president, Ate Beni, who was also a new member, notified the other members of the meeting, which fifteen to eighteen of them then attended. The group decided to organize a cooperative, which would buy and sell rice, and other goods as well.

To even begin their project, the women knew that they needed capital. They therefore wrote a letter (which they called a *resolusyon*) to the Mindoro Institute for Development, outlining the rationale for their request for starting capital: (a) they wished to be able to buy and sell rice in the village, since that is what they "need most" (*unang pangangailangan*), and (b) they wished to be able to start their consumer cooperative project to help themselves and their organization out of poverty. The women expressed their intent to make this initial project succeed so that they could expand their ability to buy and sell to include unmilled rice (*palay*). Palay is important for the peasant women because they need it as seed for sowing (*binhi*). Sometimes the women have to borrow palay for this purpose. Although they set some aside for the next season, when their share of the harvest is consumed long before next planting season, they must use the palay for subsistence.

This initial activity formalized a course of action that the women had already discussed informally before the June 29 meeting. For example, in my earlier conversations with them, Ate Gansa, Ate Beni, and Teka had mentioned that it is very difficult for them to find rice as well as other goods to buy in their village. Ate Beni said that the Capitan who has a store in their barrio would simply not sell rice, although he has sacks of it that he ships to a neighboring province that does not grow rice, Batangas, where he originally comes from. Teka mentioned that since transportation from Calintaan to the urban area of San Jose is very expensive, and even going to the market in the town costs them money, a cooperative in their village would be really useful. Ate Gansa likewise mentioned that sometimes they simply could not find rice to buy in the village when they need it. On another occasion, in the group sessions during the leadership training of this local chapter, the women informally brought out that they would like to start a cooperative where they could sell rice and other goods they usually need without having to travel to the town, thus saving transportation expenses. Moreover, they mentioned that "rice is a need of the poor" ("pangangailangan ng mga mahihirap") and that such a project would be "for the good of the organization" ("para sa kapakanan ng samahan"). The collective and class consciousness indicated by these remarks is noteworthy. It shows that the women's attempt to have some degree of control over the marketing of rice in the village is one that deviates from individualistic capitalist principles. Although they recognize the need for starting capital (*puhunan*), they do not view such capital as funds to be owned by an individual who then profits from them. Rather, they see it as common property to be used for the benefit of the members of the organization, to help them in their poverty and to respond to the needs of the poor in the community. Their view stands in contrast to the principles that private traders follow: to sell rice wherever and however they can to maximize their profits.[10]

This attempt of the local chapter in Calintaan to set up a consumer cooperative in order to have some control over the marketing of rice in their village was not a new idea within the peasant movement in Mindoro. Part of the program of the KMP in Mindoro was to set up cooperatives through which the peasants could establish alternative and collective modes of economic relations. An example was their attempt to set up a warehouse and rice mill in Magsaysay, which was aborted by the military. And some of the women who are now members of the local chapter of KAMMI in Calintaan had been part of local chapters of the KMP, whose plans for consumer rice cooperatives were defeated by the systematic military harassment in 1987. It is clear, therefore, that the peasantry in Mindoro, both men and women, persist in finding collective ways in which they can assert some control over what they produce. This broadens the concept of agrarian reform beyond the basic idea of "land to the tiller." Agrarian reform can radically alter the structure of land ownership, but it can also resist and transform other economic power relations, which exert concentrated and dominant control over the produce of the land.

Resistance to Usury

As mentioned in Chapter 3, usury is one aspect of the interlocking power structures in which peasants' lives are enmeshed. In the absence of government subsidy for farming, usurers become the peasants' source of production capital. Without laws to regulate it, usury has been largely under the control of landlords, traders, and other people in villages or rural areas who have money to lend.

Ate Loy, who at the time of my fieldwork was an elected national officer of AMIHAN, was once a peasant organizer in a village in Mindanao. She told me she used to denounce (*binuburgar*) usurers in their local church, which made them angry with her. Usurers, she said, were not following the will of God: "If we are going to base it in the Bible, practicing usury is not a help to your neighbor."

Ate Loy explained that she attempted to initiate with her former group in Mindanao a credit cooperative as a concrete alternative to usury. She submitted a proposal to the Women's Studies Resource Center in Manila, and her group was able to get some funding. The women pooled their resources during harvest time so that the organization could eventually have its own funds. Some members were able to borrow badly needed money. Vigilantes harassed their organization, however, and the women were frightened. Hence, despite the fact that funding was made available and they were already enjoying some success, they were unable to continue the venture.

In the case of KAMMI in Mindoro, there is a desire to develop a credit cooperative out of a consumer cooperative. This was expressed, for example, by some of the women in Calintaan, who thought that if they succeeded in forming their consumer cooperative they would have funds for a credit cooperative as well. But one constraint that the women experienced was the lack of a sufficient amount of money to begin with, and they see now that it will take some time before they can develop a credit cooperative.

Likewise, the village chapter of KAMMI in Magsaysay attempted to organize a credit cooperative as an alternative to usury, but they lacked the financial resources to maintain it. With no outside funding, they attempted to rely on savings alone. Given their poverty, however, the members could not in a short time gather the large amounts of money that they needed in order to circulate funds among the members, especially since production loans may require thousands of pesos. Relying simply on their meager resources was not sufficient. This implies that state intervention and external support are needed to make such alternatives succeed.

Although the Land Bank provides agricultural loans, only rich peasants have been able to make use of its resources, since it requires collateral for loans. Landlord-usurers are in a better position to make use of this formal bank credit, and in some instances they loan the money they receive from the bank through usury. I see this as an indigenous feudal articulation at the village level of what Rosa Luxemburg calls "finance capital" (Brewer 1980), which ties the Third World political economy to capital accumulation. And within the context of privatization of formal credit, which has few state or community controls, the formal financial market and the informal credit system of usury again intersect in feudal-capitalist economic relations.

Thus far the government has made no serious attempt to make peasants the main beneficiaries of agricultural development. Yet despite the everyday constraints of poverty and militarization, peasant women still envision credit cooperatives that they can call their own. While their actions do not directly pressure the government to rechannel its financial resources for their benefit, they do indicate the women's desire to empower themselves and to resist the capital accumulation that exploits them. Their actions also indicate the desire of the women to change a situation that subtly makes them party to their own exploitation: as one of the peasant women says, "If there are no poor willing to be exploited by the rich, the rich will have few means to create wealth."

Alternative Health Care

In the villages where the women live, there is inadequate professional health care. A health worker in Calintaan said she met an eighty-six-year-old woman who had never once seen a doctor. Generally there are no facilities to provide village people with emergency medical care. Where the village is remote and transportation is difficult, the people generally do not get the necessary immediate medical attention. The government has not paid much attention to this human and social need in the rural areas, especially in the barrios. The few public hospitals are located sometimes in towns but mostly in cities, and they are usually understaffed, lacking in modern facilities, and overcrowded. There are better-equipped private hospitals, but the poor cannot afford to pay for their expensive services. Although I saw military headquarters in the places I visited in Mindoro, I did not see any public clinics set up by the government, except in the town of Magsaysay where there was a family planning clinic. A signboard announced free vasectomies, and a poster said "Magplano ng Pamilya Para Masagana" ("Do family planning in order to progress").

Medicines in the Philippines are very expensive, since most of them are imported. Even nonprescription medicines are costly. The poor, whose incomes are inadequate even to buy enough food, are hardly able to buy the medicines they need to prevent common sickness, such as flu or diarrhea, from developing complications. Ate Lorena told me the story of a poor peasant (who asked to be a katulong on the farm they till) whose wife had died from flu within a few weeks of delivering a baby. Although the products of the transnational pharmaceutical industries find a good outlet in the Philippine market, they are beyond the reach of many among the poor class, especially in rural areas.

In response to this inadequacy of health care in the villages, KAMMI undertakes health training. The women learn how to prepare medicines, using local herbs and medicinal plants. Some of these plants can be found growing around the village, and women can plant them in their yards. The peasants refer to the preparation of herbal medicines as "pagluto ng gamot," which means literally "cooking of medicine."

One herbal medicine that the women have found effective is *makabuhay*, a medicinal plant that grows in the village. The women cook the leaves of this plant, from which they make an ointment that they preserve in small bottles, plastic containers, or wrappers. Applied externally, it cures itching. I have used makabuhay ointment myself, and it relieved the itchiness of insect bites. Some of those who provide the technical training in herbal medicine to the members of KAMMI say that they prefer to use makabuhay ointment because it does not leave a blemish on the skin as some strong medicines sold in drugstores do. Although the cure may take some time, they say, from their experience the results are better because makabuhay ointment does not have antibiotics that can weaken skin resistance to other diseases. I saw women use makabuhay ointment on the skin rashes of their babies and young children. Since the ointment is not strong, like some drugs, they say, it is safe to use it on tender skin. Especially in the villages, where minor skin diseases are common, this local resource has become very useful.

Another medicinal plant available in the village is what the women call *tsang gubat* (forest tea), which can be found growing in the woods and can also be planted around houses. Tsang gubat, according to the women, is good for curing diarrhea. I have tried it and found it effective. The women preserve the plant by drying its leaves and twigs, and then wrapping them in small quantities in plastic bags. These dried leaves and twigs are boiled in water to make hot tea. To cure diarrhea the tea is taken at least three times a day. Tsang gubat can also be used nonmedicinally as a beverage similar to herbal teas.

The women know of many medicinal plants that are available in their villages. When I revisited KAMMI, I learned that some members have started communal farming of herbal plants. Some Filipino doctors who are trained in Western medicine know nothing about these local herbal medicines. For example, when I mentioned them to a doctor who lives in San Jose, she said she was unfamiliar with such medicine. Although she lives in Mindoro, she has never been to the villages and so has little understanding of village life. The medicines she prescribes to her patients are of course Western made and expensive.

Although there are limitations to what herbal medicine can do, some of the women I talked to found their expertise in this area useful. One of them told me, "This herbal medicine, it really helps solve the problems of the mothers. Since we began cooking herbal medicine, we do not go to a doctor often anymore, since it is effective anyway."

In the context in which the Philippines becomes a market for medical products that are restricted in Western countries, such as the U.S., KAMMI's harnessing of local medicinal plants is in fact a form of resistance against dependency on Western medicine and medical technology. It is also a practical alternative to the government neglect to provide minimum medical services in the villages.

Yet, because of the political context in which this collective activity takes place, the women are constrained by the suspicion and labeling of the repressive government. The military is suspicious of any group of people holding meetings, even this health project. And rightly so, since the politicization of health is an important aspect of the peasants' situation. Ate Jo, of the local chapter of Magsaysay, says, "Like our cooking of medicine ("pagluto ng gamot"), they suspect that we might be supporting the New People's Army with it." Since one strategy of counterinsurgency in the Philippines is to paralyze the New People's Army by severing all civilian support, the military's suspicion of "cooking medicine" is a deliberate form of repression. For members of KAMMI, however, learning about herbal medicine and spreading their knowledge to as many people in the village as possible is a positive response to the people's immediate need for health care that is within their means.

In Calintaan, some of the members of the local chapter of KAMMI contributed significantly in setting up a Health Center in their village, in coordination with community workers who provide health education in Calintaan. Ate Gansa says: "If we are going to think about it, I was the one who really sweat in putting up that Center. I would walk, go to each of the people just to make sure we would be able to set up the Center."

The Center has become a place where the village people can gather to learn about and prepare herbal medicine, organize training sessions on dental care, or get medicines for routine ailments that do not require hospitalization. Some of the women who have already completed the health training course take turns in running the center, attending to the needs of whoever comes for help. All these activities provide an opportunity for the women to acquire skills and develop confidence.

Cooperative Income-Generating Projects

The common experience of inadequate income has also become a focus of KAMMI's organized action. The women seek collective income-generating projects in order to create additional income. Because they are the primary caretakers of their families, they will do everything they can to find ways to put food on the table. These women have never experienced the concept of a "family wage" for a husband or father. Their husbands' or fathers' incomes have never been adequate for their needs. So although the man is still generally considered the head of the Filipino family, peasant women, whether married or single, play a significant role in providing for the economic needs of their families, or at least in helping them to survive.

Some of the leaders of KAMMI are aware that by seeking to provide for this basic and immediate human need, they can begin to gather other peasant women into their organization. Some of the new members that I talked to confirmed this when they said that one reason they joined KAMMI was *pangkabuhayan*—to improve their livelihood. Such projects are also a strategy for organizing the women. Because it meets an immediate need, it is an effective initial activity to bring women together.

The members of one village chapter of KAMMI have organized a collective sewing project to earn money when they are not doing farm work. The women demonstrate their creativity and resourcefulness by using fabric remnants (*retasos*), which they can get cheaply from factories in urban areas, sometimes even Manila, to make half-slips, children's clothes, and blouses. I bought one of these when they were selling them at a provincial leadership training in San Jose. Although the women are very creative in making something useful out of these remnants, they are limited by their lack of sewing machines. Only one person could sew at a time on their single machine, so others did hemming and cutting. The project was looking for funding to buy additional sewing machines.

Through this sewing project the women come to relate to the market in a different way. They sold their product through personal contacts, a kind of informal trading that saved them money because they did not have to maintain a central store. This type of selling seems to be effective in a village or rural community where relationships are more personal than they are in a large metropolitan center. Sometimes the consumers of the women's products were members of KAMMI and their families, though of course not all the members could afford to buy them, since they themselves lacked money for food. The women therefore looked for buyers beyond their immediate contacts through the organization.

The women divide among themselves the earnings from the project, setting aside 10 percent for an organizational fund that they can draw upon for whatever purposes the group sees fit. The women thus help both themselves and their organization. And this is what makes KAMMI's income-generating projects more than just a survival strategy; they are transformative, because they not only meet immediate economic needs, but also serve the organization's political ends as well. Here, then, is a concretization of the idea that the personal is also political.

This local chapter was able to begin its sewing project because the women were able to get initial capital from the Women's Desk of the Mindoro Institute for Development. Nongovernmental organizations, staffed by professionals who can write grant proposals and secure funding for grassroots collective projects such as this, can become the partners of peasant women in many of their endeavors.

On the provincial level, KAMMI hopes to raise or acquire enough money to provide starting capital for local chapters' socioeconomic projects. They envision that such funds would be borrowed without interest and repaid under easy terms, so that as many local projects of as many local chapters as possible could be financed.

In Calintaan, another village chapter of KAMMI organized a collective, income-generating project to make dried and salted fish. The women would salt and dry the fish, wrap them in clear plastic, and sell them by the package. Again the women partly relied on informal marketing to sell their product. For example, at the end of July 1989, Ate Ara took approximately one hundred packages to Manila, where she sold them at the AMIHAN National Council conference. I myself can attest to how well the women prepared the fish. Everyone who tasted it said it was better than what they could buy in the public market.

Cooperative income-generating projects normally begin with training sessions, where peasants learn things they may find useful in managing their project successfully, such as simple accounting or relevant technical information. These training sessions are tailored to the particular project the women are planning.

Social Reproduction: From Women's Private Responsibility to Collective Concern

The peasant women perceive that there exists a sexual division of labor in the family, which relegates social reproduction primarily to themselves (see the discussion of Beneria in Chapter 1). Thus, child care is another issue that can become a target for collective action.

Some of KAMMI's local chapters have worked to set up day-care for their children. One good example is the day-care project that a village chapter in Sablayan organized in 1988. Ate Ara, who worked very hard in coordinating the project, said she contributed quite a lot of money "just to have the project going" ("para lang maipatuloy ang proyekto"). When they could afford it, other mothers also contributed money or materials for the building of the day-care center. The fathers helped in building it, by providing labor, for example.

When the day-care service began in 1988, the initial enrollment was about thirty-four children. The mothers assumed responsibility for providing a meal program for the children. The day-care teacher, who was also from the village, received a monthly allowance from the Mindoro Institute for Development, at the request of the local chapter.

But once again militarization sought to constrain KAMMI. According to Ate Ara, the military labeled the project a "day-care center of the New People's Army," warning the people not to go to the center. Because of this, many parents became apprehensive, and the enrollment decreased. Ten children were immediately removed, and another ten withdrew one by one. Only seven children remained in the program and were able to graduate.

Yet this local chapter persisted in pursuing the day-care project because it was responding to a local need in the village. Eventually the enrollment increased to fifty-five children. The felt need somehow enabled people to stand up to the fear caused by the military's psychological strategy of repression. With the increase in enrollment, the need for resources also increased. Even though the day-care teacher was getting an allowance, she spent most of it on materials for the children or for teaching. The mothers still shouldered the feeding of the children. Under these circumstances, it was decided to divide the day-care program into morning and afternoon sessions to accommodate the growing demand. In addition, a yearly fee of fifteen pesos was required. The village members of KAMMI requested the local government to provide a large table for the children, and it agreed to do so. It also agreed to their request to provide the day-care teacher with an allowance of 240 pesos a month. That the chapter was able to get the local civil government to respond to some of the needs of the center was a good strategy, for it provided legitimacy to the project and thus helped to counter the black propaganda of the military.

In June 1989, the fifty-five children graduated. The occasion provided the peasant women with an opportunity for cultural expression. The local chapter organized a graduation ceremony. They hired a sound system for 110 pesos, of which 90 pesos were provided by Ate Ara. Ate Ara also composed a song for the parents to sing during the program. The song captured the history of the project, the difficulties they had to overcome, and their joy in seeing their children graduate. It gave credit to those who supported the project, recognized the contribution of the mothers who provided food for the children, and appealed to everyone to continue upholding (*itaguyod*) the day-care center and the organization of the peasant women in the village through continued united action. The song goes thus:

Uphold the Day Care
The Organization of Mothers
Here in Paetan.
It's only now I learned
Day Care is good,
It is here that I found out
In the Organization of Mothers.
All the hardships here
We have overcome
When we see and experience our
Children's first graduation.
At first there was dismay,
And I was disturbed
Because they said
This was not what it claimed to be.
But in reality they did not know
D.S.W.D., Mindoro Institute, and baranggay officials
Supported us in everything.
And for the food
The mothers assumed responsibility.
That is why we must have unity all the time.
Let us work together,
Uphold the Day Care,
The Organization of Mothers
Here in Paetan.

[Itaguyod ang Day Care
Samahan ng mga Nanay
Dito sa Paetan.
Ngayon ko lang nalaman
Day Care pala'y inam,
Dito ko natagpuan
Sa Samahan ng mga Nanay.
Lahat ng kapaguran
Dito ay nalunasan,
Nang makita at madama ang unang pagtatapos,
Ng ating mga anak.
Noong una'y nayayamot, at
Dahil sa sabi nila
Ito raw ay bugos.
Ngunit di nila alam
Na sa katunayan lang
Ang D.S.W.D. ang siyang gabay
Ang Mindoro Institute,
At Baranggay Officials
Sila ang sumuporta sa lahat na ng bagay.
At sa pagkain naman
Ay sagot na ng mga nanay,
Kaya't tayo ay makaisa sa lahat ng oras.
Tayo ay magsama-sama.
Itaguyod ang Day Care
Samahan ng nga Nanay
Dito sa Paetan.]

At the time of my fieldwork in 1989, the success of the day-care project in this village was providing a good example for other village chapters. Some mothers in the local chapter in Calintaan were also informally talking about the possibility of setting up such a center, since there were so many children in the area. When I visited their village in 1996, I saw the simple building they had begun to construct. The men helped the women by doing the heavier construction work. But to complete this project, the members need continued funding and operational expenses, as well as a day-care teacher and money for her honorarium. The project came to a standstill when the Mindoro Institute for Development withdrew its funding. The challenge for this local chapter seems to be how it can revive the project by tapping other sources of support, both within and outside the community. Landlords could be challenged to support day-care centers; this would make them subsidize the social reproductive work that is linked to the work on their farms. Government officials and agencies, as well as church groups, could be asked for support; this would make social reproductive work a public responsibility, not just the private burden of women. There are women and men in the community who are potential day-care teachers. After some training, they could take turns working with or teaching the children. A private or public school system in Mindoro might be tapped to provide paraprofessional training for day-care teachers. Perhaps this is something that MIND, as a support institution for KAMMI, could explore.

In another village, there were also many small children, so the local chapter was contemplating setting up a day-care center as an initial activity to revive KAMMI in their village. And in Mamburao, a new local chapter had a plan to start a day-care center. The women held a preliminary discussion of the project, and members volunteered to contribute materials to build the center. There was some delay in formalizing the project, however, because the women had farm work that required immediate attention.

The peasant women see a value in setting up day-care centers for children. Some of the KAMMI members I talked to during my second visit to Mindoro said that the children who had gone through the preschool programs performed very well in primary grades.

The collective efforts by some local chapters of KAMMI in setting up these centers indicate that the women are beginning to view social reproduction as a community rather than individual responsibility. The grassroots politicization of child care can procure local government support, as indicated by the experience of the local chapter in Sablayan, but the initiative must come from the women and they must persist despite military labeling and other difficulties in order to bring about positive results. The experience of these women shows the importance of grassroots organization in effecting social change.

That the setting up of day-care centers has been primarily a women's issue has paradoxically limited their success. While such projects make child care a community issue, they do not directly challenge the ideological definition of child care as a "woman's domain." For example, the social maintenance of the center in Sablayan, which included such tasks as cooking the meals for the children, was provided mainly by the mothers. The fathers were not normally involved in such work.

Ideological Forms of Resistance: Education and Consciousness-Raising

Paolo Freire, who has worked among peasants in Latin America, argued in his *Pedagogy of the Oppressed* (1970) that education and consciousness-raising, what he calls "conscientization," are important elements of the process of liberation among oppressed peoples. Conscientization refers to the process by which people become more critically aware and gain deeper understanding of the forces that oppress them. This critical awareness can move them to act to change the oppressive situation. But Freire emphasizes that the process of building critical awareness takes place in the context of action-reflection-action, what he calls "praxis," in which people reflect about their experience.

Frantz Fanon (1968) also contends that material conditions of exploitation alone are not enough to move people to act, but that people's deeper understanding and awareness of the situation that oppresses them also play an important role in their resistance. This is further supported by James Scott in his *Weapons of the Weak* (1985), in which he finds that the forms of informal resistance among the peasants he studied in Malaysia include "ideological resistance" (p. 304). By this he means that they respond not only to objective conditions of their experience but also to the "normative understandings" and interpretations they have about these conditions (p. 305). Scott, however, emphasizes the intrinsic interaction between material conditions and ideational interpretations: the peasants' views, though varying, derive from their experience of the material conditions of their everyday lives.

My discussion so far has focused mainly on KAMMI's forms of resistance directed at or responding to the material conditions of poverty and exploitation. But KAMMI's politics also include "ideological resistance." One form their ideological resistance takes is education and consciousness-raising, which the peasant women call *pag-aaral* (study sessions). In the context of KAMMI's politics, this basically means arriving at a critical understanding of (1) the situation of peasant women in relation to that of the Filipino peasantry generally, and (2) the politics of development and underdevelopment that impact on their everyday lives and those of all Filipino people.

As mentioned in Chapter 3, repression is also ideological. It involves not only military violence directed against political action that seeks to change existing power relations, but also the repression of ideas and the prevention of an awareness and understanding of current events. It involves as well the distortion of facts and the justification of the existing order. The politics of underdevelopment in the Philippines are partly maintained by ideological justifications of the kind of development legitimized by the state. The following account shows how KAMMI, by integrating education and consciousness-raising in its politics of resistance, counteracts this ideological repression and resists the politics of underdevelopment in the Philippines.

The Basic Orientation Seminar (BOS)

One of the ways in which KAMMI makes education and consciousness-raising an integral part of its organizational politics is by requiring new members, or the women in any new village chapter, to undergo a Basic Orientation Seminar (which the peasant women refer to as BOS). Four themes compose the BOS curriculum: (1) the situation of the Filipino peasantry as a whole; (2) the particular circumstances of peasant women in the economic, political, cultural, and family spheres; (3) the importance and types of peasant organizations; and (4) an overview of KAMMI: what it is, what its goals and programs are, and how one can become a member.

The discussion of the general situation of the peasantry comprises agrarian problems experienced by both men and women. These are: (a) concentration of land among a few landlords, resulting in landlessness or inadequate land among the peasantry; (b) usury; (c) high land rent for landless peasants; (d) traders' or trader-usurers' control of the peasants' produce; (e) foreign agribusiness corporations' control of agricultural production; (f) the low wages of an increasing number of landless agricultural workers; and (g) their political constraints in organizing. Land is identified as the major problem of the Filipino peasantry, but all the above problems are viewed as causes of poverty.

Although in this general discussion the contribution of peasant women in agricultural production remains invisible, and the concept of peasantry is genderless, in the discussion of the particular situation of peasant women, the BOS curriculum highlights the following issues: (a) the significant contribution of peasant women in production, (b) the wage differential between men and women agricultural workers, (c) the insensitivity of modern farm technology to the role of women in farm work, (d) the contribution of women to the family economy by combining child care and household-based income-generating work, and (e) the absence of peasant women's rights commensurate with their significant roles in the economy and the family (such as the titling of lands in the husband's name only, the lack of peasant women's tenancy rights independent from their husbands, and the nonparticipation of peasant women in decisions relating to farm work).

The BOS presents to the trainees the view that peasant women's roles are not only economic and familial, but also political. It stresses the silencing of peasant women in decision-making bodies of the state, from the village to the national level. And it recognizes the impact of military repression and violence on these women and their families.

The BOS also introduces women's issues in the social and cultural spheres: (a) the lack of access to education of both men and women as a result of poverty, but also the preferential status of male members of the family when it is decided who should receive education beyond the primary and elementary level, (b) the ideological definition of a woman's place as primarily in the home, which deprives women of other opportunities, (c) the impact of inadequate medical and health services in the village on the reproductive and general health of women, such as the absence of medical care during pregnancy and childbirth, (d) patriarchal relations in the family and the sexual division of labor, with women doing most domestic work in addition to farm work, (e) the lack of recognition in society that peasant women's domestic work is also productive work, and (f) the limiting nature of the church activities that most women engage in, since they do not politicize them toward changing their social condition.

With this BOS overview of the particular situation of the peasant women, KAMMI contributes to a broader understanding of the peasantry in the Philippines. This experience of peasant women is usually not reflected in the way the KMP—which is open to both men and women, though it is largely dominated by male leaders—publicly articulates the problems of the peasantry.

Finally the BOS stresses to the trainees the important role organization can play in changing their situation. It points out that one cause of the persistence of poverty in both the community and the nation—and of the particular hardships experienced by peasant women—is lack of unity and organized effort. The curriculum distinguishes two kinds of peasant organizations: "samahan *para* sa magbubukid" (organization *for* the peasants) and "samahan *ng* mga magbubukid" (organization *of* the peasants). The first is defined as an organization that is started from the top by some agency, not so much in the interests of the peasants but rather in the interests of that agency. The second is an organization started by the peasants themselves, with both leadership and membership coming from the peasantry; it truly serves the interests of the peasants, and its goals and principles are defined by its own members. The BOS stresses that KAMMI is an organization *of* peasant women that serves their interests.

For peasant women who are just beginning to be politically involved, the BOS is the start of a new consciousness about women's rights and their place in society. Ate Celita, for example, says, "When I went to the BOS my husband did not give me permission. But I learned in the BOS that women's rights must be struggled for." This new consciousness may grow as these women become increasingly involved in the peasant women's movement. That there are different levels of political consciousness among the members of KAMMI indicates that such awareness is a process rather than static.

Leadership Training

Another significant aspect of KAMMI's work in education and organization is its leadership training. On June 13–15, 1989, KAMMI held a training seminar for seventeen leaders from its local village chapters. The seminar, in which I was a participant observer, was held in San Jose. The women generally came to this meeting because they wanted to learn "more about what it means to be a leader," "how to be a good leader," and "more about methods of leadership," and "to understand more about how to become a leader of a community."

Contrary to the popular notion that village peasant women have little interest in ideas, I have observed that these women leaders were eager to learn from this seminar. Some of them came with their young children, leaving their families for three days, to attend. Some came from distant villages. Still others had to cross rivers on *bancas* (rowboats) because it had rained the previous night and the water was high. Jeepneys can cross some of the rivers in Mindoro in good weather when the water is low, and the women prefer to use them because the fare is cheaper than that of the banca. Despite very limited resources, then, these women spent money to come to this training.

Facilitated by the staff members of a nongovernmental organization supporting KAMMI (I shall call it NGO), this leadership training seminar consisted of the following themes, addressed in this order: (1) sharing of the peasant women's experiences, (2) analysis of the Philippine national situation, (3) historical overview of the women's movement in the Philippines, (4) principles of social analysis, (5) concept and styles of leadership, and the roles of leaders, and (6) principles of organizing.

Sharing of Peasant Women's Experiences.

The sharing of experiences among peasant women leaders, especially when they come from different chapters, becomes an important part of their coming together. They not only learn from each other's experiences, but they gain a sense of connectedness—a sense that each local chapter is not alone in its struggle.

One issue that excited the whole group was the difficulty of organizing. Ate Juanita outlined her difficulties with the barrio captain (the highest local government official in a Philippine village): "My problem is the captain (*kapitan*), he does not want his power challenged. He is reluctant to give us a permit to hold seminars. He says to the people that our women's organization is an NPA organization." Ate Lowe added that women's organizations threaten those in power: "The captain thinks that if the peasant women become progressive his power will be lessened." And Ate Laya added that in her village "it is really like that, we have to go through the captain first in getting a permit."

Others shared the difficulties they experience as leaders under militarization. For example, Ate Lorena told the group how the presence of the CAFGUs affected the leadership in her local chapter:

Our problem is that the CAFGUs are already there, they have forced our organization apart. 1986 was the start of our organization. I am the only one left. The other leaders went into hiding, they went to other places. Some leaders were arrested and they were killed. My brother was also arrested by the military; they did not kill him, but they tortured him. They asked so many questions. Why do we come to MIND, why do we join the KMP. The suspicion about us is that half of our family are already members of the NPA. They bombed our village. Then we had to leave. In fact, again there was another military operation in our village. The military ambushed some people, they are in the funeral parlor (*puneraria*). Militarization is a big obstacle to our action.

Before we already had an organization, but it fell apart because of militarization. Those of us left behind started another organization again.

Ate Laya said she had a similar experience:

What they have experienced, I have also experienced. The military asked me so many questions. Why am I at MIND when I am also working in the church? Why are you with MIND, are they not NPA? I answered them, if they are NPA, then why are they not in the mountains? They asked me, what are you teaching there? I answered them, why are you so meddlesome (*makulit*)? The way to answer their questions is to answer them straight.

In these verbal exchanges, the leaders were expressing their own concepts of power as they experience it in the immediate context of their actions. They have found that local state power is negative; it is an obstacle, though not an insurmountable one, to their own collective empowerment.

By having an opportunity to come together to talk about their experiences and difficulties, these leaders are able to gain a sense of the problems they share. And this is important in developing a collective feeling among the local chapters—a sense that they are bound together as one force, not isolated. This is a source of their strength and empowerment. Thus, Ate Laya continues, "We cannot do any action ("Hindi tayo makakagalaw") here if we do not federate." By sharing experiences, the leaders realize the potential for growth of their federation, and how the idea of a peasant women's organization is being received by potential members. Ate Laya talked excitedly about the other women in her area, who are interested in attending the BOS: "I have talked to other women who would also like to have the BOS, but they have not been given a seminar. They are looking for this kind of seminar, the BOS." Leaders also learn from each other's organizing strategies. Ate Sarisa, who is a new leader and is just setting up a village chapter in her area, said, "We were able to organize our chapter in the village. Since we did not have a voice in our village government [*baranggay*], we thought of setting up a day-care center together as a beginning project. The members are already willing to contribute to the project."

That these leaders come together to share their experiences indicates that despite militarization, even at the risk of their lives, peasant women find creative ways to bond together. If a tactic of repression is divide and rule, then these women are resisting it from below. Sharing is a source of their strength, for it breaks the isolation that repression wants to breed. It is in the sense of being in a community that they find the courage to struggle.

Analysis of the Philippine National Situation.

Analysis of the national situation is usually a major component of leadership training. Such training is given to peasant women who have already undergone the Basic Orientation Seminar, so the analysis here is on a higher level. It also provides a context in which a collective discussion of issues can take place. This part was facilitated by a man named Carlos. Ate Gloria, a national leader of AMIHAN who accompanied me to Mindoro at the time when this leadership training was held, also joined the deliberations.

Carlos began his presentation by asking the women what they would like to talk about first, "the political or the economic situation." Ate Lorena responded, "Economic." In an attempt to make the concept of "economic" and "political" more concrete, Carlos commented, "The issue closest to the stomach is the economic situation. The issue closest to the mind is the political situation." Ate Lorena, who does not see this dichotomy between the economic and the political, then argued, "If you have no stomach you have no mind." Carlos continued anyhow, "The issue closest to the stomach is the increase in prices of all goods, for example the price of rice." By bringing up this issue, Carlos touched on something that was close to the everyday lives of the women, for rice is the resource to which they relate as producers and consumers. Carlos connected the price increase to the development policies of the IMF and the World Bank: "The increase in prices is the result of the conditions the IMF and the World Bank have placed on the Philippine government so it could borrow more money. This is contained in the Letter of Intent (LOI). These conditions include (a) import liberalization—free entry of goods into the Philippines with low or no tax, (b) increase in the Value Added Tax (VAT), and (c) devaluation—the value of the peso has de-

creased from fourteen pesos to a dollar under Marcos to twenty-one pesos to a dollar under Aquino."

Ate Gloria, an AMIHAN national leader, then interjected a concrete
illustration: "With one thousand dollars, Americans can already buy so
much rice, but with one thousand pesos we can only buy very little."
Carlos continued, putting the blame on President Aquino: "Cory said
that she would change this, but she did not change it. What she is doing
is just perpetuating what Marcos did." Ate Lorena affirmed this but
added that their suffering has gotten worse: "During Marcos's time we
were already having a hard time, but now with Aquino we are suffering
even more. Now the price of soap is 11.50 pesos, before it was 9.50." Ate
Gloria brought up the impact of inflation on them as women: "This affects us women much more." Without commenting on what Ate Gloria
said, Carlos continued with facts on the Philippine national budget:
"Let us examine the national budget. Let us look at these figures [they
were written on a big Manila paper]. The national budget for 1988 was
172 billion pesos. This was allocated to the following: (1) social services
(20.6 percent), which equals 35.45 billion pesos, (2) economic services
(20.3 percent), which equals 34.936 billion pesos, (3) foreign debt payment (40.2 percent), which equals 69.184 billion pesos, and (4) others
(18.9 percent), which equals 32.526 billion pesos." Ate Lorena, who has
witnessed military bombings in her village, added a category that was not
reflected in the statistical facts Carlos presented: "The government expenses in firing guns also come from us." Carlos continued his presentation of facts, this time touching on the foreign debt and budget deficit
in the Philippine public treasury: "Let us look at the data on the budget
deficit. We had a budget deficit of 25 billion pesos in 1986, 23.48 billion pesos in mid 1987, and more than 22 billion pesos in 1988. This is
based on the approximate government expenses of 172 billion pesos and
an estimated income of 150 billion pesos. The budget for the military is
6.6 percent of the national budget in 1987—an increase of 12.1 percent
over the 1986 budget." Carlos pointed out that it is the Filipino people
who are paying for the government's debt, and that its increasing foreign
debt is a result of a dependent Philippine economy—an economy that is
export-oriented and import-dependent. Ate Gloria pointed out the relationship between foreign debt and the increase in prices: "If we are going to analyze it critically, the 40 percent that we pay for the national
debt, we are actually the ones paying for it through the increase of prices.
We are the ones who are buying the goods." Ate Sarisa even saw the
subtle connection between debt servicing and the consumer market:
"We pay for the debt indirectly when we buy goods." Ate Lorena added
that they also pay for it through the increase in some government taxes:
"Just take for example the fee for residence tax. Before we paid three

pesos, then six pesos; now we pay ten pesos." Ate Lecia saw the unfairness of this: "We do not even have jobs yet, and we are paying for this debt." Ate Lorena, who is also active in her church, further observed that "even the fee for baptism has increased."

At this point Carlos explained why there has been an increase in prices. His explanation was critical of the law of supply and demand that traditional economists often refer to in explaining price fluctuation. He emphasized the connection between the increase in prices and the debt trap the Philippine economy is in: "Prices of goods increase not because of natural effects of supply and demand—that when there is more demand and there is little supply the prices go up. This is not the real reason for the increase of prices, but the imposition of the IMF and the World Bank on our economy. We are borrowing money in order to pay for what we borrowed."

Carlos then explained the source of the Philippine budget deficit in the international division of labor within market capitalism and expansionism: "Why do we have a budget deficit? The reasons are the following. First, because as an agricultural country we specialize in producing raw materials like sugar, bananas, pineapple, coconut, fruits, corn, abaca, and tobacco. The First World, which are the rich nations, want us to specialize in these raw products, and they will take care of other finished goods. We are made simply to feed the world, creators [*tagapaglikha*] of the food for the world [*pagkain ng mundo*]. We are also made into simply suppliers of raw materials, for example the raw materials that we find in Mindoro: chromite, greenstone, blackstone, copper, iron, and nickel. Second, the reason why we have a budget deficit is because we are made to be simply a market for the manufactured goods of the rich nations. Since they have a surplus of goods in their nations, they must export these goods, otherwise that becomes only an idle capital." Cristina joined in, explaining what Carlos said in more concrete terms: "We buy these manufactured, finished goods at much more expensive prices. Already included in the price are the labor and other materials needed to manufacture the products." Carlos continued, touching on the core-periphery economic relations in the global political economy: "That is why this is what the First World [*mga maunlad na bansa*] wants, that we remain in this situation."

This deliberation provoked Ate Lorena to ask a practical question: "What are we going to do?" Ate Gloria responded with an appeal to economic self-reliance: "We must be the ones to make other products from the raw materials that we have." Carlos offered "alternative education" (*alternatibong edukasyon*) and "organization" as steps toward change. Bella elaborated: "By alternative education we mean the kind of education that we can make use of." Ate Gloria also brought out the importance of organization: "We will not be able to liberate ourselves [*hindi tayo lalaya*] if we are not organized." Carlos continued relating organization to con-sciousness-raising and demands for agrarian reforms: "Strength of unity (*lakas ng pagkakaisa*) of Filipinos is what we need. We need organization that will change the minds of the different sectors. The organization must demand genuine agrarian reform. For instance, what are the prob-lems of peasants?" Ate Lorena immediately answered, "No land." "No land to till—that is the root of our poverty. Ninety percent of the popu-lation is poor," Carlos affirmed.

But Ate Gloria, who understands the complexity of the peasants' prob-lems, raised the question, "If we have true agrarian reform, can we say that we are already liberated [*malaya*]?" Ate Juanita, quick to see her point, responded, "No, we would still have so many problems, like medi-cine." So Carlos brought up the concept of integrated development, which combines agrarian reforms with national industrialization, for ex-ample: "The second solution is national industrialization. We may have land, but if we still import pesticides, fertilizers, we are still not yet truly free. The HYV that peasants produce is a result of the control of our economy by multinational corporations. Sometimes the seeds are being contracted with the multinational corporations. The seeds of unmilled rice [*butil ng palay*] will become truly Filipino if genuine land reform is implemented alongside national industrialization."

But Carlos did not point out the woman question in his discussion of development, and it again became the task of Ate Gloria to broach the issue: "Land reform is just one step toward the solutions to these prob-lems. There might still be discrimination against women. It must be recognized that we are a force in agricultural production, and that we have a right to own land. We must have a voice not only at home but also in the nation [*bayan*]." Ate Sarisa then added, "We are not yet visible ['Hindi pa tayo nakikilala']. We are still being looked down on because we are women. We are still expected to take care of men." Carlos at-tempted to support the women's concerns and said, "The men are able to work in the fields because they are freed from housework. That is why the contribution of women must be recognized." Ate Gloria ex-panded his view, touching on the invisibility and nonrecognition of peas-ant women's work: "We must be recognized not only by the men, but by the whole society. We, as women, are being used by landlords, without pay." Others brought out that the traditional concept of "peasant" is "male," although peasant women also work in the landlords' farms. Ate Lorena said, "When your husband dies, you also do not get support from the landlord to work on the land. Even among landlords, it is seldom that it is the woman who manages the land." Ate Gloria gave an example: "We already have had this experience with the case of Isabela. When her husband died, the landlord did not allow her to till the land, because according to him she was not capable of managing it. That is why we must fight for that." Ate Lorena affirmed this: "I was told by our landlord that I have no right to meddle ['wala daw akong pakialam'] because he is going to get the land that we are tilling." Ate Juanita also expressed her sense that the peasant woman has no identity separate from that of her husband: "When our husband dies, we are considered nothing ['bali wala na kaming kuwenta']." Ate Laya expanded this to point out the lack of recognition of all peasant women: "Even if you are a woman without a husband, you are also nothing."

At this point, Carlos took the chance to move the discussion to the next issue in his agenda. He presented statistical information on the level of poverty in the Philippines, which he had culled from government documents and handwritten on a big Manila paper: "Let us look at these figures on the poverty line. In 1983, 45 percent of the whole population was under the poverty line. In 1985, 65 percent of the whole population was under the poverty line, and 85 percent in 1989. In 1989, 160 pesos per day was the average income a family of six in Manila needed; 100 pesos a day for a family of six in rural areas." Carlos explained the concept of "poverty line" in a way that the peasant women would understand: "If families are living on the poverty line, this means that they are able to buy new clothes only once a year, have only three meals a day, and are able to educate their children only until high school. Other essential needs, like a house, are not included here. Living below the poverty line means that families sometimes have only brunch, only one meal a day, sometimes just coffee." Ate Lorena added her own concept of the poverty line: "It means therefore that out of 100 people, 85 are hungry [gutom], only 15 are filled [busog]." Ate Lalay, from her own experience of poverty, added: "What we earn is not even enough." Cristina tried to relate the impact of poverty to the role of women in the family as generators of additional income for basic needs: "Peasants earn only one thousand pesos. The two thousand pesos that need to be put up are the responsibility of the woman who must look for other means of income." Ate Laya affirmed this: "The responsibility placed on the women is greater." And Ate Sarisa agreed, touching on the sexual division of labor in meeting family needs: "That's right, the men think only of the fields [bukid]."

Carlos moved the discussion to an analysis of the political situation, focusing on human rights violations under the Aquino government. He presented statistical data on human rights violations, comparing the early period of the Aquino regime with the later part of the Marcos reign. Carlos concluded that militarization has intensified, despite the toppling of Marcos, and asked, "Why is militarization intensifying?" Ate Gloria cited the connection between the desire of the landlords to protect their land and the spread of paramilitary troops in the villages: "The vigilantes are also one instrument of militarization. The vigilantes spread when the Comprehensive Agrarian Reform Program [CARP] of the Aquino government was approved. That is why the vigilantes are a protection for the landlords. It is the landlords who have control over the vigilantes." Ate Sarisa mentioned Almeda as one example of this kind of landlord, who makes use of paramilitary troops to protect his land.

Cristina contributed the idea that the present militarization in the Philippines is now a "total war policy" in which the U.S. government is involved: "This thing they call total war policy, in this policy the government will use some social approach, that is, they will use some of the social programs of the government in winning the people. This is what they call WHAM (winning the hearts and minds of the people). It is the United States that gave this policy to us. We will be the ones to fight each other, while the U.S. supplies the arms." Carlos pointed out that there is no longer a middle road in political action, according to the politics of militarization: "The danger here is that there is no opening for us to be neutral. For the government, if you do not support the military or vigilantes, you are for the left. Here in Mindoro, militarization is also widespread; the vigilantes have also spread."

Ate Lorena then brought out the impact of militarization on the peasant women's work: "Because of militarization, working on the farm has become more difficult for us." Carlos continued, pointing out that militarization is a way for the Aquino government to legitimize itself: "To consolidate her government, Aquino wants the military to unite and everyone to support the government." But Ate Gloria argued that various groups would vie for power in the next presidential election in 1992: "But now we can see that there are factions in the government. For example, in the coming elections, we must use deep critical analysis. That is why we must be prepared." Carlos went on to cite the financial burden of the elections on the people: "The expenses for the election, we will be the ones to pay for them." Ate Gloria ended the deliberation by pointing out their only defense against being deceived by government leaders: "Our weapon is our vision, a critical thinking [*malinaw na pag-iisip*] in all these happenings." Ate Laya agreed: "Let us open our eyes."

In these deliberations on the national situation, two patterns can be observed. First, Carlos made no attempt to incorporate the woman question into his analysis, despite the fact that he was talking to peasant women. Carlos's presentation is typical of those of most male activists in the Philippines who are involved in the mass movement for national liberation. They still commonly believe that the question of women in development is not a national issue, that it is relevant only to women, and that bringing up the gender question will divide the national liberation movement, whose goal is to consolidate and unify all forces from different sectors and classes.

Second, it was always the peasant women who attempted to bring women's issues into the discussion. Ate Gloria, an AMIHAN national leader who happened to attend this training session only because she accompanied me to Mindoro, was particularly assertive in bringing the woman question into the analysis of the national situation. And the peasant women of KAMMI were particularly assertive in bringing the analysis down to the level of their concrete experience.

The dynamics of their discussion raise three issues: (1) that peasant women have an important contribution to make in the analysis of national issues, (2) that analysts of the national situation have something to learn from the experience of peasant women, and (3) that asserting the woman question in analysis of the national situation is part of the peasant women's politics of resistance within the peasant movement as well as within the national liberation movement. Cynthia Enloe (1989) recognizes the struggles of women activists in Third World countries such as the Philippines to bring the woman question into the politics of national liberation movements, for the dominant thinking is still that the woman question should be addressed only after national liberation is attained. The assertiveness that the peasant women showed in this part of the seminar is just one indicator of their struggle within the national struggle. Part of the silencing of women, both in the politics of underdevelopment and within the liberation movement, is the denial of their own interpretations in analysis of national issues. This silencing helps perpetuate a world system that is maintained by the exploitation of women's productive and reproductive work. Thus, we should consider what Enloe says: "It is worth imagining . . . what would happen to international politics if more nationalist movements were informed by women's experiences of oppression" (1989, 64).

History of the Women's Movement in the Philippines.

Cristina was the facilitator in the presentation of the next topic. She addressed two themes: the impact of colonization on the status of Filipino women, and the evolution of women's organizations in the Philippines and the role women played in them.

Cristina presented Western colonialism as the origin of patriarchal ideologies in Philippine culture:

Before the Spanish colonizers came, we had a primitive, communal way of living. Private ownership was not the norm. Women had a relatively equal status with

men. Women were consulted in decision making in the community. When the
Spanish colonizers came, there was a change in our social order. Here came
the patriarchal culture—the idea that the father or the husband is the head of
the family. The woman was expected to be a martyr.

Cristina's view represents one perspective on the history of women's oppression in the Philippines. It is the nationalist feminist view, which puts
emphasis on the assumption that Filipino women's oppression began
during the colonial conquest, when the relative equality they enjoyed
in precolonial times was suppressed by the patriarchal ideologies about
women that diffused into Philippine culture alongside a material change
in the social order. The present articulation of gender and class has
roots in the colonial and neocolonial history of the Philippines. A second
perspective emphasizes that a sexual division of labor that existed even
before colonial conquest was the seed of the gender inequality that further germinated in the colonial and postcolonial periods. This view lacks
an analytical connection between productive and reproductive work of
women, however. A third perspective emphasizes that there is a connection between production and reproduction in the subordination and exploitation of women, and that women's experience of the nature of such
exploitation will differ depending on their class position.

All these perspectives reflect an attempt to reconceptualize Filipino
women, given the historical matrix of their exploitation, oppression, and
subordination. Filipino women activists who try to link feminist politics
to the national liberation in the Philippines tend to follow the nationalist
feminist perspective. AMIHAN's documents indicate that it too follows
this perspective, which therefore filters down to KAMMI. The nationalist
feminist perspective finds support in Cheryl Johnson's study of Yoruba
women. She takes the view that "the solution to the problem of women's
general lack of political and economic power in Africa is not just a question of the position of women vis-à-vis men in their respective societies, but also a question of the position of the societies in which women
find themselves vis-à-vis their former colonizers" (Johnson 1986, 237).
Within the nationalist feminist perspective, the same can be said of Filipino women, especially of the peasant and working classes.

There was an attempt in this part of the training session to situate the
emergence of AMIHAN and KAMMI in the history of the women's movement in the Philippines, to demonstrate that women's organizations in
the Philippines are not just emerging now. Their coming together has a
historical precedent. Cristina, for example, traced the evolution of the
major thrusts of Filipino women's organizations back to the 1800s:

In 1890, upper-class women in the Philippines began to organize. By 1893 Logia
de Adopcion was organized under the leadership of Teresa Tecson, who was then

fighting against the Spanish colonial rule. In 1896 the Filipino people revolted against the Spanish colonial government. The women were involved in the revolution. Gabriela Silang was one of the women revolutionary leaders against Spanish domination. In 1899, Asosacion de Damas de la Cruz Rojas was set up more for humanitarian purposes. Its work was similar to that of the Red Cross. The major part of its work was to provide emergency help to victims of calamities. In 1902 the Philippine Women's League of Peace (La Liga Filipina) was formed under the leadership of Carmen Poblete. The nature of their work, however, was directed toward helping the American government suppress dissent.

In response to Cristina's presentation, Ate Gloria emphasized the historical precedents of the present women's struggles: "Even before, there was already a struggle of women; it is not only now that they are emerging." Ate Laya agreed: "Before there were already women's organizations. It is not only at this time that they are beginning." Ate Gloria, however, brought up the connection between the nature of some of the early women's organization and the colonial mentality: "Before there was no direction toward the liberation of women. They thought that the American colonizers were friends of the Filipino people."

Cristina continued tracing the evolution of women's organizations in the Philippines, this time from 1900 to the present, situating the emergence of AMIHAN and KAMMI historically:

By 1905, the Association of Feminista Filipina was born. Its major work was directed at demanding labor law reform, land reform, and rights of women prisoners. They demanded educational reforms and changes in the workplace, and addressed other national social problems. In 1906, the Association of Feminista Ilonga was organized, and they were the first to put forth the issue of women's suffrage.

Then in the 1960s, the MAKIBAKA [Malayang Kilusan ng Bagong Kababaihan] was founded. It saw the problems of Filipino women within the context of national problems and issues in the Philippines. This group went underground after its members were harassed during the Marcos military regime. In 1984, GABRIELA was organized, followed by the organization of AMIHAN in 1986. KAMMI formally became a chapter of AMIHAN in 1987. GABRIELA is an alliance of all women's organizations in the Philippines; it is a national federation of women's organizations all over the country. It includes all women's organizations from the different sectors: peasant women, students and youth, church women, urban poor women, professional women, women workers. They are members of GABRIELA if they promote the issues of the federation. AMIHAN is the national federation or alliance of peasant women's organizations in the Philippines. KAMMI is a local chapter of AMIHAN. Although AMIHAN is federated with GABRIELA, AMIHAN has a distinct structure of its own because it is a sectoral organization of peasant women.

Cristina learned what she presented here from a seminar of GABRIELA that she attended in Manila. Here we see how ideas in the women's movement are diffused. Ideas, therefore, have a place in the women's movement, as they do in any other movement. It can be said, without going into an argument on the Hegelian and Marxist perspectives, that ideas do influence political action and change. Consciousness of the historical background of one's organized action can provide direction and a sense of continuity or rootedness. But this historical consciousness is also a process that can develop as one becomes involved in political action. This is indicated, for instance, by the fact that the peasant women leaders who have been involved in the movement for a long time have a greater awareness of the historical precedence of the current women's movement in the Philippines than those who are just beginning. The building of this historical consciousness is part of their attempt to recapture their nationhood, which was nipped by colonial subjugation.

Leadership.

The peasant women think of leaders as those who undergo and organize training for the organization (*pagsasanay*), lead in implementing organizational activities (*pangunguna*), raise critical consciousness in themselves and among the members of the organization (*pagpapalawak ng kaisipan*), facilitate decision making in the group (*taga-saayos*), and take the lead in getting things done (*pagpapasunod*). Adding to these ideas, Mira presented a theory of leadership (*pamiminunu*) that differs from the patronage politics of traditional political leaders in the Philippines. "Pamiminunu," she said, refers to "the methods, ways, or style of running or administering an organization so that it pursues its goals, not through the use of power or influence of wealth and fame, but through gaining the respect and trust of the members." Pamiminunu, Mira further explained, differs from the concept of *pamumuno*, which refers to "the ability of a person to lead a group of people including herself toward achieving the goals of the organization." One can be considered a leader (*pinuno*), Mira continued, if one "has the knowledge, experience, and correct attitude toward the dynamics of leading the organization." Touching on the concept of legitimacy in leadership, Mira explained that a pinuno can be officially part of the formal leadership (*namumuno*) if she has been "elected and assigned by the members to a position in order to perform a responsibility."

Without speaking in sophisticated language, the peasant women articulated their own concept of leadership roles, which is actually a concretization of Mira's theoretical explanation of leadership. For these women, leadership roles include (a) activating the organization, (b) providing direction toward the efficient concretization and implementation of the organization's goals and program of action, (c) sustaining the interest, persistence, and unity of the members, and (d) acting and leading based on the interests of the members, not just the interests of one person or a few individuals in the organization. The peasant women see that to fulfill these roles, leaders must possess certain qualities: (1) Social skills: "Leaders should not be the first to destroy the reputation of their members," "Leaders must give and receive feedback (*magpunahan*)," "Leaders must treat others equally" ("pantay-pantay na pagtingin sa kapwa"), "They should treat others as their equals," and "A leader is like a mother who must treat her children equally." (2) Knowledge: "Leaders must be knowledgeable" ("may sapat na kaalaman"). (3) Personal virtues: A leader is "understanding" (*maunawain*), "trustworthy and loyal; no one will follow a leader if members do not trust her," "responsible," "principled" (*may paninindigan*), "courageous" (*hindi takot, matapang*), "is respected by members because she also respects them."

Mira added something that the peasant women did not mention: "A leader must be fair in distributing benefits of the organization by not giving preferential treatment to relatives." I never heard the peasant women say that kinship relations interfered with their organizational politics, and the subject did not emerge in my informal interviews either. There are cases of nepotism in the Philippines, wherein relatives of state officials receive preferential treatment or acquire wealth and power through their kinship connections. For example, relatives and close friends of former president Ferdinand Marcos and Imelda Marcos "all prospered through access to government credits, contracts, and their ability to manipulate government permits required of foreign investors, often becoming Filipino partners in joint ventures or licensing arrangements" (Wurfel 1988, 237); President Corazon Aquino herself "made no attempt to replace patronage politics" (ibid., 340). By mentioning the expectation that public leaders must overlook kinship when allocating organizational resources, Mira was pointing out an alternative style of public leadership that KAMMI must strive for. That the peasant women seem to have a sense of this alternative leadership is evident in their concept of *pantay-pantay* (equality) in the way a leader must relate to others.

To identify and become more aware of their own styles of leadership, the peasant women were given a training exercise: one group was assigned to create a drawing depicting a home and family (*tahanan at pamilya*), a second group was to draw the situation of women in the economy (*pang-ekonomiyang kalagayan ng kababaihan*), and a third group was to draw the political life of women (*pampulitikang pamumuhay ng kababaihan*).

The products of this exercise revealed their concepts of a woman's place in the family, economy, and politics. The first group drew, they explained, "the woman suggesting to her husband that it was already the opening of school, and they did not yet have money for their children's tuition. So the woman looked for another means of income, such as raising a pig and selling it." This drawing indicates that the role of the woman in the family contributes to its economic welfare. In the experience of these women, it is generally they who look for other means of making money to supplement the inadequate income of the family, and especially to provide for the education of their children. The drawing also indicates the high value the women, like most Filipino families, place on education for their children. They will seek every possible way to earn additional income for this purpose. So when poor peasant families are unable to send their children beyond high school or even grade school, it is not because they do not value education; it is because poverty and a lack of government support make educational opportunities unavailable to the poor.

The second group drew a woman tending a cooperative store that she had set up in the front part of her house. The women interpreted their drawing in this way:

A woman must not just be tied to the house [*bahay*]. She must have a means of income, even if she usually stays at home [*bagamat namamalagi sa bahay*]. If women are part of production, they also have a right [*karapatan*] to sell [*maibenta*] their own produce. This way we are able to help in meeting the needs of the family and in preventing the exportation or "going out" [*pag-labas*] of our own produce. This way we are able to raise the livelihood of peasant women. By selling our own produce directly to the community, we are helping lower the prices of important basic products. Then we will be able to get away from importing fruit, like apples, from other countries.

This interpretation indicates the women's consciousness of their place in the Philippine economy. They see their economic activity on the village level in relation to larger issues. They are aware that they need to produce and to create a market that is more oriented to local needs and that maximizes the utilization of local resources.

The third group drew a group of women having a meeting (*pulong*). They interpreted their drawing thus: "Our drawing shows women joining and participating in political discussions [*usapang pampulitika*], and women participating in discussions about the local situation. They are expressing how they feel about women's rights in the political sphere ['karapatan ng kababaihan sa larangan ng pampulitika']. This shows that it is not only men who are capable of leadership, but also women." This interpretation indicates that the peasant women, having already been involved in organizational politics, view their political participation as a right (*karapatan*), and being a leader as being political. They also appreciate women's capacity for leadership; it is, they believe, not an ability with which only men are endowed.

Through this training exercise, the women were actually teaching each other, and perhaps changing each other's views about a woman's place in society. By talking together about their ideas and presenting them in a visual form, the women were actually articulating a redefinition of their roles in the family, economy, and politics.

After the women's presentations, Mira introduced them to a second level of analysis, this time involving the process that evolved in each group as they went about accomplishing the first task collectively. She posed the following question: How did you as members or as leaders feel about what happened in your group?

The first group said that they did not finish the drawing. They were still trying to figure out what they must do, and the leader of the group took over and the members just followed her. The members said that they felt insulted, confused, surprised, and hurt when the leader did this. The leader said she was amused (*natuwa*), but also felt a bit afraid (*natakot*). Mira drew out the idea that the dynamics of this group illustrated "autocratic leadership" (*makapangyarihang pamumuno*), wherein only the wishes of the leader are followed, the leader does not accept mistakes, and she puts herself at the center of the group, stifling the participation of the other members.

The second group was commended as the most orderly. The members said that there had been teamwork and unity. Each of them participated in deciding how to accomplish the task, and the leader gave each a sense of importance by appreciating her work. The leader reported that she realized that even if you do not command, you can let a group do its work by a "soft way of talking" (*malumay na pananalita*). She said she also realized that she could be a leader in spite of herself ("puede na pala akong isang lider kahit na ganito lang ako"), which was understood to imply that although she did not have a great deal of formal education, she realized she could be a leader. The peasant women identified the style of leadership in their group as "democratic leadership" (*malayang pamumuno*).

The third group reported that they did not feel their leader was helpful to them in accomplishing the task and they felt bad about it: "The leader told us, it's all up to you what you want to do." They said they felt envious of the other groups where the leaders were helpful, and they felt even worse when they saw their own leader helping the other groups but not their own. The leader of the group said that her conscience bothered her when she learned how the group felt, but she also said that each member learned how to use her capacity to be a leader. The style of leadership in this group was identified as "pabaya" (there is no literal English translation, but Mira explained the meaning as "no deep concern for the organization"). One peasant woman, however, argued that this style of leadership may not always turn out badly, that it can in fact at times lead to members learning to stand on their own feet ("matutong tumindig sa sarili niyang paa"). But another woman contended that a leader who is *pabaya* needs to be replaced.

After having identified the different styles of leadership, Mira ended the session with a question: "Can we reflect and think about which type of leader we are?"

Principles of Social Analysis.

Nila facilitated the next discussion, which focused on the concept of change, the relationship of change and the belief in a predestined future, analysis of social problems and change, and the process and nature of change.

Despite the fact that the quality of life of the peasant women in Mindoro has not been improved by any significant structural changes in the political economy, the peasant leaders in the training session were optimistic, agreeing with Nila's statement that "all things change." Ate Lorena's response, "Yes, people can change in their character, views, and attitudes," eloquently articulates their optimism. "People can change" is an abstraction of their experience of personal change resulting from their community and political involvement with KAMMI, as their testimonials illustrate. Ate Sarah, for example, said, "Before we were not yet aware [*hindi pa tayo noon namumulat*]. Our consciousness changed. Before we were not yet organized and had no education [*pag-aaral*]. We did not yet know what was happening around us, and we did not yet have awareness about women." Ate Laya, who is active in her church, acquired a new understanding of "church" (*simabahan*) through her political involvement with KAMMI. She now sees the "church" as one that actively responds to social situations in the community: "Before, my awareness [*pakaalam ko*], because I was working in the church, was simply to pray and read the Bible. But I became aware [*naunawaan ko*] that the church must not isolate [*hindi dapat umiwas*] itself from the situation in the community [*kanayunan*]. My perspective [*pananaw*] changed when I joined [*sumalo*] this organization." Others learned social skills as they became more involved in the activities of KAMMI. Ate Lorena, for instance, learned diplomacy in dealing with others: "Before, when I was not yet with the organization, I would easily get irritated. But now I first try to understand, and say words that will not hurt [*hindi makasira*] my members. I realized that too much leniency [*sobrang pag-uunawa*] without discipline is also not good for the organization. What is good is that there is change in all aspects of your life when you are part of the organization."

The increased awareness of the peasant women influenced their behavioral response to certain situations that contradict their new understandings of gender relations. For example, Ate Lalay learned how to assert herself with her husband: "Before I did not know how to talk [makipag-usap] to people. I was always submissive [sunod-sunuran] to my husband. But now, not anymore, we now decide together." Another said: "My husband did not want me to come to the seminar, but I came." And Ate Juanita, a very young peasant woman who became aware of the sexual division of labor in farm work, even learned to plow the fields, although her father gets angry when she does it because he thinks it is a "man's job."

As the peasant women get to exercise leadership, they also become aware of other skills they need to possess. Ate Sarah learned the usefulness of verbal skills: "I realized that when people ask you questions you must be able to answer them well." Ate Lorena realized the importance of other skills in their work: "We must be resourceful and patient in gathering information or knowledge [mapagsaliksik] in order to understand our situation."

Most of the peasant women who attended this training pointed to KAMMI's educational sessions, training, and seminars as the source of their increased awareness: "In my joining educational sessions [pag-aaral] I also learned a lot"; "Before I did not like to join organizations because I thought the people would just gossip about me. But when I went to the seminar I learned a lot of things"; "At first I did not know the situation of women. But gradually I began to understand it since that time Ate Lorena spoke in the seminar."

Thus, as these peasant women leaders became more involved in the politics of their collective struggle, their views about themselves, and their perceptions and responses to the world around them, altered. This personal experience of change served as a basis for their conceptualization and theorizing about change. They understood the idea that people's consciousness of the social world and their views about themselves can change because they have experienced this personally. They theorized that their experience of change came about through the organization, through their association with others in the organization, and through the educational sessions (pag-aaral). However, the opportunity to come together and collectively reflect on and articulate their ideas about their experiences is necessary for them to make sense of what they have undergone. Fr. John Doherty, a Jesuit sociology professor of mine in the Philippines, said: "Once you are able to talk about your experience and reflect about it, you begin to own that experience and allow yourself and others to learn from it." An opportunity for a peasant woman to talk about her experience allows her to "own" that experience; transferrable knowledge can be the result. There is a conscientizing element in being able to talk about experiences together.

The peasant women's capacity to make abstractions about or conceptualize their experience of change disputes the common stereotype among those who occupy a higher social position that peasants have little interest in ideas—that they have a "low level of thinking." Middle-class people tend to look down on the intellectual capacities of peasants because they have little education. But the peasant women's articulations show that they are capable of theorizing from their experiences.

Having undergone personal change in their lives and having gained increased critical consciousness of the world around them, the peasant women do not believe in a predestined future (*takda ng kapalaran*). Contrary to the assumption of Oscar Lewis's "culture of poverty" theory that poor people have a fatalistic view about life (1959), the peasant women are aware of their poverty but do not believe it was foreordained. Ate Juanita said, "For me, our future is not predestined. Like us being poor, that is not predetermined. We must work hard." Ate Lorena, who is active in her church, reflected on the role of God in their future: "It is possible that God does not predetermine our future. Doing belongs to people, mercy belongs to God ['Nasa tao ang gawa, nasa Diyos ang awa']. We are the ones to make our future, our situation in life." Ate Laya, who is also active in her church, affirmed this: "No, our future is not predestined because God gave people the freedom [*kalayaan*] to reflect [*magpasya*] and to act [*gumawa*]." Since they believe the conditions of their lives are not unalterable, they think they can shape their future by planning. "If you do not plan your life, you will not know the different ways and things that must be done," says Ate Lorena.

Contrary to another popular notion about poor people, these peasant women are anything but lazy; in fact, they see themselves as among those who must work hard (*magsikap*) in order to progress (*para umunlad*). Ate Lucy, for example, said: "For me our condition in life is not predestined. Because if your situation in life is poor, then you must work hard to make progress." Benedict Kerkvliet (1990, 169–70) gives a similar account of poor people's views in his study of a Philippine village in Central Luzon, which he named San Ricardo:

When poor people discuss the course of their own lives, one pronounced theme is industriousness. Laziness is not part of their self-image. On the contrary, poor people see themselves as always "on the move" (*kumikilos*), looking for ways to improve their standard of living and exploring various avenues: they travel to distant places to work, attempt to make extra cash through petty trade, [and] buy small goats and pigs to sell.

The peasant women have faith that people are endowed with the capacity and freedom to shape the world they live in. They are hopeful that through action they can achieve progress and improve their situation. And this is probably another source of their persistence in their struggle as peasant women, despite the difficulties they experience. They come together because they believe they can change their lot. And their interest in understanding the social situation that affects them is part of how they seek change.

But simply understanding the situation, without taking action, is not enough to effect change. Ate Lorena poignantly said, "Even if you know the problem, if you do not do anything about it, then nothing will happen." They do not think of change as having a single cause. A situation can change "because of oneself" (*sarili*), "because of experience" (*karanasan*), "because of action" (*pagkilos*), and "because of education" (*pag-aaral*).

Nila, the facilitator of this topic, presented the concept of internal and external factors in change. She explained these factors as if they were dichotomous, which was difficult for the peasant women to understand. It did not seem important for them to identify when factors were internal or external. And rightly so, for in reality there is no clear distinction between the two, since they interact in any situation. Ate Lorena nonetheless sought to apply the concept: "We can also analyze the leaders and members of the organization. What are the leaders good at and weak at? We must also regularly analyze our members. If we see what they are good at, we can put them in a position where they can be good at it. We must also consider a member's time, how much time she has." Nila added: "In analyzing members, we must also consider their class origin, know the region where they come from so we can know their customs, know what percentage of the population is women, and know the occupations of the women." There was no actual discussion on how to gather such information, however.

Nila further introduced the idea of studying contradictions (*tunggalian*) in analyzing a social situation, the importance of seeing how a particular situation relates to "the larger system or structures in society," and the concepts of "quantitative change" (for example, an increase in the number of organized peasants) and "qualitative change" (for example, change in agrarian relations or land reform). Although she tried to illustrate these general points with concrete examples, her presentation was theoretical and her style of facilitating didactic; she did not evoke the experiences of the peasant women, through which they could actually contribute to the analysis. There was a moment when the peasant women began analyzing: Nila said that to examine problems in their local chapters they must relate them to "broader issues," and she asked the question, "What are the problems that are arising in your chapters?" In response, the peasant women mentioned "lack of funds" for carrying out their organizational work, and "fear" of the "military," their "husbands," and the "barrio captain." Ate Lorena, a provincial leader, contributed her analysis: "Financial difficulties are the root problem. For example, you want to go to meetings but you do not have money for transportation." But Cristina, one of the professionals providing support for KAMMI, rejected this important problem that the peasant women were raising: "Well, if everything will be coming from us, then we will not be helping you anymore because you will become dependent. After all, there are other projects." After this statement, Ate Ara and Ate Lorena kept quiet for a while, as if embarrassed by what Cristina had said. But instead of withdrawing from the discussion, Ate Lorena said, after gaining back her composure, "OK. Let's talk about major problems." Although the women's analysis of their own actual problems was now subdued, Ate Lorena still tried to bring up the issue of lack of funds and its consequences for maintaining the interest of members at the beginning of a project: "For example, in our chapter, at first there was funding for the project, but then, when there was only a little funding, some members were not interested anymore and they left." Nila responded: "It is not only funding that is the problem, it is also education. For example, in setting up cooperatives, it is not only funds that are needed but also knowledge of accounting. Otherwise the organization will not know if it is gaining something it could distribute to the members. The problem of lack of education should not be seen in isolation from the other aspects of the organization." Ate Gloria, a national peasant leader of AMIHAN, affirmed Nila's statement: "In my view, it is lack of education [*kulang sa pagaaral*]. We do not just look at the financial aspect." Nila's and Ate Gloria's responses were geared more toward selling the idea of the importance of education in organizational work than toward actually analyzing the financial situation of local chapters as an organizational problem.

The lack of financial resources that the two peasant women mentioned here is actually a practical problem with which they must cope in their everyday organizing work. Although their financial difficulties are clearly viewed by some to be subsumed under the peasants' need for training and education, the peasant women feel it is one of their major problems, and they talked about it even outside this training session. From the perspective of the peasant women, money is concretely related to other things that they want to do, whether it is to start a socioeconomic project or to organize a study session: "You want to go to meetings but you have no money for transportation." Being poor, this is something they experience more than the middle-class women who may also be doing organizing work. The lack of resources that the village peasant women experience in their organizational and political work is related to broader issues of class formation in the Philippines (through which peasant women are impoverished) and of allocation of state funds (to which peasant women have virtually no access). Foreign development aid that the government gets, for example, does not trickle down to village organizations like KAMMI, with political change agendas. Instead, such aid is partly used for counterinsurgency in the villages, and it benefits mostly businessmen and landlords who have government connections. These interrelated issues have policy, organizational, and tactical implications.

The peasant women found their leadership seminar useful. Some of them said that they learned something that they did not know before the seminar. Others said that their understanding of organization and of how to organize correctly was broadened and improved ("lumawak ang kaisipan ko na magagamit ko sa pag-oorganisa"). Some said that they were happy that KAMMI is beginning to revive again.

The peasant women were also very candid about what they found hard to understand. Women mentioned as difficult the topic on "how to do social analysis," some terms like "*kantitatibo*" and "*kalitatibo*," and the topic on how to analyze contradictions (*tunggalian*). One said that the presentation on the national situation in the Philippines ("pangkalahatang pananaw sa pambansang kalagayan") needed more explanation.

Most of the women believed this kind of *pag-aaral* is valuable, however, and they recommended that the training seminars be continued. Hence, although through actual organizing the peasant women can gain practical knowledge, they also see that formal training like this can be useful. First, it helps them conceptualize their own experience, learn from that of others, and then broaden their practical, experiential knowledge with the theoretical knowledge of others. But the real test of the practical value of formal, theoretical training sessions like these lies in whether the peasant women in fact found them helpful in their organizing work. Their usefulness is not something that can be easily and immediately assessed.

To conclude, this discussion on some of the ways KAMMI integrates education and consciousness-raising in its politics brings up a few points. First, it indicates some of the sources of the increased awareness of the peasant women about their situation and how it relates to the larger issues in Philippine development and underdevelopment. Their awareness develops as they talk with each other about their concerns and concrete experiences, as they become more and more involved in the different levels of organization, and as they are exposed to other sources of information, educational sessions, and discussions of issues. Their awareness increases as they have the opportunity to relate with other peasant leaders outside of their local village, with national leaders who are more politically aware and critically conscious, and with people who may not necessarily come from the peasantry but are involved in working to support the peasant movement or are engaged in the larger movement for change and social justice in the Philippines.

Second, as members of the working class, peasant women come to women's organization not entirely devoid of feminist class awareness. Some of the comments they articulated in their deliberations show that they have an understanding of the relationship of gender and class, although they may not express this awareness in academic language.

Third, the peasant women develop concepts of leadership and what being a good leader entails through their experience. I found their way of articulating these concepts, and the language they used to express their own intellectual abstractions, very powerful because these come from their conceptualization of their own experience. It is this knowledge from below that still needs to be appreciated by those who construct concepts of development and politics in the Third World. None of the leaders spoke of military might or dominance as a characteristic of leadership. What they spoke about was a good leader being able to create a sense of equality with others ("pantay-pantay na pagtingin sa kapwa"). Important qualities of leadership, they said, were having strong principles and the courage to stand up against oppression, having a critical vision and broad understanding about the local and national situation affecting them, and being able to accept one's mistakes. Some also said that good, democratic leadership can mobilize members to act in order to accomplish a goal without having to command them.

Fourth, education and training sessions, such as leadership training, develop the peasant women's confidence: "I realized I could also be a leader, even if I am just like this"; "We should not be ashamed if we have no higher education, because we are also learning, studying like the teachers." Thus, training helps them acquire a better self-image, which in turn helps them to reject society's stereotype of peasant women as being "of low education" (mababa ang pinag-aralan). In the Philippines, where people with little education are looked down on, a peasant organization like KAMMI, which serves as what some of the women call "school" (paaralan), has a very significant educational value at the grassroots level. But the women here conceive of pag-aaral (education) not as formal education, but rather as educational sessions that may prove useful in transforming their situation.

Fifth, educational sessions are an important part of KAMMI's politics because they serve as alternative sources of information. They provide views and analysis of the Philippine situation that the mainstream media may not. As the peasant women discuss issues together, they give personal meaning to these issues and learn different ways of viewing them. They relate their personal experiences—such as the increase in prices—to larger issues—such as foreign debt. This process is part of political consciousness-raising, which is an important component of political action, since one cannot change a situation one does not understand.

Chapter Five
AMIHAN's National Politics of Resistance

We set up a separate women's organization because the participation of women in production is very important. Women hope and we want to make sure that our demand for true land reform is heard. The KMP alone cannot do it. Peasant women must have participation. Peasant women have particular demands as peasant women. There will be no true land reform if half the peasantry does not own land. We, the peasant women, will ourselves be the ones to carry the issues particular to peasant women.

—An AMIHAN national leader

The national politics of AMIHAN, like that of KAMMI, confronts the interlocking power structures in the Philippines that affect peasant women's everyday lives. AMIHAN promotes alternative development policies, which, if given legitimacy by the government, could bring about fundamental agrarian reform that is sensitive to the situation of peasant women. The existence of AMIHAN as a national federation indicates the attempt of peasant women to stage their struggle on a national level, to give a stronger voice to their demands.

AMIHAN: Distinct but Linked

Before the formation of AMIHAN in 1986, there was already a national federation of peasants comprising both men and women: the Kilusang Magbubukid ng Pilipinas (KMP, or Peasant Movement of the Philippines). The KMP was organized in 1985 in response to the need for a strong national organization that would advance the peasant struggle by generating a militant political force. Its members include small owner-cultivators, tenants, peasants, women, rural youth, subsistence fisherfolk, and farm workers. As of 1988, the KMP had approximately 800,000 members from the rural sector, with fifty-nine provincial and six regional chapters nationwide. Leadership in the KMP is largely male dominated.

The need not only to make visible the role of peasant women both in production and in the peasant struggle, but also to recognize its importance resulted in the formation of AMIHAN. The founders of AMIHAN saw that their goals could be achieved through an independent peasant women's organization, which would have an adequate awareness of the particular situation of peasant women and would further their demands in the process of agrarian change. According to a national AMIHAN leader who played a major role in the founding of AMIHAN, a separate peasant women's organization would give importance to the role of women in production. It could also bring forth issues and demands particular to peasant women in the struggle for true agrarian change.

AMIHAN therefore serves as a vehicle for peasant women to push for agrarian change—change that will benefit the peasantry but at the same time will attend to the needs of women in particular. For example, under the present feudal-patriarchal system of land ownership, land titles are given only to men. From the perspective of AMIHAN, a genuine agrarian reform must guarantee peasant women the right to own land. AMIHAN thus believes it has an important role in bringing about agrarian change that will address the patriarchal practices woven into the feudal relations of production. It will perform that role through the collective action of peasant women.

Hence, AMIHAN stresses the importance of both local and national organization. But while its main task is to nationally coordinate and federate peasant women's organizations, it recognizes that its foundation is building strong local organizations in the villages where the peasant women conduct their everyday lives. AMIHAN continually reorganizes its structure in concretizing this vision, sometimes to correct past mistakes, and sometimes to respond to emerging situations.[1]

AMIHAN serves as a center for analyzing and raising national issues relevant to true agrarian reform and other aspects of peasant women's lives, using the perspectives of peasant women. Through national conferences, members of local chapters are able to meet peasant women from different regions of the Philippines and to learn from them what they are doing. During these conferences they share their problems in organizing and get insights on how to deal with them. They also study national issues, with AMIHAN defining its official stand on an issue after it has been critically analyzed. Each AMIHAN representative states her understanding of the issue and what she thinks the stand of AMIHAN should be; then together they define the official position. Sometimes it is apparent that the representatives are not yet ready to take a stand on an issue. In this case they postpone the decision until there has been further analysis. (An example of this kind of deliberation is discussed later in the chapter.)

Though it is a distinct organization sensitive to the peasant women's needs, AMIHAN believes that its struggle is linked to that of the broader peasant movement, as represented by the KMP, and that the peasant movement must also address peasant women's issues. One national leader of AMIHAN puts it thus: "The vision of AMIHAN on the KMP [is that the] KMP and AMIHAN must have a relationship that can be likened to marriage, because both are carrying one issue, and we want the KMP to help in raising awareness of the situation of peasant women."

AMIHAN sees itself as linked not only to the national peasant struggle but also to the women's movement as a whole. It is federated to the women's movement through the nongovernmental, multisectoral, inter-class organization called GABRIELA (the National Coalition of Women's Organizations in the Philippines). AMIHAN sees its role in GABRIELA as advocating the particular situation of peasant women, who comprise the majority of Filipino women. The liberation of this sector of the population, it believes, will contribute significantly to the liberation of all Filipino women.

The Struggle Within the Struggle

AMIHAN struggles with structural articulations of gender and class not only in Philippine society, but also within the peasant movement itself. For example, at the time of my fieldwork, AMIHAN national leaders were striving to make KMP national leaders more open and to have them give due importance to issues particular to peasant women. From the point of view of AMIHAN's national leaders, creating a separate organization for peasant women and raising gender issues strengthens the whole peasant movement and broadens its base. National KMP leaders, on the other hand, tend to view the raising of gender issues as divisive within the peasant movement. From their perspective, AMIHAN should raise issues particular to peasant women within GABRIELA. Although AMIHAN national leaders do not dispute this, they believe it is important that the KMP's agenda for change and its framework of analysis of the Philippine situation include the ways in which the larger social structures and development policies affect peasant women. AMIHAN national leaders want KMP national leaders to understand that "feminism" means "struggling for their rights" as peasant women, and that feminist issues should not be given negative connotations. One AMIHAN leader,

Ate Loy, described this struggle within the struggle. She spoke of her desire for peasant women's leadership in the national peasant movement to be given greater recognition:

The KMP has not yet really carried the issues of peasant women. We have not yet been given importance. Even in speaking in rallies, we are always made to go last, and we are given only a short time; we are almost forgotten. Like here in the midnight prayer service, we have no speaker. One reason is that they still see us as weak leaders. They want us to be under them. There is still no real support for our actions. Since the start of AMIHAN, the KMP has not been as helpful to us as they have been to other sectors, because their view is that we must ask help from GABRIELA. But in the regional chapters, the relationship is all right between men and women. It is only here on the national level that we are being looked down on. But when KMP leaders were in Europe, they told us that the people they met there said that they should not come to Europe again without a peasant woman with them to speak about the situation of peasant women. Only then did they help me to go to Europe on a speaking tour about the peasant women's situation. Why are we being underestimated by the KMP national leaders? Do they think we are not yet as articulate as they are about the issues? A feudal attitude is still there. On one occasion, they did not invite us to their National Council Assembly. I wrote to them and asked them why they did not invite us. Question mark was the answer they gave me. Why is it that on the national level the relationship is not good, when in fact it is on the national level that we must tighten our relationship. They say that it is a priority that it should start in the regional chapters.

She indicated that most KMP national leaders lack an understanding of "feminism," and she argued against their view that a separate national peasant women's organization would divide the peasant movement:

They say AMIHAN is "feminismo." We told them that "feminismo" means struggling for our rights. What is wrong with struggling for your rights? They do not yet understand an orientation toward women. We must have a dialogue with the KMP to make the relationship closer. Why don't they give us the chance to speak before big groups? You are just coming up to the stage, and they already tell you to shorten what you will say. Another national AMIHAN leader has had the same experience. KMP national leaders look down on us. There is one national leader in the KMP who comes to us, he is supportive of us, but he has no power . . . because others still worry about "who is going to be left at home" and that they will lose force or their mass base. But in my view it will strengthen the force or mass base if the local membership is both KMP and AMIHAN.

Despite this, peasant women keep joining AMIHAN. We are increasing our regional organizations. The peasant women in Cebu who have organized themselves want to be linked with AMIHAN.

There are actions of the KMP that we do not know about. This affects united action.

While these peasant women struggle within the peasant movement for due recognition of their own analysis and experience of gender and class in the conceptualization of alternative development policies and the politics of change, they must also struggle within the women's movement. For example, the national leaders of AMIHAN want to assert the peasant women's issue in the women's coalition under the umbrella of GABRIELA. They argue that the majority of women are peasants, and that the poverty of rural women and their families is related to urban poverty and prostitution in the U.S. bases, which were issues that they observed GABRIELA had focused on. But since GABRIELA is a multisectoral coalition of women's organizations, with members of different social classes, it has a tendency to subdue issues fundamental to peasant women.

Alternative Views on Peasant Women and Agricultural Development

The current government approach to agricultural development is mainly geared toward increasing production through the use of Western technology without changing the relations of production. AMIHAN believes that changing the feudal and semi-feudal modes of agricultural production is fundamental to the liberation of peasant women both from poverty and from exploitation as peasants and as women. It advocates genuine land reform as a major step toward changing the Philippine feudal and semi-feudal system. AMIHAN states in its official document, *AMIHAN Praymer: Ang Tunay na Reformang Agraryo—Binhi ng Kalayaan ng Kababaihang Magbubukid* (AMIHAN Primer: Genuine Agrarian Reform—Seed of Peasant Women's Liberation):

Feudalism exploits and oppresses peasant women, the majority of women in the Philippines. Feudalism prevents the progress of women in the economic sphere, their participation in decision making in social policies, their intellectual and cultural growth. Land reform that will dismantle the feudalist system is a big step toward the liberation of women because it will remove many obstacles to their progress. That is why it is the responsibility of women to push for land reform as part of their liberation—their liberation as peasants and as women. (p. 67)

But AMIHAN is aware that agrarian change that simply makes peasant women beneficiaries rather than active political actors cannot guarantee benefits that address their particular needs. Only by becoming collective social actors in the process of agrarian struggle can they bring their own agenda to bear on the direction that genuine agrarian change will take. Thus, AMIHAN promotes peasant women's leadership in the process of agrarian change through peasant women's organizations. It asserts that peasant women must struggle against all obstacles that preclude their full political participation in the process of agrarian transformation. It promotes the feminist development perspective: agrarian reform that pays special attention to the situation of peasant women will benefit everyone, both men and women. But in AMIHAN's view such reform cannot be achieved without the full participation and leadership of peasant women.

Agrarian development, therefore, from the point of view of AMIHAN, is conceived both as a *process* and as an *end*. As a process, agrarian development must ensure equal participation of peasant women and men. As an end, it must change the feudal relations of production in a way that will benefit equally peasant women and men by seriously considering the oppression, subordination, and exploitation of peasant women. Without these two aspects, AMIHAN believes, agrarian change is not genuine, will not have a community-wide impact, and will not benefit women. Only by simultaneously confronting both gender and class, which together are woven into the feudal relations of production, can land reform be genuine. This view of agrarian change relates to the everyday lives of peasant women and is an articulation of an agenda for change that would be responsive to both peasant women and men on the national scale.

The Congress for a People's Agrarian Reform: PARCODE as Alternative to CARP

Agrarian development policies of past and present government administrations have been unresponsive to the needs of the peasantry as a whole, and even more so to those of poor peasant women. A current example is the government's Comprehensive Agrarian Reform Program (CARP), or Republic Act 6657, which has been widely criticized by the KMP, AMIHAN, and other sectors. Their criticisms led to the formation of the Congress for a People's Agrarian Reform (CPAR), of which AMIHAN was a founding member. On June 25–26, 1988, CPAR called for a multisectoral conference in Quezon City to legislate the People's Agrarian Reform Code. Over six hundred delegates—representing a broad spectrum of peasant organizations, sectoral groups, political alliances, nongovernmental organizations, and agrarian reform advocates—responded. The conference produced the People's Agrarian Reform Code of 1988 (PARCODE), which was intended to be an alternative to the government's Comprehensive Agrarian Reform Program. The peasants criticized CARP, saying it is "pro-landlord," "puts the burden of land reform on the peasantry," and contains "loopholes" (*mayroon mga butas*) favoring landlords. The Philippine Peasant Institute (1989, 6–9) identifies some of these loopholes: (1) the variable retention limit, which landlords can manipulate to retain more than the five hectares they are allowed to keep if they are covered by CARP, (2) exemptions of private agricultural farms (such as livestock, poultry, aquaculture, vegetables, flowers, cacao, and coffee) and rubber plantations from being covered by the law for ten years after it becomes effective, (3) permission for landlords to transfer titles for more land than is allowed by the retention limit, for three months after the law becomes effective, (4) absence of a provision compelling landlords to obey the law (i.e., compliance is voluntary), and (5) valuation of land based on market value, not productivity, making the price of land more favorable to the landlords.

CARP, formulated by the landlord-dominated Philippine Congress, and PARCODE, formulated by people's organizations, have basic differences. While both legislative documents talk about agrarian reform, they differ in their conceptualization of it. The following examines the basic differences between CARP and PARCODE and shows how PARCODE provides an alternative to CARP.

Land to the Tiller.

Unlike CARP, wherein the basic principle of land distribution is just compensation for the landlord on the basis of the current market value of his land, the fundamental principle of agrarian reform in PARCODE is "land to the tiller." "Land to the tiller" essentially means that only those who can directly till the land have the right to own it. Those who choose to retain land must make it productive by themselves, without tenants. PARCODE chapter 1, section 3, "Retention Limits," states:

Based on the principle of owner cultivatorship, *no person, family, corporation and/ or association (except farmers' and fisherfolks' cooperatives or associations) may own/retain directly or indirectly any agricultural land except that which s/he is cultivating directly* [emphasis mine]. The land retained by such person or family shall vary according to factors governing a viable family-size farm, such as commodity produced, terrain, infrastructure, soil fertility, and others as determined by the local People's Agrarian Reform Council (PARCON) but in no case shall retention exceed five (5) years from the effectivity of this act.

The right of the tiller to own the lands which they till shall be superior to the retention right of the landowner, and tenancy relationship shall not be permitted in the retained landholding [emphasis mine].

Any sale, disposition, lease, management contract or transfer of possession of private lands covered by this law, executed after February 2, 1987 by the landowner, shall be null and void, unless made in favor of qualified beneficiaries as defined in Section 6 hereof.

No sale, disposition, lease, management contract or transfer of possession of private lands executed by the original landowner prior to February 2, 1987 shall be considered valid unless it has been registered with the Government prior to such a date or unless said transaction is not inconsistent with any provision of this act.

PARCODE's basic principle of "land to the tiller" therefore aims at dismantling the feudal relations of agricultural production that create an unjust and inequitable system of land ownership and use. CARP does not guarantee to effect this fundamental change, since it follows the principles of "voluntary land transfer" and "voluntary offer to sell" on the part of landowners; the government, for its part, may or may not purchase the offered lands for distribution to peasants. Executive Order No. 229, "Providing the Mechanisms for the Implementation of the Comprehensive Agrarian Reform Program," chapter 3, "Land Transfer, Utilization and Sharing," states:

Section 8. Voluntary Land Transfer. Landowners whose lands are subject to redistribution under this Order have the option of entering into a *voluntary agreement for direct transfer of their lands* [emphasis mine] to beneficiaries, under terms and conditions acceptable to both parties and subject to the approval of the DAR. . . .

Section 9. Voluntary Offer to Sell. The government shall purchase all agricultural lands it deems productive and suitable to farmer cultivation *voluntarily offered for sale* [emphasis mine] to it at a valuation determined in accordance with Section 6. Such transactions shall be exempt from the payment of capital gains tax and other taxes and fees.

Inclusion in Land Reform What Is Exempt in CARP.

To make agrarian reform truly comprehensive, PARCODE includes lands other than agricultural lands that can be put into productive use, such as "military reservations," idle and abandoned arable lands "including church and school owned lands," and "all other agricultural lands which have been converted to non-agricultural uses" to evade land reform (PARCODE, chapter 1, section 2). CARP exempts these lands (section 3, Executive Order No. 229). That PARCODE included lands used by the military reflects the view that peasants cannot effectively struggle for genuine land reform under a militarized government. A comprehensive agrarian program must include the dismantling of the military and challenge the class interests that militarism serves. PARCODE thus directly confronts the possibility of CARP being used as part of the government's strategy of low intensity conflict. In low intensity conflict, the government may give in to some reforms or make concessions while at the same time intensifying militarization. Using the military to implement these reforms or concessions through civic action is a way to construct a liberal facade for the government and a benign image for the armed forces. In CARP, the Armed Forces of the Philippines and military government agencies may be involved in the implementation of land reform (section 5, d and m, of Executive Order No. 129-A, "Modifying

Executive Order No. 129, Reorganizing and Strengthening Department of Agrarian Reform and for Other Purposes").

Multinational Corporations and Filipino Control of the Political Economy.

While CARP has left the important issue of multinational corporations and their major control of the Philippine political economy unaddressed, PARCODE has made it a special concern. PARCODE greatly reduces the corporations' control of the political economy and places them under the collective ownership and management of the Filipino direct producers. PARCODE chapter 3, section 15, no. 1, "Special Concerns," states: "All lands currently under the control of transnational corporations must revert back to Filipinos, in a period of two years in accordance with Sec. 9, and their ownership and management transferred collectively to the direct producers. All improvements found in the land like factories must also be given to the beneficiaries."

Peasants' Political Will and Collective Participation.

Unlike CARP, PARCODE regards peasants not as passive beneficiaries but as collective political actors who must play a major role in all levels of decision making and policy implementation. PARCODE's initiatives toward "people's control and ownership of the production and marketing of commercial farm inputs" must be legitimized and accorded government support (PARCODE chapter 3, section 13, m; chapter 2, section 6). Peasant collectives, such as cooperatives and other organizations, must go hand in hand with land distribution, since they will serve as vehicles for the participation of peasants in agrarian reform (PARCODE chapter 3, section 10). Hence, under PARCODE, it is the political empowerment of peasants that will guarantee their access to the economic benefits of an agrarian transformation.

Equal Rights for Rural Women.

CARP has made peasant women invisible. Even its language renders them nonexistent. When it refers to a peasant, CARP uses "he." In PARCODE, however, peasant women visibly exist. PARCODE guarantees that "all women members of the agricultural force" must be "assured equal rights with men to ownership of the land, equal shares of the farm's produce," and equal representation in "decision-making bodies" (chapter 3, section 15, no. 5). In the distribution of land to rural women, priority is given to "widows, single women parents, abandoned women, single women heads of the family" (chapter 2, section 7).

Agrarian Reform Funding and Foreign Debt.

Funding for CARP depends largely on foreign loans, thus putting the Philippines further into debt. The foreign debt increases more than $1 billion yearly. Already $26 billion in 1986, it is expected to rise to $38 billion in 1998. Most foreign funds for CARP go to "support services" such as the purchase of foreign agrochemicals like fertilizers and pesticides, and the purchase of grain and postharvest technology—all products of transnational corporations. Major lenders are the International Monetary Fund, the World Bank, and U.S. AID (Research and Policy Studies Desk, Philippine Peasant Institute, 1989). With the structural adjustments that the IMF and World Bank prescribe as conditions for loans, CARP entrenches the multilateral development aid agencies' control of the Philippine political economy. Already reflected in CARP is the privatization scheme, a major requirement of IMF loans. In CARP, privatization takes the form of selling public sector enterprises to private business as a way to raise funds for CARP and as a form of incentive for landlords to invest in industrial ventures in a free enterprise economic arrangement (Proclamation No. 131, "Instituting a Comprehensive Agrarian Reform Program," section 8; Executive Order No. 229, "Improving the Mechanisms for the Implementation of the Comprehensive Agrarian Reform Program," section 6). PARCODE, on the other hand, confronts the issue of foreign debt. Funding for agrarian reform shall be "sourced primarily from the amount that shall be saved by the national government in the event that debt services be reduced from its present level, or a moratorium on or repudiation of debts be declared" and "from a decrease in the budget for national defense" and other uses of local resources (chapter 6, section 20). Hence, PARCODE reflects the view that agricultural development and change must lead to self-reliance, rather than perpetuate dependency that puts the Philippine political economy under foreign control.

Legitimation of Land Occupations.

Organized peasants in rural areas, such as Mindoro, Laguna, and Negros, have used the strategy of land occupation to make idle lands productive (see Chapter 4). This is a grassroots initiative to implement land reform despite government inaction. CARP imposes sanctions on such initiatives: it "permanently disqualifies" peasants involved in land occupations from being beneficiaries of land reform and takes away their right to own land (Executive Order No. 229, chapter 6, section 22). PARCODE, on the other hand, safeguards and legitimizes this peasant initiative: "The occupation of private or public lands prior to the effectivity of this order shall not be a bar to being a beneficiary to this program" (chapter 2, section 7). CARP's sanction against land occupation provides the basis for the peasants' criticism that the government's land reform is part of low intensity conflict or counterinsurgency strategy.

In the final analysis, PARCODE demonstrates an ideological and organizational resistance, and offers an alternative, to the current ideology of agricultural development in the Philippines. PARCODE, as a grassroots initiative, reflects the capability of Filipino peasant women and men to formulate legislation. The formation of the Congress for a People's Agrarian Reform (CPAR), which gave birth to PARCODE, indicates that the grassroots organizations it comprises can indeed devise a mechanism for meaningful participation in policy making. CPAR conducted a campaign to obtain signatures in order to pressure the government to recognize PARCODE. AMIHAN, for example, facilitated petition signing among its chapters. But it remains to be seen whether the government will move to legitimize PARCODE by incorporating it into the development agenda.

The basic differences between PARCODE and CARP also indicate how the social and economic class of policy-making bodies influences the development policies they define. The policy-making body that produced CARP was dominated by politicians from the landed class; hence, it sought to protect its class interests. The members of the policy-making body that produced PARCODE come from the ranks of the working class and from the broad alliance of organizations seeking social justice in the Philippines. Hence, PARCODE contains a change agenda that represents the interests of the poor majority. It attempts to bring about fundamental change in the power structures and agricultural development policies that CARP seeks to preserve under the guise of reform and concessions.

Lastly, PARCODE's inclusion of, and CARP's lack of, the peasant women's change agenda shows how the gender and class composition of policy-making bodies can influence their sensitivity to the particular situation of peasant women. Of the 204 members of the Philippine Senate, only 2 are women, and they are landlords themselves. AMIHAN's influence in the formulation of PARCODE indicates the importance of the collective participation of peasant women in defining agricultural development policies. As long as the legitimated policy-making bodies in the

Philippines continue to exclude peasant women's grassroots organizations from the formulation of state policies, they cannot adequately represent the particular needs of peasant women.

AMIHAN's Alternative Agenda of Agrarian Reform

Continuing Education on Women and Agrarian Reform.

AMIHAN recognizes the importance of continuing education on women and agrarian reform. It recognizes, too, that although it has reached quite a number of peasant women, it needs to expand its educational programs. At its National Council convention in July 1989 in Quezon City, delegates of the different chapters of AMIHAN received and studied the AMIHAN primer on genuine agrarian reform, entitled *AMIHAN Praymer—Ang Tunay na Reformang Agrario: Binhi ng Kalayaan ng Kababaihang Magbubukid* (AMIHAN Primer—Genuine Agrarian Reform: Seed for Peasant Women's Liberation). They took copies of the primer back to their respective chapters, to use them in their local education programs or activities.

The primer contains four main sections, each with cartoon (komik)-style illustrations. The first analyzes why the feudal and semi-feudal system is the basic problem of peasant women, what its historical roots are, and how it particularly oppresses peasant women. The second analyzes why the implementation of genuine land reform is the fundamental way to change the feudal and semi-feudal system, and describes the objectives of a true land reform based on the perspective of women. The third sets forth the essentials of land reform that peasant women must struggle for, based on a feminist perspective. And the fourth explains why the Filipino women's movement as a whole must support the struggle (*pakikibaka*) of peasant women for true land reform.

Alternative Land Reform.

Since the need for genuine land reform is a national issue that affects the peasantry as a whole, AMIHAN has formulated a comprehensive alternative agenda for land reform that differs from the government's Comprehensive Agrarian Reform Program (CARP). This alternative program, which is described in the *AMIHAN Praymer*, confronts not only the issue of gender equality in the access to the primary resource of land and its produce, but also the issue of political empowerment of peasant women through collective social formations. According to AMIHAN, women's ownership of and control of agricultural resources and their organizational empowerment in the process of land reform are crucial to the conception and implementation of agrarian change. The following specific proposals in the *AMIHAN Praymer* reflect these views.

First, AMIHAN believes that the feudal exploitation of peasant women will basically end with free land redistribution to peasant women and men as couples (legally married or not), or to single female heads of families. Free distribution of land equally to men and women will not put the burden of land reform on the peasants' capacity to pay amortization; hence it will guarantee an end to the feudal relations of production. In AMIHAN's perspective, such free distribution is just, because the peasants have already paid for the land through the exploitation of their labor (*Praymer*, p. 28). But AMIHAN is aware that men have traditionally controlled decisions on land and its produce. Hence, it believes that peasant women must also have equal decision-making power with regard to land titled to couples (p. 28).

Second, AMIHAN stresses that those distributing free land must be sensitive to the fact that some peasant women are the heads of their households, either because they are widows or because they are abandoned or separated. They must be given priority in the early phases of agrarian change (p. 35).

Third, there must be a mechanism by which women can safeguard their benefits. Peasant women can create that mechanism through the formation of agricultural cooperatives that will collectivize not only ownership but also decisions regarding land. These collectives must provide education for women, so they acquire the knowledge and skills they need to participate fully in collective decision making regarding their newfound ownership and rights (p. 36). AMIHAN is of course conscious of the fact that the patriarchial decision-making structure in the family limits women's full participation in community collective action. Therefore, along with community collectivization of decisions regarding land must go a democratization of the decision making in the family (p. 36). But certain individual family decisions should not take precedence over the collective decisions of peasant organizations about the distributed land. For example, if a peasant couple can no longer till their land, the decision on what to do with it must be made by the peasant cooperative to which they belong. The collective decision must uphold the principle that distributed lands cannot be sold or mortgaged by the individual beneficiaries, but must be returned to the peasant cooperatives (p. 37). Thus, AMIHAN's view breaks away from the concept of land as a private property and embraces instead a concept of land as a community property. This perspective strikes at the very essence of feudalism, in which land is concentrated among a few, who make the decisions regarding its use. This perspective also reclaims the indigenous concept of land ownership, which was lost to colonialism's privatization of land.

Because of the significant impact of usury on the lives of peasant women, AMIHAN's ideology of genuine land reform includes eventual abolition of this practice. This could be accomplished by (a) promoting credit cooperatives, (b) ensuring equal access of peasant women to formal credit systems, (c) increasing government subsidies on farm production, (d) forming peasant cooperatives, including women's cooperatives, where women have adequate access to formal credit systems, (e) canceling debts, (f) empowering peasant organizations to set up fair rules to regulate the informal credit system, (g) using alternative farm inputs that do not result in a high cost of production, and (h) encouraging peasants to save (pp. 50–51). Some of these proposals are already being implemented by AMIHAN's local chapters, such as those of KAMMI (see Chapter 4).

From the point of view of AMIHAN, usury is a result of the feudal mode of production and of the commercialization of agriculture, with foreign corporations having monopoly over the prices of such resources as fertilizers, seed, machinery, and pesticides. AMIHAN sees that usury will end when the income of peasant families increases as a result of free land distribution, farmers' cooperatives, and their control of agricultural production and marketing. While it may take time to totally eradicate usury, AMIHAN believes certain regulatory steps could already be taken. Among its recommendations are: (1) peg the annual interest of government banks at 12 percent and make credit available to peasants at low interest rates, (2) lower the current interest rates of local creditors to 30 percent, and (3) reassess current debts based on the peasants' ability to pay (pp. 47–50).

AMIHAN's alternative program of land reform calls for an end to feudal forms of exploitation of peasant women because they are women. First, women's free domestic service in the landlords' or usurers' household as payment for debts must be stopped. And second, peasant women's organizations must be empowered to collectively confront landlords' sexual abuses by providing the support systems needed for peasant women to bring such cases into the open (p. 54). Often victims of sexual abuse do not make their cases public because of fear or shame. In AMIHAN's view, sexual abuses arising from feudal relations must be treated as a public concern.

AMIHAN realistically acknowledges that distribution of free land to the tillers may not be completed quickly; instead, a transition period may be necessary. They see three conditions that may affect the rate of land distribution. First, the level of organization and consolidation of peasant organizations may vary. Second, it may become necessary for big landholdings to be given priority in the distribution of land. And third, the system for payment of landlords may not be settled yet. Even during a transition period, however, some reforms must already be in place, such as: (a) a 50 percent reduction in land rent from its current rate, or a reduction to 10 percent of the harvest after all production expenses are deducted; (b) a reduction in the rent of farm animals and machinery, based on a rate peasant organizations agree on; (c) the establishment of provisions in which peasants will not be made to pay land rent in cases where destruction from military operations and natural calamities is at least 20 percent of the expected harvest (pp. 44–46). These reforms can immediately ameliorate the poverty and extremely exploitative economic relations in the everyday lives of all peasants. Hence, AMIHAN on the national level, like KAMMI on the local level, combines both reforms and radical change in its agenda of agrarian development. Its members do not see these two levels of change as contradictory: reforms can serve as a transition toward more radical change.

Although the free distribution of land to the tiller is basic to AMIHAN's concept of land reform, the organization recognizes the fact that there are situations when land must be paid for before it can be distributed. In such cases there must be conditions to govern the purchase of land. (1) Nondespotic and nonabusive landlords will be paid for their land. They will be allowed to retain some land if they till it themselves; they cannot use tenants to till the land for them. (2) Rich peasants will be required to sell excess land to the government for distribution to landless peasants. (3) Landed farmers who placed their land within the peasant cooperative system will be allowed to retain some, under the same conditions as nondespotic and nonabusive landlords. (4) In general, selective compensation will be used to determine the price of land that will be placed under land reform (pp. 42–43).

AMIHAN's alternative program of land reform also addresses the issue of economic imperialism in the form of external control of the Philippine political economy by transnational corporations. AMIHAN supports PARCODE's provisions that plantations owned and controlled by foreign corporations must be nationalized, and that peasants who lost their land to agribusiness transnationals through landgrabbing must be given back their land or be justly compensated.

AMIHAN proposes that agricultural corporations forcibly, illicitly, or deceitfully acquired by Marcos and his cronies must be confiscated; they may then be transformed into farm cooperatives, or they must be placed under state ownership and control. In AMIHAN's plan, corporate farms and plantations that may not be covered by free land distribution must set aside 20 percent of their landholdings for their farm workers to use for subsistence production and family needs. In coconut plantations, peasants must be allowed to intercrop for their subsistence, while in sugar, pineapple, coffee, and other plantations, 20 percent of the land must be placed under the control of an agricultural workers' union (p. 40). In this way AMIHAN apparently allows for the continuance of existing export crop production, but insists that it be combined with a subsistence production that could respond to the needs of the agricultural workers and the local market. This way cash crop agricultural workers can have something to fall back on during a slump in the world market. At present, the government's agricultural development policy has no such provision. For example, the sugar plantation workers and their families suffered from hunger when the demand for sugar decreased in the world market.

AMIHAN believes that the rights of agricultural workers in corporate farms must be safeguarded by strong unionization of both regular and seasonal workers. Unions for women agricultural workers must also be promoted. AMIHAN views the following as basic rights of agricultural workers: (1) work security for all farm workers and permanent work for seasonal workers; (2) just wages, and just pay for overtime work and tedious tasks; (3) decent housing for workers; (4) free health care; (5) vacation leave, sick leave, and maternity and paternity leave; (6) free day care for the children of agricultural workers, and educational benefits for them; (7) accident and death benefits; (8) the right to inspect the books of farm corporations to determine their financial situation; and (9) free acquisition of corporate lands, for workers' unions and their families to use to provide for their daily needs (pp. 61–62). The last right is being exercised through the peasants' occupation of idle lands in Mindoro (see Chapter 4). In the present land reform program of the government, these rights are not addressed.

AMIHAN's alternative land reform program also promotes the unionization of contractual agricultural workers who do not work on corporate farms or on large plantations of big landlords. Such unions can protect them from exploitative dealings of contractors and recruiters, and can assert their right to just wages and benefits (p. 63).

Genuine land reform, AMIHAN believes, is integrated with changes in other sectors of the economy, such as national industrialization. The *AMIHAN Praymer* states, "It is necessary that national industrialization must take place simultaneously with genuine land reform" (p. 20). But national industrialization, AMIHAN emphasizes, must be sensitive to the particular situation of peasant women, so that they derive some benefit. Technology must be appropriate for women in that it lightens their workload, and farm machinery must be made in such a way that it can be used by both men and women.

AMIHAN believes that genuine land reform must also include improvement of social services. For example, land taxes collected after successful land reform shall revert back to the communities in the form of, for example, health services, schools in the villages, day-care centers, and other services that will lighten women's work at home (p. 37).

Overall, then, AMIHAN's program of land reform is comprehensive, integrated, redistributive, and feminist. It is comprehensive because it addresses local, national, and international issues that are excluded in development policies currently legitimated by the Philippine government. It is integrated because it is conceived within the context of related changes in the social political economy. It is redistributive because it basically aims at redistributing resources and power from where it is presently concentrated to the direct producers of agricultural wealth. It is feminist because it demands that the process of land redistribution must actively involve peasant women and promote their equal access to and control of basic economic resources and political decisions.

Arriving at a Collective Political Position on Development Issues

One important aspect of AMIHAN's politics is the way in which it takes a collective political position on development issues. For example, on July 23–25, 1989, during the AMIHAN National Council meeting in Manila (in which I was a participant observer), regional and provincial representatives from twenty-two chapters analyzed some major development issues and deliberated collectively on what the official stand of the organization should be. The following discusses how the National Council arrived at a political position on some major development policies and government programs. It is important to show this process because it indicates AMIHAN's attempt to put forth a collective voice, perspective, and analysis of issues that have an impact on peasant women's lives.

The Foreign Debt Crisis.

On July 23, the National Council held a study session on the Philippine foreign debt crisis, and the members discussed what AMIHAN's position should be. The session began with a talk on foreign debt and its impact on the peasantry by a staff member of the national office of the KMP, Tonio. This was followed by an open forum. Then the executive director of AMIHAN, Tina, briefly touched on the impact of the foreign debt on women.

Tonio first presented some statistical facts: "The Philippine foreign debt in 1989 is $29.7 billion, equivalent to 107 billion pesos. The Philippines has paid 90 billion pesos for its 1989 debt. This is 44 percent of the 220 billion pesos in the Philippine fiscal budget in 1989, and 35 percent of the national income from export." After giving these facts, Tonio related the foreign debt to the Letter of Intent (LOI), which stipulates the conditions of the International Monetary Fund (IMF) and the World Bank for their loan package to the Philippines:

The LOI program is in effect from 1989 until 1992. What are the contents of the 1989 LOI? They are: (1) continued implementation of deregulation policies and import liberalization, (2) implementation of an austerity program to increase savings and control expenditures in order to pay the foreign debt and recover deficits, and (3) attracting foreign investments and encouraging private investment in the control of the economy. Before the 1989 LOI was approved, 1,217 items were to be deregulated—this means that their prices would be decontrolled—and uncontrolled importation of 1,700 items were to be allowed beginning in March 1989. The World Bank has targeted 2,300 items for deregulation.

Tonio then traced the history of IMF deregulation in the Philippine economy and its impact on agricultural development:

In 1981, there was also an LOI for eleven industrial projects. In 1984, the program for agriculture came out. In 1984, with the LOI, the deregulation in trading started; government control of commerce was removed. The effect was increased prices of fertilizers and pesticides. There was import liberalization. The Fertilizer and Pesticide Authority, which had price control authority, was abolished. In 1984, the price of fertilizer per bag was 104 pesos; in 1985 it increased to 300 pesos per bag. With government control removed, multinational corporations gained control of production and marketing of fertilizers and pesticides. Atlas and Philphos, for example, control 39 percent of the market. The unrestricted entry of imported goods also began in 1984.

Tonio specifically pointed out the impact of the LOI on the peasantry. First, he analyzed its effect on rice production; for example, higher production costs increase poverty and debt bondage among peasants, which further reinforce usury. This situation, he said, results in reduced production, creating a rice shortage:

What are the effects of the LOI on the peasantry? First, in the production of rice, material inputs in production, which now compose 35 percent of the total production cost, will be left to the free market. That is, when fertilizers and pesticides are in demand during the planting season, their prices will be higher, and after the planting season, when there is less demand for them, their prices will be lower. For example, now that the planting season is almost over, the price of fertilizer has gone down from 200 pesos to 175 pesos per bag. Second, in the situation where peasants have no production capital and the majority do not own the land they till, an increase in the price of production inputs means (a) further bondage through usury, and (b) a decrease in production, because some peasants will reduce the amount of land for farming and decrease their production inputs. This will decrease the peasants' income and share in the harvest, as well as lessen the rice stock in the market. Our annual rice stock should be 6.2 million metric tons; we are short 800,000 metric tons. Our present rice stock is good only until August 1, 1989. In 1985 we borrowed 200,000 metric tons from Indonesia, and we paid for it in 1989 in kind. What is often said to be rice "export" to

Indonesia because we had "excess" rice production was not really export; it was a payment for debt. Third, the consequent liberalization of credit benefited the usurers, who borrow from agricultural banks and then in turn lend to peasants. Peasants usually are not able to borrow money from rural banks.

Another effect of the LOI that Tonio pointed out is the decline in the National Food Authority's (NFA) ability to procure and market rice, which was intended to stabilize its price:

In the procurement of rice, the National Food Authority (NFA) was able to buy only 9 percent of the total rice harvest during the time of Marcos, and only 4 percent during the Aquino regime. In 1989, the most recent harvest, it has not been able to procure any rice. In 1988 the NFA set aside 700 million pesos in order to buy rice from California. In the world market, the price of rice is cheaper, because some big industrialized countries have surpluses.

With the deregulation of the NFA, according to Tonio's analysis, private traders are able to have greater control of rice procurement and marketing, consequently increasing its price:

Traders have gained significant control of the procurement of palay. Yesterday, in a conference, they said they control 91 percent of the procurement of rice. The average daily consumption of rice is 16,800 metric tons, which is 100 kilos per capita annually. The NFA releases an average of 1,362 metric tons per day, while the private traders release 15,438 metric tons every day.

Tonio also discussed the relationship between import liberalization, which was one of the conditions of the IMF and World Bank, and the creation of the preconditions for cash crop production, causing local food insecurity:

The importation of flour has been increasing. We are being led toward the production of cash crops, rather than staple food. This is one of the strategies of the IMF/World Bank: to create the conditions that would lead to cash crop production. Decreasing government subsidy for staple food production and marketing can also lead to more land becoming idle and abandoned, resulting in food insecurity.

Tonio's presentation was followed by an open forum. The peasant women raised the following questions and additional points:

Question: Isn't the Department of Trade and Industry supposed to control prices of goods?
Tonio: The Department of Trade and Industry is vested only with price monitoring power, which means that it cannot enforce price control measures.
The government gets 88 percent of its revenue from consumer

taxes, indirect taxes on goods and services that citizens buy. The people's real wages do not catch up with the increase in prices of goods and services, although there might be a slight increase in wages.

Question: What is the role of the U.S. in this debt crisis?

Tonio: The U.S. is the biggest borrower in the world. The Mini-Marshall Plan, also known as the Brady Plan and now generally referred to as the development aid plan, actually promotes a free market economy in which government control on private enterprise is minimal. The conditions attached to development loans can impose the principles of a free market economy on the political economies of a country dependent on aid. This is related to the nature of the relationship between an imperialistic country and a neocolonial nation.

Question: What are some actions that we can take? What are the solutions?

Tonio: Price control is not the solution to our problem. The solution lies in the unified position of the peasantry and other sectors. We can also demand certain agricultural policies, such as an integrated agricultural loan fund, subsidized production fund, or rolled back prices. To implement a subsidized production program, the government would need $5 billion dollars to buy pesticides and fertilizers, which would be given free to farmers. The government also would need to set aside $5 billion for credit subsidies, which would take the form of writing off peasants' debts from agricultural banks. We can also demand a rice calamity fund—subsidized buying and selling of palay. The Task Force Bigas (Task Force on Rice) has in fact brought out this issue. We need at least 20 billion pesos to subsidize a rice calamity fund that will be profitable to the peasants.

Peasants can demand continued subsidies on production, which can eventually become self-sustaining. This means that eventually peasants must be the ones to procure and market palay or rice by means of cooperatives. In turn this will open up new jobs. We can also organize mass action. Strategies for mass action may include a mass campaign that will pressure the government to stop sending rice from the rural areas to Manila.

Question: How is foreign debt related to CARP?

Tonio: All these issues are related to genuine agrarian reform. Under CARP, the Philippine foreign debt will increase. How will the government pay the landlords for their land? They intend to borrow. The 3 billion pesos that is budgeted for the Department of Agriculture does not include a subsidy for peasants.

Since Tonio did not include in his presentation the impact of the foreign debt crisis on women—which is a typical problem with the KMP's framework of analysis—Tina presented some aspects of this issue, such as the exportation of female labor to pay foreign debt, and the extreme inadequacy of the type of social services that benefit women: "One effect is the feminization of labor, particularly in the form of exporting women's labor as payment for external debt. Filipinas are cheap labor abroad. Two-thirds of Philippine laborers abroad are women. The other effect is cuts in social services, aggravating malnutrition and a high mortality rate among women and children. Many women have died from lack of medical care during childbirth." Tina further pointed out how ordinary people pay for this foreign debt as consumers, since development policies and decisions of the government do not solve the debt crisis:

For every 1 peso, 60 centavos go to the payment of the Philippine external debt. It is the consumers, we, who pay this foreign debt. Every time we buy goods in the market, we pay indirectly for this debt through the taxes on goods. Because these debts accumulate interest, our debt increases even if we do not borrow for a certain period. The development policies of the government do not solve the debt crisis of our nation. There are already other nations that have declared a moratorium on their debt payments until such time as they become more economically stable. But the Philippine government said "Amen" to the IMF–World Bank policies.

She did not really address the particular ways in which the debt crisis affects Filipino peasant women. Instead she threw the issue back to the women, asking them to reflect on its specific impact on them.

Then Tina asked the question, "What is the position of AMIHAN on the debt crisis?" Some of the women radically suggested debt cancellation, since the people who are paying for it have not really benefited from it: "Do not pay. We did not benefit from it." "What benefits did the peasants get from the foreign debt? None!" "Do not pay. We did not benefit from it." "Those we have not benefited from we must not pay. That which benefited the people we must pay."

Since approximately 40 percent of Philippine export earnings go to foreign debt servicing, one woman moderately suggested, "Limit our payment for the debt to 10 percent of our export earnings." A couple had a clever idea, striking the connection between foreign debt and price increases: One said, "We cannot avoid paying for the debt. Every time we buy, we pay for it. What if we do not increase prices?" The other suggested, "Return the price control law." A few saw the connection between debt payment and cuts in social services, resulting in greater poverty ("We became poorer"). They proposed, "Give priority to social services and other projects for the people" and "Reduce the military budgets and give the funds to social services." Two of the peasant women saw the relationship between foreign debt and imperialism in the Philippines; they suggested, "Resist the exploitation of foreign imperialism" and "Change the U.S.–Aquino imperialist system." But this would mean changing the Philippine government so it would incorporate the progressive people's organizations and recognize the peasant women, so some said: "There must be a coalition government," "There must be people in the government that come from the people's organizations, especially in government agencies for peasants," and "Why are we not recognized, if peasant women have the capacities?"

The Philippine Development Plan for Women.

The Philippine Development Plan for Women (PDPW) is an example of how the "integrationist" perspective (see Chapter 1) can be translated into a policy and program within a type of development based on modernization. Santos and Lee (1989, 58–59) wrote a critique of the PDPW. It is wrongly premised on the integrationist perspective, ignoring the fact that women are already integrated in development but "are not benefiting from it." PDPW's "potential to benefit women is circumscribed" by the nature of development the government promotes.

PDPW was one of the development issues that the AMIHAN National Council took a political stand on. On July 24, 1989, it arrived at its position through the following process:

First, Tina provided background information on PDPW and the importance of studying it:

What is PDPW? During the Aquino administration, a five-year development plan for women was set up under Executive Order No. 348, officially called the Philippine Development Plan for Women (PDPW). Partly this was brought about by the fact that there were people with feminist consciousness who secured government positions during the Aquino administration. The government set up the National Council on Women (NCW) to implement PDPW. The NCW is linked with NEDA (National Economic Development Agency). Solita Monsod, who was then connected with NEDA but has since resigned, was one of those who formulated PDPW.

Tina then explained how PDPW is related to other government development plans:

PDPW is not separated from programs of other government departments. PDPW is based on the Medium-Term Development Plan (MTDP) of NEDA, which is a development plan for the entire country. MTDP contains a five-year development plan for all sectors of the economy, for example, housing and agrarian reform. Part of MTDP contains a plan for the progress of women. MTDP provisions deal with import liberalization, CARP, trade relations, foreign debt payment, government programs for social services, multinational corporations, and the

OMNIBUS Investment Code, which contains provisions on how to attract foreign investment into the Philippines. PDPW is linked to the national development plan of the government.

Tina discussed the manner in which PDPW was formulated, citing the lack of real input from women's organizations when it was designed:

It was formulated by many people through several consultations. In fact, GABRIELA and AMIHAN representatives were there, too. But GABRIELA and AMIHAN did not know that PDPW was going to be formulated out of these consultations, since when we were called to these meetings they told us that it was a forum. PDPW was launched on March 8, 1989, at Malacanang at the same time that one of our AMIHAN national leaders was speaking in a rally.

The PDPW document contains seventeen chapters. Tina talked primarily about chapters 1 and 2, however, because the first presents an overview and the second is relevant to AMIHAN.

What is the overall framework or vision of PDPW on women? Chapter 1 gives an analysis of the situation of women. It talks about the double burden of women. However, its analysis is not contextualized within the broader political-economic situation in the Philippines. PDPW says that women are poor because they are subordinate to men and because men earn higher wages than women.

To summarize the first chapter, Tina emphasized that PDPW encompasses various aspects of women's lives:

The following are the objectives of the PDPW program: (1) individual help: establish support mechanisms for women such as day-care centers and programs to train women to be more assertive; (2) household and family: promote shared parenting, so that child care is the responsibility not solely of women but also of men; (3) socio-cultural: promote nonsexist education and analyze the different forms of discrimination against women; (4) economic: promote equal wages for men and women, and promote women's right to own land; and (5) political: set up legal mechanisms for the implementation of the provisions of PDPW, such as formulating laws that stipulate sanctions and punishment for noncompliance.

Tina then described chapter 2, which concerns agricultural and agrarian reform, as well as how PDPW and CARP are linked:

Chapter 2 of PDPW, which deals with agricultural and agrarian reform, contains the following: (1) the ways in which rural women could be integrated into rural development, (2) how women can share in the fruits of progress, and (3) how an increase in women's participation can ameliorate poverty. CARP (Comprehensive Agrarian Reform Program) is the mechanism by which PDPW can achieve these three objectives. PDPW views CARP as the solution to peasant women's problems, so it aims at mobilizing peasant women in implementing CARP. Under the Marcos government, the agrarian reform program P.D. 27 made no mention of peasant women.

Within five years, 1.2 million grassroots women will receive orientation on the objectives of PDPW by managers and technicians. An additional 5.2 million families will be given education and training. PDPW's strategies consist of the following: (1) a women's orientation program; (2) promotion of PDPW in rural areas; (3) strengthening the participation of women through research on ways in which women can be used in government projects, and through monitoring and inter-agency networking between nongovernmental organizations and government agencies; (4) promotion of income-generating projects; (5) providing for women's access to credit; (6) promotion of women-oriented technology; (7) building of infrastructural facilities in rural areas; (8) promotion of research on women; (9) training of women in information and media services; and (10) promotion of women's organizations.

Tina pointed out that there is a close connection between CARP and PDPW, with the former becoming the "implementing mechanism" for PDPW:

With regard to land reform, the target of CARP is to give emancipation patents within five years to 1,981,498 farmers. It is expected that 5.9 million women will benefit from this. Under CARP, the certificate of land transfer is called an eman-cipation patent. The objectives of PDPW in using CARP as its implementing mechanism are (a) to integrate women into CARP, (b) to mobilize women in the implementation of CARP and in the organization of cooperatives, (c) to make women partners of the government in implementing CARP, and (d) to coordinate government agencies in organizing peasant women. PDPW's strategies to achieve these objectives include (a) recruiting peasant women into government organizations, (b) increasing production, (c) providing jobs when it is not plant-ing season, (d) improving the education and training of women, and (e) setting up ways to monitor PDPW projects.

After the above background was presented, the representatives in the AMIHAN National Council stated their own positions. Most of the women were skeptical about how PDPW would truly benefit them under a repressive government, and they perceived it as not truly addressing fundamental issues, such as feudalism and militarization:

- In my opinion it is garbage.
- My answer is an answer to the answer. Is it good? Yes, it is good only on paper.
- We cannot be sure that it is good.
- In my view, the ideas in PDPW were taken from us, but theirs are limited.
- I do not believe in it. They do not deal with feudalism; that is the most important.
- The three problems of the country that we are addressing are not there. Feudalism and imperialism are not being talked about.
- This is not the solution to remove low intensity conflict. We must focus

on the major problem of peasants. What do we want to remove? The
system of feudalism. Is that the solution to our problem?
- It is not good in all its aspects. Is it good in essence?
- In general, it is not good!

Others were critical about its implementation:

- It looks good, but how about its implementation. If it is really people-
oriented, why not course it through people's organizations that are
people-oriented?
- We cannot expect benefit for all, because only 1.5 million are targeted
as beneficiaries; whoever is more influential and close to the government will be the ones to benefit from it.
- They are giving solutions, but it is like a dole. What kind of education
are they going to provide?

The peasant women criticized PDPW as a tool of the government to
garner their support for CARP, the government's land reform program
of which they were very critical. They thought PARCODE (the People's
Agrarian Reform Code), which was formulated by the peasants themselves as an alternative to CARP, should have been the program attached
to PDPW:

- I am not in favor of PDPW. It is just a way to implement CARP, and we
know what CARP is.
- How can this be implemented if it is linked with CARP?
- The issue of CARP is the loophole in PDPW.
- It should have been PARCODE, not CARP.

The peasant women also questioned the lack of genuine peasant participation in the way PDPW was formulated: "There should be participation of peasants here"; "We were not consulted; we were not allowed
to participate."

They felt slighted by the fact that PDPW has a provision to appoint
managers to organize peasant women, even though AMIHAN is already
organizing them: "They ignored AMIHAN"; "Why should it be the managers who will be the organizers for PDPW?"

The Manila-based national leaders of AMIHAN, who were invited by
the government to come to a meeting, said they felt manipulated, since
they were not aware that the meeting would be used to formulate the
provisions of PDPW: "When I went there it was not clear to me that they
were going to make this book about PDPW"; "We must be careful about
invitations we receive"; "It was as if we were made into toys." They be-

lieved that PDPW was seeking to subtly silence peasant women, now that they were radically organizing:

- For me, PDPW is not good. . . . It is riding on our program to silence us.
- Besides, it is connected with low intensity conflict, so it can be said, here are the things you are asking for.
- Now that we are already organizing, why is militarization the answer? With all these things happening now, PDPW is already blurred.
- Why is this [PDPW] coming out at this time, when women have begun resisting? This is one way to silence us.
- I asked them what they will do about militarization. They did not answer me.
- This is just a pacifier. Why did they not answer the question on militarization?
- It is as if . . . we women must now be silent.
- Because we are already shouting, we are now making noise. Oh, here it is, be silent now. Are we going to allow ourselves to be silenced?

They also thought that PDPW is a means for the government to solicit foreign aid as well as to create a good image for itself: "It is just a way to get much money; women will be used in order to solicit money. The contents and concept of the book came from us. We were used in order to facilitate the borrowing of money from other countries."

Three of the peasant women thought they might as well consider how they could exploit PDPW to their own advantage: "That will be implemented anyway. How can we benefit from it without allowing ourselves to be used?"; "There are some particular aspects about it that are good. What we should watch for is if the implementation is not good"; "There are particular aspects of PDPW that we can use"; "What they have said is true. We have seen that we cannot rely on this being the solution to our problem. But we can use it in legitimizing our organizing work for women. We can use some of its provisions."

Women and Development Aid.

On July 25, 1989, the AMIHAN National Council also deliberated on the issue of women and development aid. Mila, a member of GABRIELA, gave background information on the theme. She informed the peasant women that there is a network of women's organizations, organized in 1988, whose main interest is women in development. These organizations looked into the impact of development, including the issues of foreign aid and the debt problem, on women in the Philippines. They found that part of the funding from CIDA (Canadian International Development Agency) went to support paramilitary troops, the CAFGUs, in Negros. Women's groups therefore became concerned about accepting external funding.

Mila introduced the concepts of "Third World" and "First World" in a simple way that could be understood by the peasant women. Her explanation was premised on the dependency perspective: "In the international scene, we have First World nations and Third World nations. The First World consists of rich nations and the Third World consists of poor nations. In both of these, there is an elite class and '*masa*' (the masses). Change begins from the masa. The First World is rich because it exploits the Third World."

Mila compared the ideology of development in the First World with the liberation movement in the Third World:

The First World has an ideology of development that is based on capitalism and imperialism. It is capitalism and imperialism that brought progress to the First World, so they view this as the kind of development that will also make the Third World progress. But in the Third World there emerged liberation movements that have a new and different ideology of development. Their idea of development is one that is participative, that includes the participation of the *masa*—one that is mass-oriented [*linyang masa*].

Here, two AMIHAN national peasant leaders interjected their own understanding of First and Third World relations: "There is a contradiction between the First World and the Third World. There is no progress in the Third World." Mila then continued, tracing the changes in the way policymakers thought about development, and citing criticisms of the integrationist perspective on development:

In the period of the 1940s through the 1960s, America's Marshall Plan was conceived and implemented. The basic goal was to achieve economic growth through maintaining a war economy. After the world war, the main thrust of the United Nations was reconstruction.

In the 1970s, the idea of a "basic needs approach" to development emerged as a way to deal with poverty in the Third World. The basic issues raised were housing, food production, and education. But at the end of the decade the Third World had not progressed. It was during this period that Vietnam won its war, however, and this was a big slap in the face of the United States.

In the 1980s, there emerged an awareness that development is different for women, men, and children. There evolved the concept that women have the right to participate in development. There were feminists who lobbied in the U.S., calling for "integration of women in development," though they had no critical perspective or had not analyzed the nature of development presently taking place. This was also the ideology of the United Nations. The response of the women's movement was: Why will you integrate Third World women into development, since they will be exploited? What must be done is to change society.

At this juncture, two women leaders commented on First World development aid: "Rich nations want to help poor nations so they can benefit from it." Mila picked up on this idea:

There are different kinds of aid. It can involve money, material, service (like volunteers), morals (like campaigns), commodities (like relief, fertilizers, pesticides, rice surplus), or exchanges (like technical cooperation). Sources of aid can be (a) progressive countries like the United States, Canada, Japan, and West Germany; (b) global institutions like the United Nations; or (c) development aid agencies like the World Bank, the International Monetary Fund, and the Asian Development Bank. Types of aid can be nongovernmental (i.e., aid comes from nongovernmental institutions) or official (official development aid [ODA], in which funds come from governments and are given to governments). Global institutions such as the UN give aid to the Philippine government, but 10 percent of that aid goes to nongovernmental organizations. Official aid for country programs is given to governments, but 10–15 percent is for NGOs.

To Mila's question of why First World nations give aid to Third World countries, some of the peasant women gave answers that revealed their understanding of who mainly benefits from the politics of development aid: "Because they gain much from interest"; "They do not want to smell bad to the people [i.e., they want to create a good image]"; "That is just a cover. Some of the aid goes to buying helicopters. Much of that also goes into their own pockets"; "Why do they give aid to NGOs if they are against NGOs?" Mila added to their comments by citing the political and economic nature of "tied aid" (Payer 1974), which imposes conditions on the Third World that will benefit transnational corporations and the First World market: "Why do they give aid? The reasons are mainly political, economic, or commercial. With the giving of aid go certain conditions for the recipient country that will benefit multinational corporations. There are also surplus goods in the developed countries, like rice, that they want to market in the Third World." She also linked development aid to counterinsurgency in the Philippines, explaining how the people are made to support it through their taxes:

Aid is also given to support the government. For example, in the Philippines it was during the decade of 1970 to 1980 that aid increased—the period when Marcos declared martial law. In 1986, when Cory Aquino came into power, funding agencies looked for socioeconomic projects to fund. Some of these monies went to financing the CAFGUs, which is what happened in Negros. By financing these socioeconomic projects, funding institutions and the government are able to get information under the guise of gathering data, such as who the members of the organization are. These aid agencies are beginning to be afraid of the resistance of the NGOs. That is why they are now helping. Their real intentions have been exposed.

Essentially, it is the citizens' taxes that serve as financial sources for these development aid agencies.

The peasant women then commented that official development aid is given only to NGOs that are already organized, and thus is not really useful in initiating new peasant women's organizations, where funding is most needed: "Aid for livelihood projects are given to those that are already consolidated"; "NGOs are now being encouraged, but where there are already chapters, it is there where they come in."

Mila concluded by posing some questions that AMIHAN must consider seriously:

Official development aid politically supports the Aquino government. Since Aquino came into power, we have accepted invitations for joint projects with the government. This is a scheme to weaken the NGOs. PDPW is a big problem. Funding agencies are asking what we think about it and whether we are going to join it.

What is our position on development aid? Should we accept it? Why? Yes or No? Under what conditions, or on what basis?

With regard to ODA [official development aid], what are the principles that should guide us in dealing with ODA? What programs or activities of AMIHAN must be supported? What other tasks do we still need to accomplish?

At this point, the members of the AMIHAN National Council voiced their positions. One woman was totally against accepting foreign development aid. The rest thought that since official development aid will be given to the government, regardless of whether they reject it, it might be all right to accept it, on the condition that: (a) no conditions shall be imposed on them; (b) the aid should go directly to the grassroots organizations, not through an institution, to make sure that it benefits the peasants; (c) grassroots organizations accepting this aid know the nature of the agency giving aid; and (d) grassroots organizations be firm in applying their principles in using the aid. During this deliberation, some of the peasant women's statements (presented here in the order they were mentioned) illustrated this stance:

- Official development aid does not reach the hands of the peasantry. It is the middle forces who are able to have access to it. It must be given instead to people's organizations directly. If it is given to us directly, we can be sure that it will benefit the peasants.
- The government officials are already squabbling over the money; the same with the nongovernmental organizations. The issues are graft and corruption, and that aid must be directly channeled to grassroots nongovernmental organizations.
- It might be all right to accept aid, but we must stick to the principle that we must have a say in its policies. But official development aid sets up conditions.

- We must clearly understand the principles and basis for accepting aid. If we are going to accept aid, it must be given directly to people's organizations.
- Aid must go directly to the people's organization, not through an institution anymore. Whatever principle the giving of aid is based on, it must be a people-oriented one.
- We must really know what the nature of the agency giving aid is. We must be certain about what their principles are.
- In my opinion, we must accept, but they should not dictate to us. We must be the ones to design our plans.
- The aid that we receive is a debt; we will be paying for that. But we must not lose our principles, so they should not impose conditions on us. They are treating us like children, so that we will not shout, so that we will not protest.
- In addition, we should accept, because even if we don't take it, they will give it anyway. But we must not give up our principles.

This stance reflects the dilemma of whether or not to accept development aid. For this particular issue, the delegates of the AMIHAN National Council decided to do the following in order to arrive at a political position: (1) campaign for a fact-finding mission on how the government is using aid, and at the same time investigate how aid relates to the situation of peasant women's organizations; (2) conduct research on and document the experience of AMIHAN chapters with development aid, or their participation in programs funded by official development aid; (3) organize consultations on the issue; and (4) conduct internal educational campaigns on official development aid.

This decision indicates that the AMIHAN National Council does not automatically take a political position on a development issue. There is serious study involved in the process. Members recognize the need to use research, documentation, and reflection on their experiences as a basis for defining the official stand on issues. This is the organization's way of making informed decisions.

Arriving at a collective analysis of and political position on a development issue is an important part of AMIHAN's politics, for it then serves as a basic principle that is considered in making other organizational decisions. It is a manifestation of AMIHAN's political will in asserting grassroots Filipino sovereignty and the peasant women's role in defining that self-determination. It is a political act that seeks to redirect a technocratic formulation of development policies to reflect the viewpoint of peasant women. It is a struggle toward gaining women's right to have political control of policies that affect their lives, as well as the lives of the majority of the Filipino people.

Mass Protests

In a village, collective land occupation can be considered a militant action. In an urban area, a mass demonstration, which brings people to the streets to publicly protest against government policies, can also be considered a militant action. AMIHAN, with a national office in urban Manila, organizes and participates in mass demonstrations relevant to its agenda for change. Almost every day during my fieldwork, there was a demonstration or rally in Manila, for it is the most urbanized region of the Philippines, and is also the location of the Malacanang Palace (the executive house of the Philippine president), the Philippine Congress, the United States Embassy, and other major government agencies and departments. According to Ate Laly, an AMIHAN national leader, an average of three demonstrations a week took place in Manila. There did not seem to be this many in Mindoro.

Demonstrations and rallies publicly dramatize issues that are not given a fair amount of attention by the government-controlled media. They become the context in which AMIHAN's political position on development issues is publicly articulated. They indicate the increasingly open organized resistance to the politics of underdevelopment that is coming from all sectors. They are a manifestation of the fact that official development policies do not reflect the people's alternative agenda, and that other development perspectives are arising from below.

The following is a personal account of the two mass demonstrations that I participated in with some AMIHAN members in Manila. These demonstrations, as part of popular politics, were not only a public context in which AMIHAN could contest development policies based on peasant women's experience, but also occasions for AMIHAN to offer its alternative concept of agrarian development, with an analysis that makes peasant women more visible. Because the issues that AMIHAN advances in public have been collectively studied and analyzed internally, on both local and national levels, mass demonstrations go beyond sloganeering and are not simply sporadic outbursts of emotional anger against the existing system. They are indicators of the peasant women's and other sectors' organized resistance to the politics of underdevelopment in the Philippines. At the same time this politics of underdevelopment shapes AMIHAN's local and national politics of resistance.

The July 24 Rally.

On July 24, 1989, President Aquino was scheduled to give the State of the Nation address. Progressive groups organized a rally in Manila to give an alternative state of the nation address. The themes of the rally were the foreign debt crisis and militarization. Delegations representing organizations in various parts of the country attended, though most were from Luzon, because Manila is then accessible by land transportation. The approximately five thousand demonstrators assembled at the Welcome Rotunda near Quezon Boulevard around one o'clock in the afternoon and marched to Mendiola in front of the Malacanang Palace. The AMIHAN National Council was holding their meeting at this time in Quezon City. Its seventeen delegates, who represented chapters in different parts of the country, all joined the rally, and I participated with them. The delegates prepared placards with slogans reflecting AMIHAN's political positions on the issues related to the theme of the rally. These slogans show how the women relate larger national issues to their concrete situation or experience as peasant women. Some placards denounced militarization, something they have directly experienced: "Detachments and checkpoints in the rural areas are not needed. They are the ones that must be sent away, not the citizens"; "Dismantle the CAFGUs in the rural areas"; "Stop military abuses against peasant women in rural areas"; "Dismantle total war in the Philippines"; and

> Military, CAFGUs, Vigilantes
> During military operations
> It is innocent women that they attack
> They growl like tigers.
> Liars!
> Stop doing this to us!!!

Other slogans protested against the policies of the IMF and their impact on peasant women: "LOI adds to the hardship of peasant women. Foreign debt adds to the poverty of peasant women." The representative of KAMMI wrote a poem about foreign debt on a placard and carried it to the demonstration:

> Women of Mindoro
> Their heads are aching
> Because of high prices of all goods
> Foreign debt
> need not be paid
> because it did not benefit our nation

The June 9 Rally.

On June 9, 1989, I took part in the rally led by the KMP, in which AMIHAN participated. This rally was held in commemoration of the massacre of thirteen peasants who were among the demonstrators at

Mendiola, in front of the Malacanang Palace, in June of 1987, during the second year of President Corazon Aquino's administration. Various organizations from Manila and the provinces came to this rally. Ate Ludy (an AMIHAN leader) and I estimated the huge crowd to be at least five to eight thousand people. There were delegations from Bataan, Quezon, Nueva Ecija, Pampanga, and Negros. From their banners I could identify some of the different organizations involved: the KMP, AMIHAN, KMU (National Union of Workers, May 1st Movement), BAYAN (a national coalition of progressive groups), SAMAKANA (an organization of urban poor women), religious groups, and GABRIELA.

I joined AMIHAN's march with other sectors from Luzon. We began to assemble at one o'clock in the public park in front of the Manila Post Office, and from there started walking to Plaza Miranda at about two. On the way, Ate Loy, an AMIHAN national leader, led the march. She rode on a yellow and red jeepney, with a banner of AMIHAN. As we marched, she used a loudspeaker to speak out against the government's land reform, CARP. Her voice thundered for the bystanders to hear.

When we arrived at Plaza Miranda, many people were already there with their banners. A student on the roof of the underpass in front of Quiapo Church, in the vicinity of Plaza Miranda, was speaking about the youth's and students' solidarity with the peasants. He spoke vehemently against the government's land reform. There was another speaker from a labor organization, as well as a woman evacuee from Negros who testified about the sufferings of those who had been displaced because of military operations there.

From Plaza Miranda, we proceeded to Mendiola, near the Malacanang Palace, the seat of the Philippine government. Before we started, however, the demonstrators chanted, "Huwag matakot! Huwag matakot! Magkapigbisig, makibaka!" ("Do not be afraid! Do not be afraid! Join hands in struggle!"). Someone shouted over the loudspeaker, "Handa na ba tayong patungong Mendiola?" ("Are we ready to proceed to Mendiola?"). The whole crowd answered with determination, "Oo!" ("Yes!"). My brother, who had volunteered to escort me, suggested that I not go to Mendiola because it was there that the peasants were massacred during their demonstration two years before. But I said, "No, we must join the people."

I happened to march with the delegation of peasant women from Bataan, a province in the central part of Luzon, a five- or six-hour drive from Manila. We crossed our arms and held hands as we marched to Mendiola, and Monica, the woman to my left, said to the eight of us who were supposed to walk together, "Whatever happens we must not separate from each other." I had never met these women before, but I felt one with them, as if there was one vision that was uniting our steps.

At Mendiola there was another program of speeches and nationalist songs. Determination and anger against the government's policies marked the tone of the speakers: the peasant, the worker, the urban poor woman, the religious. They all spoke against the government's development program, including the land reform program, militarization, IFM–World Bank policies in the Philippines, and U.S. imperialism.

As the program went on, all of us—young and old, women and men—sat down on the streets. The media tend to present poor people as easily manipulated to join mass protests, but the ordinary people around me did not appear as though they had been simply cowed into participating in this event. They were conscious not only of what they were doing, but also of the risks they took in being there. They had come anyway.

I was impressed by the courage of the women and men who spoke. I thought, these are the real people, who love life and who are willing to offer their lives for a cause, for a change that will improve the lives of many, not only themselves. Then I was no longer afraid. I was in the midst of a struggling people willing to give life to many, by giving their lives for a vision they hope to see realized someday. Here was made concrete the theory that if there is anyone who will persist in the struggle for revolutionary change, it will be the peasants and workers, men and women together who pay the price of underdevelopment. Once they are politicized and can critically analyze issues, they demand a fundamental social transformation, addressing issues and development policies.

The themes of the rally were: *pagkain* (food), *lupa* (land), *kalayaan* (freedom), and *kapayapaan* (peace). All of these were developed by the speakers and echoed in the slogans and streamers of the different sectors. Some of the placards and streamers carried by the peasants said: "Itaguyod ang PARCODE" ("Uphold PARCODE"); "Itakwil ang CARP" (Reject CARP); "Itakwil ang LOI" ("Reject the Letter of Intent"); "Ipaglaban ang tunay na reforma sa lupa" ("Fight for genuine land reform"); "Alisin ang militarisyon sa kanayunan" ("Stop militarization in the rural areas"); and "Isang taon ng CARP, isang taong pahirap sa kababaihang magbubukid" ("One year of CARP, one year of added suffering for peasant women"). AMIHAN carried a big streamer: "Kababaihan magkaisa, Ibayong isulong ang tunay na reformang agraryo, Itakwil ang CARP" ("Women unite, Together push for true agrarian reform, Reject CARP").

During the rally, both AMIHAN and the KMP, like the other groups, gave out written statements to demonstrators, bystanders, and motorists. The KMP entitled its tract "Resist the False Agrarian Reform and Fight Against the Increasing Poverty Under the US-Aquino Regime." AMIHAN entitled its "CARL, a Burden for Peasant Women." While both AMIHAN's and KMP's statements touched on issues that affect the peasantry, only AMIHAN's addressed the particular experience of peasant women. Hence, without AMIHAN's participation in this rally, peasant women would again have been made invisible in the analysis and public articulation of the impact of development policies and programs on the peasantry.

In its written tract, AMIHAN contested the government's claim that the Comprehensive Agrarian Reform Law (CARL) would be the priority of the Aquino government: "June 10, 1988, is a historic day because of the deceit and disloyalty that the Aquino government has perpetrated on all poor peasants. This was the day on which Cory Aquino signed the Comprehensive Agrarian Reform Law [CARL] into law as a major program and a priority of the government." AMIHAN supported this contention with an analysis of CARL:

CARL HAS INCREASED THE EXPLOITATION OF PEASANTS. One year of experience under CARL indicates there is no hope for progress. It cannot solve the problem of landlessness of more than 8.5 million peasants. Like the other land reform laws in the past, it makes no provision for free distribution of land to landless peasants. Peasants will pay for the land to landlords, at a price set by landlords and the government. This does not take into consideration the inability of peasants to pay the yearly amortizations owing to poverty, with the end result being the confiscation of their right to farm on the land.

AMIHAN further contended that in its one year of implementation, CARL had not demonstrated any inclination to change the control of land by landlords and foreign corporations. Instead it enabled landlords and government officials to enrich themselves:

Moreover, in its implementation CARL has many loopholes that perpetrate the continuing monopoly on land by landlords, plantation owners, and foreign corporations.
    Corrupt officials and opportunists in the government have also taken advantage of CARL, resulting in graft and corruption, as in the cases of Hacienda Alberto, Gatchitorena, and other confiscated property of Marcos.

AMIHAN's statement did not give details here, but the KMP's tract did. The KMP cited Hacienda Luisita, the large haciendas owned by President Aquino's clan, as the first irregularity in CARL. It exposed the devaluing of one-third of Hacienda Luisita's land assets, which President Aquino claimed she would distribute to the agricultural workers on her hacienda through a stock-sharing scheme, therefore charging her with "cheating" the peasants. And the KMP rejected Aquino's claim that Hacienda Luisita was a "model agrarian reform," because of this irregularity and because the stock-sharing scheme does not actually transfer ownership and control of land to the peasants.

The weaknesses of Aquino's agrarian reform, on which the crocodiles in and outside the government are feasting, have been uncovered. Because of its comprehensive loopholes that allow profiteers to exploit CARL, awful irregularities are what the Aquino regime can boast about in this first anniversary of CARL. First is the irregularity in Hacienda Luisita. Does the government have the face to boast of this as a model agrarian reform, when in fact it is just a grand show to deceive the people about its circumventing the distribution of large tracts of land of the Cojuangcos and its hiding the real value of the assets stolen from the agricultural workers in the sugar plantation? In the scheme of stock distribution in CARL, only one-third of the entire value of land assets of Hacienda Luisita will be distributed to its agricultural workers, based on the value of 33,000 pesos per hectare when in fact the actual value is close to 60,000 pesos per hectare. About 162 million pesos have been hidden and taken from the workers of Hacienda Luisita by the relatives of President Aquino, who are owners of this hacienda.

The KMP's statement also gave details on government corruption in the Garchitorena land deal. This time the irregularity did not take the form of devaluing land assets. Rather, there was an extreme overpricing of barren, cogonal lands (producing cogon, a coarse grass used for thatching) that landlords sold to the government:

The other irregularity is the overpricing of lands that were being sold to the government by landlords. The Garchitorena land deal is one example. If in Hacienda Luisita there was the undervaluing of the real price of land in order to decrease the value of stock for distribution to the beneficiaries, in the Garchitorena land deal there was the 80 to 90 percent overpricing of barren, useless, and cogonal land sold to the government, supposedly to be distributed to the peasants. The Department of Agrarian Reform agreed to buy the land at 33,000 pesos per hectare when in fact the actual value was less than 5,000 pesos per hectare.

In addition to all this corruption within CARL, the KMP exposed that the government budget for its implementation had been increased, although there was a decrease in the amount of land designated for distribution: "With all these irregularities, it is not surprising that the bankrupt CARL has inflated its budget from 120 billion pesos in 1988 to 330 billion pesos currently. The other miracle that occurred is the decrease in the size of sequestered land identified for distribution to the peasants. From 60,000 hectares in April 1987, it decreased to 2,500 hectares. Where did the rest of the land go?"

While the experience of landowners and state officials with CARL was one of taking advantage of its loopholes, the experience of peasant women, AMIHAN contends, is one of increased subjugation:

CARL HAS FURTHER ENSLAVED PEASANT WOMEN. If this law has further entrenched the exploited position of poor peasants, it is perpetuating even more the slavery of peasant women. The Aquino government has shown no serious desire to liberate from poverty and oppression the majority of women, who are part of the peasant class in the Philippines. Landlords and capitalists view peasant women as slaves who are paid a wage, slaves who pay rent on their land, slaves whose labor could be used as payment for debt, and slaves to their flesh.

AMIHAN asserted that CARL perpetuates the "enslavement" of women because it devalues and maintains the invisibility of women's significant contribution in production and their major role in the survival of peasant families:

It maintains the position of peasant women only as a supply of supplemental labor in production, a source of cheap and unpaid labor, although in reality women have major roles in the production process.

Peasant women carry most of the burden for the survival needs of peasant families, such as food, housing, and social services. To survive they often fall into debt bondage.

AMIHAN also discredited the empowering element of CARL, since it is introduced along with intensification of militarization in the countryside, exacerbating the misery of peasant women:

CARL AND TOTAL WAR, COMBINED TOOLS FOR EXPLOITATION AND REPRESSION IN THE RURAL AREAS. While the Aquino government entices the peasants with sweet promises, it responds to peasants' resistance and protests with an iron hand. Zoning, forced evacuations and resettlement (hamletting), food blockades, strafing, bombings, salvaging, and other forms of militarization continue. This adds to the suffering of women. They are the ones who are left to work on the farm, who suffer the military's anger, who experience sexual abuse, hunger, and family dislocation.

AMIHAN further questioned the effectivity of CARL, since the government's economic program opens natural resources and the Philippine market to the exploitation of foreign investors:

CARL IS PART OF THE DEFECTIVE ECONOMIC RECOVERY PROGRAM OF THE AQUINO GOVERNMENT. This is one way to maintain the Philippines as a source of cheap raw materials and a market for finished or manufactured products of big foreign capitalists. It has given incentives and security to big foreign capitalists to build and manage large plantations, mines, fisheries, and so on in the rural areas.

Such a development framework, AMIHAN asserts, does not result in "economic progress" for poor peasants:

This system always results in a foreign trade imbalance, since it is the foreign capitalists who are able to set the price and quantity of export goods. Consequently, this brings no economic progress to the Philippines. The effects of this situation fall on the shoulders of poor peasants and citizens, like what has happened in Negros.

AMIHAN pointed out the role of the International Monetary Fund and the World Bank in promoting this externally controlled economic program:

While the persistent trade imbalance and foreign debt continue to plague the country, they are worsened by the government's implementation of LOI and the dictates of the IMF–World Bank, which is primarily controlled by the imperialist United States. The bad effects of this can immediately be felt in the price increase of basic goods and services, tax hikes, an increase in the prices of pesticides and other things needed for agricultural production. On the whole, the economic program of the Aquino government is favorable only to big landlords, foreign capitalists, and large Filipino capitalists.

AMIHAN's statement did not consist only of criticism. It also offered alternatives: free redistribution of land to peasants, restrictions on foreign corporations and plantations, public subsidies for peasants' production, and democratic participation of peasants in policy formulation:

GENUINE AND COMPREHENSIVE AGRARIAN REFORM, NOT CARL, IS THE DEMAND OF PEASANTS. It is only just that these lands be distributed freely to landless peasants. They are lands taken away from peasants, large lands under the control of big landlords that have long been paid for with the peasants' taxes, idle lands, lands confiscated from Marcos and his cronies. It is just that foreign corporations and plantations be nationalized. It is only right that peasants have a say in the formulation of policies that affect their lives. It is only just that the government provide production subsidies to peasants.
Land to the tiller—this is what will gradually liberate the poor peasants, and especially the women. It will slowly dismantle the feudal system that exploits and oppresses peasant women. That is why it is their primary interest to struggle for genuine and truly comprehensive agrarian reform.

But this alternative agenda will not come from the top of the power pyramid. Hence AMIHAN calls for the united action of all peasants and women, and the support of all sectors and classes in Philippine society:

All of these can be achieved only with the united action of all peasants and the support of all classes and sectors in our society.
WOMEN UNITE!
SUSTAIN THE STRUGGLE FOR GENUINE AGRARIAN REFORM!
JOIN THE MOVEMENT FOR THE LIBERATION OF PEASANTS AND WOMEN!!!

Nonpeasant groups who joined the rally to show their support for the struggle of the peasantry also gave out leaflets to bystanders. *PINALAKAS KA* (United Force of Rural Youth), an organization of rural youth with members throughout the Philippines, mimeographed their statement, which contained illustrations that tried to appeal to younger age groups. The first section contained an illustration of a little girl giving a public speech criticizing the International Monetary Fund and the Letter of Intent. The second section illustrated President Aquino responding to the question of what benefits the LOI and the IMF program would bring the Filipino people. Aquino was caricatured as asking the people to make sacrifices as prices go up, for "the sake of economic recovery." The third section illustrated a farmer asking President Aquino how the LOI will affect poor peasants. It showed President Aquino responding that it would increase the price of rice, put more peasants into debt, require them to mortgage more of their harvest, increase the price of their means of production, and increase taxes on goods, thus making poor peasants poorer. The fourth section commented on how the Aquino government hurried to set up the LOI in order to create the conditions necessary for the United States to grant the $10 billion loan that the Philippine government will use to pay its foreign debt and to implement CARL. The LOI, it argued, is therefore doubly bad in that it not only brings more hardship to the poor majority but also supports the "anti-peasant" land reforms of the government. It pointed out that CARL ensures the continued control that multinational corporations and agribusiness have over the land. And it raised criticisms regarding the loopholes in CARL, similar to those pointed out by AMIHAN and the KMP.

Church sectors, like the Christians for the Realization of a Sovereign Society (CROSS), also expressed support for the demands of the peasantry. CROSS passed out a leaflet entitled "Struggle of Peasants, Struggle of the Whole Nation," which began with a religious perspective on the issue of land:

"This is the year of your liberation; the slave will go back to his/her own home and the land that was sold will be returned to the original owner."—Leviticus 25:10

Land, as God's gift to humanity, is a grace for all, that all may live fully as human beings. Truly land is a primary source of life for everyone. That is why it is right that everyone benefit from it.

In its statement, CROSS deplored the fact that peasants, who are creators of wealth from the land, have remained poor, and that IMF policies in the Philippines have exacerbated their poverty. The tract condemned CARP and supported PARCODE. CROSS concluded its statement with a challenge to Christians to see the connection between their faith and the struggles of the peasants: "In the midst of this situation, our faith is challenged as Christians and as Filipinos to be part of the struggle of the peasants. It is only through this vision that we can show to them that we unite with them in their action."

After the speeches and songs at Mendiola, the moderator ordered the crowd to disperse ("organized dispersal," an AMIHAN leader told us). Someone announced that we should proceed to Mt. Carmel Church in Cubao, Quezon City, for a vigil (prayer service that lasts till midnight) in memory of the peasants who were massacred at Mendiola on June 22, 1987.

I was impressed by the mobilization and how well organized the rally was. It ended peacefully, although the military had stationed a fire engine nearby, which could be used to hose water on the demonstrators, and soldiers were ready with barricades and arms. The people, on the other hand, were armed only with their ideology and their stance against the development policies that exploit them and cause their poverty, oppression, and repression.

The program of alternative agrarian reform that AMIHAN and the KMP publicly articulated in these demonstrations is not simply rhetorical. These organizations are already putting their words into action. Redistribution of land to the tiller is being implemented at the village level, through the strategy of land occupation. The problem is that the present administration, like past governments, continues to ignore and even penalize grassroots-initiated efforts.

I sensed the anger of the people against the policies of the government, as well as their commitment to bring about change. As I walked with the peasant women, I believed that the people's demands were legitimate and could change radically the economic and political structures of Philippine society.

Resistance Under the Ramos Regime

But their voices have not been heard. So AMIHAN and other groups still protest on the streets. In its rally of June 6, 1996, AMIHAN continued to criticize CARP: "The eight years that CARP has existed equal eight years of evidence of its inutility for peasants. It has even become a mechanism to reconcentrate the power of landlords and transnational corporations over land, and worsen the landlessness of peasants."

Ramos's Philippines 2000 has not heeded these voices that must be heard. So AMIHAN still advocates, "Ipaglaban at isulong and tunay na repormang agraryo at makabansang industrialisasyon!" ("Fight and push for genuine agrarian reform and nationalist industrialization!")

"Genuine agrarian reform" and "nationalist industrialization" are age-old themes in the agenda of the national liberation movement in the Philippines. Under Ramos's Philippines 2000 they have become not less relevant but more urgent as the government gears up the Medium Term Philippine Development Plan (MTDP) to bring the Philippines into the circle of NICs (new industrializing countries). And the lives of the poor majority will be critically affected by further industrialization, which entails foreign loans and investments, structural adjustments of the IMF, massive land-use conversions, foreign market–oriented production, tourism and export of labor to bring about a foreign exchange reserve to pay the foreign debt, and continued militarization.

For peasant women, "genuine agrarian reform" and "nationalist industrialization" are development goals that have become more critical as increasing industrialization takes away their land and makes foreign transnational corporations the lords of Philippine land, products, and capital. AMIHAN's alternative concept of agrarian reform is challenged by massive land conversions for the industrial and commercial use of multinational corporations. Land occupation becomes even more arduous, as KAMMI has already experienced. As the interests of the Filipino landed elite and the foreign transnational lords interlock in the politics of export agribusiness, which is more aggressively promoted under Philippines 2000, peasant women must struggle against more formidable, powerful forces in their quest for land. Peasant women confront the partnership of the state, the Filipino landlord, and the foreign transnational lord.

As massive land-use conversions displace peasant women from the farm, a reserve pool of cheap labor is created for industries in industrial or export processing zones. In industrial ventures where women are absorbed, they experience exploitative working conditions that profit transnational capital.[2] Women who are not absorbed into these industries become another pool of cheap labor for tourism projects, which the government promotes to bolster its dollar reserve to pay its foreign debt. There is a feminization of labor in the tourism industry, and within this pool of labor, the women engaged in prostitution are the most exploited and unhappy.[3] Women who are not absorbed into industrial and tourism projects create a third pool of labor—export labor for overseas contract work. They become the OCWs (overseas contract workers), who are misnamed "modern-day heroes"[4] by the government because their remittances pay the existing Philippine foreign debt and the loans to fund Philippines 2000. Most women OCWs—94.4 percent in 1992[5]—are relegated to domestic service work, where many experience physical and sexual abuse from employers, violations of their work contracts, and nonpayment of wages or withholding of portions of their pay.[6] Perhaps these women are not "modern day heroes" but modern day slaves—"slavery talaga" (really slavery) was a term used by one of the peasant women I met in Mindoro in May 1996, who had come back from domestic work in Saudi Arabia and Taiwan. The women who are not absorbed into any of these labor pools will join the growing number of urban poor who make a living in the informal economy by vending, selling newspapers, laundering for rich families, working as servants in middle-class homes, or scavenging for scraps that recycling factories buy cheaply. This scenario, in which the processes making land available for transnational capital are interlocked with those creating a pool of cheap labor, propels the wheels of Philippines 2000.

For AMIHAN, "nationalist industrialization" has become more relevant and no less urgent because Ramos's Philippines 2000 program is not
nationalist. It opens up the economy even more to foreign investments
and the dictates of the IMF, entrenching foreign control of the Philippine political economy. Thus, AMIHAN publicly criticizes Philippines
2000 as a development package "in obedience to the prescriptions of the
IMF and GATT (General Agreement on Tariff and Trade), ruling tools
of imperialist countries led by the United States."

What is GATT? What is the connection between GATT and Philippines 2000? Why are AMIHAN and other groups critical of and resistant
to GATT? GATT started in the 1940s to help rehabilitate nations after
the devastation of World War II. Its goal was to regulate international
trade. In the 1990s, GATT's catch-22 is "free trade."[7] Vandana Shiva
(1992, 31) criticized "free trade" as GATT perceives it:

Agriculture and related activities are the most important source of livelihood for
Third World women. "Free Trade" in agriculture as construed in GATT aims at
creating freedom for transnational corporations to invest, produce and trade
agricultural commodities without restriction, regulation or responsibility. This
freedom for agribusiness is based on the denial of freedom to rural women to
produce, process and consume food according to the needs of the local environment, the local economy and local culture.

The signing of the GATT accord on April 15, 1994, in Marrakesh,
Morocco—bringing to a close eight years of debate among 117 countries, led by the United States, on multilateral trade—will "reduce tariffs
on industrial goods by an average of one third" and "progressively lib-
eralize trade in agricultural products."[8] PUMALAG (*Pambansang Ugnayan ng Mamamayan Laban sa GATT*, Philippine Network of Citizens'
Action Against GATT)—a coalition of grassroots organizations, including AMIHAN, opposing GATT—says that the liberalization of trade in
agriculture will flood the local market with imported farm products
from more advanced countries whose governments subsidize farm production. Being subsidized, these imported farm products can be sold
cheaper, resulting in unfair competition for the Filipino farmer. This
situation creates a local market that is more favorable to multinational
corporations and big Filipino traders who already control agricultural
trade.[9] As imported farm commodities capture the market, the country
becomes dependent on imported grains and its self-sufficiency in food is
threatened.

Dependency on foreign grain is in the making as the Ramos government cuts subsidies on the pricing of local grains, marketing facilities,
rural credit, and other forms of support for Filipino farmers. For instance, the National Food Authority (see Chapter 3) plans to stop pro-

curing rice in 1998.[10] Also, the Medium Term Agricultural Development Program of Philippines 2000 will significantly reduce lands planted with such staples as rice and corn (see the Introduction). Peasant women are most likely to feel the full force of food insecurity, since they are the ones who go to the usurers to borrow for their families' daily food consumption, and they are the ones who go to the market to get food to put on their children's plates (see Chapter 3).

Another provision in GATT that threatens the peasant women's alternative sustainable agriculture and control of the local seed variety is "Intellectual Property Rights." This provision denies peasants the right to save their own seed. Seed becomes the private property of transnational corporations, which can demand royalty payments from farmers who save it and can make farmers buy seed in patented form (ibid., 41). This provision actually legitimizes corporate theft of seeds and plant varieties from the Third World peasants who own most of these varieties. With seeds and plant varieties privatized by transnational corporations, communal farming and sharing of these seeds are likely to be controlled. The peasant women of KAMMI whom I talked to when I visited Mindoro again in 1996 are aware of this problem. They said that the herbal plants they are now communally raising and the local rice variety they are trying to preserve might someday be taken over by transnational corporations "dahil sa GATT" ("because of GATT"). They mentioned that people have visited their village to survey medicinal plants and take samples of them. The women are aware of these problems because GATT was one of the issues they discussed in their educational sessions.[11] AMIHAN has attempted to monitor, at the village level, groups who come to ask local people to gather medicinal plants for them and then buy them at very low prices.

AMIHAN's stand against GATT has gone beyond national borders. In 1990, with other farmers from Asia, AMIHAN representatives lobbied against GATT in the Uruguay Round of negotiations in Brussels. It has promoted its position on GATT in international forums, such as the Fourth World Conference in China. In 1992, AMIHAN established solidarity with Asian women by organizing a conference of peasant and rural women from Sri Lanka, Vietnam, Indonesia, Nepal, Korea, India, Japan, and the Philippines. Held in Antipolo in the Philippine province of Rizal, this conference determined a collective stance on GATT and a related issue—the structural adjustment programs (SAPs) of the IMF. It framed this stance as the 1992 Antipolo Declaration of Asian Peasant Women.

In this declaration, the Asian peasant women defined themselves as the "creators of life, nurturers of the earth and producers of food, . . . capable, rational, thinking human beings." They deplored the fact that their voices had been ignored in development policies, and felt that now they must speak. They spoke unequivocally about GATT and SAPs as imposed "mechanisms of transnational capital to maintain, expand and intensify extraction of profits" from their countries at the expense of the poor, "especially rural women." They called attention to the environmental destruction and the violation of their culture and identity caused by GATT and SAPs. And they called the IMF an "international usurer" that facilitates greater foreign control of their lands and industries. As Asian women "producers, home managers and community organizers," they consider themselves "the frontline casualties of SAPs and GATT" because they will lose ownership of their seeds and knowledge to GATT's "intellectual property rights," become hungry as SAPs and GATT deplete their "food resources," and are repressed when they demand social justice. Hence, they advocate a "cancellation of all debts" of Asian countries and the "creation of an international indemnification fund" to rehabilitate "all debt-caused destruction" in Asia. They called on all their fellow Asian sisters and brothers (a) to oppose GATT as the IMF's and transnational corporations' instrument to further control their nations, villages, and communities; (b) to defend the "last frontiers of their biodiversity"; and (c) to "strengthen" their "solidarity" in resisting and protecting themselves from the debacle of SAPs and GATT.

As Philippines 2000 gears up and peasant women are marginalized, AMIHAN intensifies its campaign to organize peasant women on all levels. As one peasant woman of KAMMI ways, "Organization is our defense." So AMIHAN resolves, despite structures of greed and exploitation, to persist in organizing and reorganizing peasant women in an effort to empower them.

Chapter Six
Reorienting Development Analysis and Perspectives on Third World Women

Why is life in the farm so hard?
Peasants plant but they get nothing to eat
The rising price of farm inputs
is slowly killing us.

In my long hours of thinking
I have come to realize that
I cannot be oppressed
If I choose to struggle.

So all of us women must unite
Struggle to advance our rights
We must unite in our cause
So we can change our oppressive society.
                              —Loreng Ayupan (1987)

This study has shown the value of using the experiences of peasant women to examine the politics of underdevelopment and resistance in the Philippines. Studying the everyday lives of the women of KAMMI helped me to reorient development analysis, and it revealed the interlocking power structures in which peasant women's lives are enmeshed.

My examination of their daily lives supports the emerging literature on women and development that is critical of the "integrationist perspective." While this perspective assumes that Third World women are poor because they are not integrated into development, my research suggests that this is not the case. They are in fact integrated in Philippine development, but remain poor nonetheless. I suggest that their poverty is a consequence of the nature of Philippine development, which exploits their roles as producers, reproducers, and consumers in order to maintain and reproduce a political economic system that (a) concentrates ownership and control of land and agricultural labor in a few who do not till the land, (b) concentrates control of the produce of the land in nonproducers, (c) links agricultural development to transnationalization of capital accumulation, (d) thrives on gendered hierarchies, and (e) feeds a military state that represses political action for change. The poverty resulting from this development in turn reproduces the social conditions that make peasant women vulnerable to exploitation.

The dynamics of this exploitation is concretely articulated in the lives of the peasant women of KAMMI, who are mostly landless and work either as tenants or as waged agricultural workers on lands owned by landlords. As rice producers who till land they do not own, the tenant women must give a large portion of their harvest to their landlords, leaving so little for themselves that it is insufficient for their subsistence. The women who work as agricultural laborers do not get a share of the harvest, are paid very low wages, and are not guaranteed work. Some tenant women, after working in their landlords' fields, then work for wages for other landlords in order to supplement the insufficient share of the harvest that they earn as tenants. Despite working this double shift, however, they remain poor. This phenomenon raises serious questions about the integrationist perspective on women and development, which assumes that Third World women are poor because they are not integrated into the wage economy. In the feudal and wage economies, the peasant women of KAMMI are made poor. But tenants and wage agricultural workers are not simply made poor in parallel ways. It is the peasant women's labor that links the different modes of production—feudal, semi-feudal, and capitalist—in the neocolonial Philippine economy today. This modifies Ernesto Laclau's theory (Chilcote 1984; Brewer 1980) of the coexistence of different modes of production in Third World economies, which he says results from colonial, transnational capital interlocking into preexisting economic relations. In his theory he does not consider the circumstances of peasant women.

The nexus of exploitation that the peasant women provide in this articulation of the different modes of production takes on a more complex form when viewed within the sexual division of farm labor, for the more back-breaking tasks are generally relegated to women. This reveals the intersection of gender and class in their lives. Furthermore, the gender ideologies that give rise to the perception of peasants as being mainly male make invisible the peasant women's significant contributions to production as unpaid wives, and at the same time help to define peasant women's paid farm work as secondary. This double or even triple exploitation of peasant women within the feudal, semi-feudal, and capitalist economic relations results in their poverty.

A closer examination reveals that there is something peculiar about the peasant women's poverty, since it is not simply a direct result of their class position in the relations of agricultural production—in this case the production of rice and the landlord system. There is also a relationship between the poverty of these women, their role as consumers of rice (their produce, over which they have no control), and the informal credit system (usury), which thrives on the poverty of peasant families and the lack of government subsidies for peasant food production. While the peasant women produce good quality rice, they cannot consume it, not only because traders market such rice outside Mindoro, but also because the women are made to buy inferior rice that landlords and traders cannot sell to the rich. This exploitation is exacerbated by the system of usury, which the women must resort to as source of production capital because of the absence of state subsidies for food production, and because they must do so to survive during *tagkiriwi*, the months when they are most poor. Since the peasant women pay their loans with good quality rice, moneylenders who are also landlords, traders, or landlord-traders are able to accumulate salable rice. These landless women again become the link between poverty, usury, and the market, since they, more than men, are involved with informal credit transactions. In the final analysis, the peasant women subsidize the production and marketing of rice, which have become the source of profit for the few big landlords and the traders who control the rice market and the informal credit system. The dynamics of this system is very different from the rationalization of the market conceptualized by Max Weber. It suggests the importance of examining the links between the capitalist market, feudal and semi-feudal relations of production, and the informal sector in the politics of underdevelopment in the Philippines. These elements come together fully and clearly in the lives of the peasant women of Mindoro.

Through "state action" (Mackintosh 1990), the Philippine government helps to maintain the exploitative terms of farm production within the feudal and semi-feudal village economy, as well as the capitalist rice market that exploits the peasant women. This "state action" is epitomized by the reluctance of past and present governments to legislate and implement genuine agrarian reforms that would radically transform the structure of land ownership. State action is also manifested in the government's decision to decrease the funding that enables the National Food Authority to procure rice. This decision capitulated to the IMF's conditions for the granting of loans, which included a privatization scheme that allowed big traders more freedom to control the marketing of rice. State action can also be seen in the absence of government subsidies for the production expenses of peasant women. While big traders and landlord-usurers have access to formal credit systems, such as the Quedan Financing Scheme, peasant women generally have none.

The productive/reproductive model, which emerged as an alternative to the integrationist perspective, finds support in my analysis. Peasant women view the "center" of their lives as the "farm" and the "home"; this is their interpretation of the concrete reality of their lives. But farm and home are not two dichotomized spheres, as the integrationist perspective implies. Nor are they the separate spheres conceptualized in the liberal feminist view of the sexual division of labor, which does not provide a clear analysis of how the reproductive role of women is linked to the politics of farm work. It is the social construction of farm and home as the center of peasant women's lives that links the home to the economy, but only insofar as the reproductive role of women maintains and reproduces the system that exploits peasants as landless producers. By creating food resources that do not benefit them, they enrich the few who own and control most of the land and its produce. This process is clearly articulated in the following ways: (a) a peasant woman maintains and reproduces the labor power in the feudal and semi-feudal economy of Mindoro, since her children generally become peasants as well; (b) a peasant woman's children perform farm labor but remain unpaid, since their contributions are not taken into account in share-cropping; and (c) a peasant woman does domestic work related to farm work, but it is unrecognized as a contribution and is not considered when her family's share of the harvest is allocated.

The reproductive work of peasant women not only maintains the feudal and semi-feudal economy, but also subsidizes the household economy that is linked to capitalist production. This is particularly so when daughters of peasant women become low-paid domestic workers in the households of wage workers employed outside the village. Hence, it is not only the peasant women's farm work that connects different modes of production, but also their social reproductive work.

The productive/reproductive analytical model does not consider the ways women's productive and reproductive roles can be enmeshed in the politics of a militaristic state. Nevertheless, the model can be useful for understanding how militarization affects peasant women's lives in the Third World. Not only are the women victimized by military operations that affect their farm work, family, and organizations, but they are also made to participate in the social maintenance of the very military that represses them and their village communities. This diverts the peasant women's meager resources, such as food, from their subsistence, adding more pressure to their already difficult situation. Indeed, they are doubly oppressed, since requiring that they help maintain the military subtly obtains their consent to the existing social order that exploits and represses them.

Furthermore, the state, by neglecting to provide adequate social services in the village, passes on to the peasant women's productive and re-productive roles the unsubsidized care of the retired labor force (the elderly) and the reserve labor force (the young).

My examination of the daily lives of the peasant women of KAMMI reveals that not only the village economy but also the critical position of peasant women in this structure are linked to the national and global political economies. It is in the peasant women's work, their place in the market, and their reproductive role that we find the exploitative connection between transnational capital and the village economy. This can be seen particularly in (a) the negative impact of the Green Revolution on farm work and the rural ecology; (b) the way that peasant women experience the impact of the IMF's "tied aid" (Payer 1974), as in the increase in the price of rice; (c) their role in the exportation of rice to pay foreign debt; (d) the way in which the United States supports militarization in the Philippines through military aid and direct involvement in counter-insurgency; and (e) GATT's transnational control of the women's indigenous rice variety, local market, and trade.

These interlocking power structures affecting the lives of the peasant women have roots in the Philippine colonial past, and they support the neocolonial present. The legacy of Philippine colonial history (see Chapter 2) continues to reverberate in peasant women's lives.

But despite these complex realities that make peasant women poor, exploited, and repressed, they have chosen resistance over submission. Defying the depiction of Third World women as simply victims of under-development (Bisilliat and Fieloux 1987) or the possessors of a fatalistic "culture of poverty" (Lewis 1959), the women of KAMMI have developed a culture of resistance. Like Salvadoran women (Golden 1991), South African women (Russel 1989), and Mozambican women (Urdang 1989), the women of KAMMI and AMIHAN challenge their exploitation and repression. They are not passive victims of underdevelopment. Showing tremendous courage against the forces of greed and militarization, they are claiming a place in the transforming social order. Part of their agenda for change is to tell their story and to offer analysis based on their experience when talking about the national situation and the peasantry in the Philippines. This book is conceived as part of their efforts to tell their story and be heard.

The organized resistance of KAMMI and AMIHAN is making peasant women more visible. The revival and reorganization of KAMMI after the 1987 systematic harassment of KMP-Mindoro brought the peasant women to the fore as they opted to separate from the KMP. The formation of AMIHAN as a national federation, distinct from the national federation of KMP, brought the peasant women's voices in the villages into the national arena and the broader movement for change in the

Philippines. And their international solidarity with other Asian peasant women in opposing GATT brought their collective voice to light on the global scene, where major development policies affecting them originate. Through their continued resistance, strengthening, and reorganization under the Ramos regime, they refuse to submit to development policies that continually ignore and marginalize them election after election. They refuse to further the programs of Philippines 2000, which disregard their interests as peasants and as women.

Although the way in which the politics of underdevelopment affects the peasant women's lives is central to creating the preconditions for their organized resistance, an examination of the politics of KAMMI and AMIHAN shows it is the peasant women's volition that brings to life their collective action. Their organization is their defense against the divisive tactics of repression, and it gives them a collective voice. Land occupation is their radical alternative to the structure of land ownership that denies them the basic right to own land, a right they believe springs from their being tillers of the land. Their cooperative income-generating projects are responses to their inadequate income and poverty. Their collective child-care projects resist the privatization of their reproductive roles. Their campaign for increased wages is their attempt to take control of their labor. Their consumer cooperatives are their response to the anarchic market, and their attempt to establish credit cooperatives resists the exploitative usury to which they have been subjected. Their struggle to protect their *suyuan*, an indigenous collective form of work, from being exploited by landlords opposes the capitalist penetration of communal forms of work still existing in their village. Their experimental attempts to bring back the traditional rice hybrid rejects the development ideology behind the externally controlled and damaging Green Revolution. Their deliberations and political position on foreign debt and IMF policies denounce forms of economic imperialism that infringe on their ability to meet their basic needs. Their village health-care projects, which harness local resources, both counteract the dependency that results from a neocolonial political economy and provide the village with the social services it lacks because of the absence of government support. Their *pag-aaral* (education/study sessions), where they discuss and analyze development issues, opposes ideological control of information by the repressive state. Their leadership training is part of the struggle to make themselves visible not only within the community but within the male-dominated peasant movement as well. Their mass demonstrations publicly express their collective demands and their political stance on the development issues that affect their everyday lives, contesting the state's official development policies, which counter such demands at every turn.

These forms of resistance imply the need to reconceptualize develop-ment paradigms—such as modernization or the integrationist perspec-tive on women and development—outside the experience of peasants, workers, women, men, and children in the Third World. AMIHAN's re-jection of PDPW (Philippine Development Plan for Women), which is premised on the integrationist perspective, is the outcome of such re-thinking. KAMMI's and AMIHAN's alternative agrarian reform program begins from the perspective of peasant women, who compose the ma-jority of women in the Philippines and in the Third World. Their politics of resistance and their agenda for change offer a grounded reconcep-tualization of development as empowerment, which such Third World feminist scholars as Audrey Bronstein (1982), Peggy Antrobus (1989), and Gita Sen and Caren Grown (1987) have begun to recognize.

Reconceptualizing development as empowerment has policy implica-tions for the everyday lives of poor Third World women, and thus is an important task in feminist scholarship. In a reconceptualization using the perspective of these women, it is they who become the theorists of empowerment, based on their history, experience, and struggle. One of the national leaders of AMIHAN stated this idea eloquently in a speech during one of her international "solidarity tours":

Empowerment for us in AMIHAN means equality and autonomy. . . . By equality we mean here that as human beings the peasant women should be given all the rights and responsibilities accorded to our male peasants. We therefore are claim-ing equal rights to resources such as land, capital, and information. And by au-tonomy we mean spaces for us peasant women to express and realize our dreams and aspirations toward the greater goal of the attainment of genuine agrarian reform and the emancipation of our country from foreign domination.[1]

She explained strategies for empowering peasant women:

We are organizing separate organizations of peasant women, not to compete or fight with the male peasants, but only because we wanted us peasant women to define among ourselves what it is that we want, what we think must be accorded to us as human beings. We do organizing of peasant women, for we believe that only through organization can they achieve our rights and demands. We do edu-cation work among peasant women, for we believe that that in itself is empower-ment. Our advocacy work is aimed at propagating the issues of the peasant women to the greatest number of people possible, which consequently will gen-erate the much needed support for the cause of the peasant women. We in recent years have women to help support, however meager, the economic needs of the peasant women.[2]

The politics of KAMMI and AMIHAN provide insights on what de-velopment as empowerment would mean from the perspective of poor Third World women. Such empowerment requires an integrated approach to development, comprising various aspects. First, it involves analyzing development from the point of view of poor Third World women, because their experiences embody the intersection of complex power structures of gender (relations between men and women and the ideologies defining a woman's place in society and her reproductive roles), race (the impact of colonialism and neocolonialism in Third World countries), and class (the position of women in the relations of production). Second, it involves redistribution of economic power in order to guarantee these women's access to critical resources so that they may lead decent, dignified lives. This could mean transforming the relations and modes of production and social reproduction that exploit women's productive and reproductive labor for the benefit of a small class of owners. Third, it involves restructuring political institutions in order that these women (a) will have the political power to participate meaningfully in policy-making bodies of the government, so they do not simply become passive beneficiaries of development programs but are active shapers of policies that have a direct impact on them; (b) will succeed in having their alternative development policies institutionalized by the national government and global/international institutions; and (c) will be able to organize freely, without military repression, for their collective empowerment. And finally, it involves the deconstruction of gendered relations, which are intricately enmeshed with the practices and ideologies of economic, political, and cultural institutions. This deconstruction is integral to the process of economic and political empowerment. For development that perpetuates or thrives on the exploitation of women and on gender hierarchies is not empowerment.

Appendix A.
Fieldwork, Culture, and Militarization: Organic Feminist Inquiry

Feminist scholarship on women in development can now begin to elaborate on this grassroots conceptualization of empowerment. This theoretical task, however, has methodological implications. It calls for tools that redefine concepts in order to "reflect women's reality" more visibly (Antrobus 1989, 194) and deconstruct theories embedded in studies premised on development perspectives that have evolved outside Third World women's experience. It calls for creative methods of fieldwork that can be employed in the militarized zones of most Third World nations, which may preclude staying in the field for extended periods. Organic feminist inquiry, which evolved in this study as I dealt with the difficulties of conducting fieldwork in militarized Mindoro, opens a door to these theoretical and methological tasks. While there may be some relationship between such an approach and works of First World feminist scholars, such as Dorothy Smith's "institutional ethnography," which evolved in a North American context, the unique contribution of organic feminist inquiry is that it arose from field experience in a Third World, militarized context.

Militarization and Fieldwork

Militarization and repression in the Philippines presented me with difficulties I did not anticipate.[1] For example, I was unable to stick to my original choice of a site for fieldwork. I had planned to work in the Bicol region, where a local chapter of AMIHAN is located, because I can speak its dialect and there was intense political activity there. But upon my arrival in the Philippines, I was told by the people who were to facilitate my research that the leaders of the AMIHAN chapter in Bicol were harassed by the military and could not secure my stay in the area. After considering three alternative sites, I finally chose Mindoro because (a) I had not been there before, (b) I could speak the local dialect, (c) there was a legal institution to receive and sponsor me, (d) the local chapter had been in regular communication with the AMIHAN national office, and (e) in the perception of the AMIHAN national coordinator Mindoro was not as intensely militarized as Quezon Province and Bicol.

When I arrived Mindoro, however, I realized that it was indeed militarized, and more intensely than I expected. In fact, I had some direct encounters with the military. On my way to the mayor's office to acquire a permit to enter its villages (as suggested by the peasant women), soldiers standing by the military headquarters adjacent to the mayor's office accosted me and my companion. One soldier called to get my attention, saying, "Miss, can we see what is inside your bag?" Afraid that they might harm us, since they were holding guns, and thinking that our resistance might trigger more trouble, we walked obediently toward them. Two of the soldiers searched my bag and subjected me to tactical interrogation, which made me very nervous. They took turns in repeatedly asking me such questions as: Why we were going to see the mayor? How did I come to Mindoro? Did I know someone in Mindoro before I came? Who accompanied me to Mindoro? What office or organization in Manila was I connected with? What was I teaching the people, to whom was I giving medicine (since I had medicines in my bag)? Why did I come to Mindoro when the political situation there was dangerous? And, How did I get to know my companion? Although the soldiers eventually released us unharmed, the experience made me feel violated, angry, and afraid.

Organic Feminist Inquiry

In an effort to conduct fieldwork that would be sensitive to the political situation and the cultural context of the peasant women's daily lives while enabling me to learn about their experience as peasants and as women, I evolved the concept of *organic feminist inquiry*. I also employed this concept—beginning from the experience of Filipino peasant women—to examine the national and global politics of development and underdevelopment, as well as the resistance it engenders. Organic feminist inquiry has several basic elements. These are: (1) being sensitive to the political context and the culture of the women involved in the study, (2) conducting research in natural settings, (3) being flexible by letting questions emerge, (4) seeking to understand the power structures in which women's lives are enmeshed, and (5) being reflexive.

Being Sensitive to the Political Context
and the Culture of the Women Involved in the Study

I learned that the political context of Third World women's lives, which includes militarization, raises ethical issues that the researcher must deal with sensitively. One issue that confronted me was the need to safeguard my informants and my data from the military and others who could harm the peasant women or use the data to justify repressive action against them. The possibility that my research could be used against the women seemed more probable to me after I learned, while in Mindoro, that the national office of the KMP in Manila had been raided by soldiers, who were searching for someone they wanted to arrest. They did not find him, but they did find a list of KMP members in Mindoro.

I thus took several measures to protect the women and my data. First, I learned how to enter the villages safely, incurring few risks for them and for me. Having no knowledge of the places myself, I relied on the peasant women's advice. For example, I took their suggestions concerning what villages I should not enter. Because a new person in a village becomes a suspect of the military, I did not want to incur reprisals on the peasant women or risk my safety in the area. Second, I did not use a tape recorder in the villages. This had both advantages and disadvantages. One advantage was that I had written data (approximately twenty-five pounds of paper) when I came back from the field; a disadvantage was that I had no other record against which I could check details. Third, I used codes to record interviews and write down my observations and other field notes that I thought involved sensitive issues.[2] I ensured that these notes could not be easily found. Fourth, I sometimes left the village in order to write. I used the place of my contact in Mindoro as a location for writing the observations I could not record while in the village. It was also the safest place to store my data, since it was located outside the village. Fifth, in recording my findings I did not name the village I was studying, and I avoided any description that could lead to the identification of a peasant woman, such as her position in the organization.

In addition to the political context in Mindoro, I had to be sensitive to Filipino village culture. One element of this culture is that relationships are more personal than impersonal. Having had some experience doing research in the United States before going back to the Philippines made me more aware that different styles of doing fieldwork are required by these two cultures. In the U.S., formality was appreciated or at least expected, but in the Philippines, people were not very comfortable when I was too formal with them. The village peasant women perceived me as too formal when I carried a piece of paper, had an interview schedule before me, or wrote down their responses. I saw that these activities interfered with their spontaneity and with my ability to establish rapport with them. The peasant women were more open when I simply talked to them informally and conversationally, without writing down what they were saying. In this way I could be more personal in my approach, the women were more trusting and open, and I could gather more information.[3] I shared this observation with some professionals who also do research in Mindoro, and they confirmed that they had experienced the same things. They pointed out that the women's reaction was not simply an odd cultural trait. The women are wary about having their words recorded because they have experienced military searches for "subversive" materials in their village. Here, militarization and culture interact in determining the way in which peasant women respond to interviews.

To respect the personalism of Filipino culture, I approached the peasant women with what I call *cultural reciprocity*. By this I refer to the desire of the peasant women to relate to people very personally and my ability to respond in the same way. For example, the first time they met me, they addressed me at once as "Ate" (pronounced ah-tĕ), a form used for someone who is kin. This is their way of expressing their acceptance of someone who is not a relative. I responded by also addressing the women as "Ate" and the men as "Kuya." Being a Filipina myself, it was not hard for me to practice this form of cultural reciprocity, and doing so helped in my being accepted and trusted. Cultural reciprocity also allowed me to demonstrate acceptance and appreciation of the village culture of the peasant women.

Conducting Research in Natural Settings

I learned that conducting fieldwork in natural settings means discovering the most respectful way to enter the field. To gain entry into the field, I used the proper channels and respected AMIHAN's standard operating procedures, such as going through the international representative of GABRIELA and the national office of AMIHAN in the Philippines, and using contacts I had in the Philippine support movement in the United States. Gaining entry and trust also meant it was necessary for me to be explicit about "whose side" (Schutte 1991; Becker 1967) I was on. That is, I had to make it clear that I was not an informer for the military, and that I was sympathetic to the progressive movement of which AMIHAN was part. These operating procedures are an important way in which the organization protects itself from the infiltration of informers who may be working for the military.

Conducting fieldwork in natural settings also means having a feel for and adapting to the rhythm of life in that setting.[4] For example, I learned that most of the time information would come out in informal conversations I had during meals with women, while walking together, while swimming at the beach with some of them, or simply when I was just hanging around. There is a practice I observed among the village people: *kwentohan sa gabi.* These are evening conversations, usually after supper, which can go until very late at night. I took these occasions to be with the women and their neighbors or relatives who came by to talk. There were times I succeeded in staying up as late as they did, but there were also occasions when I had to give in to my sleepiness. The last day I saw Ate Ara, we stayed up the whole night without sleep, just talking. I kept myself awake by drinking coffee, but for Ate Ara this seemed to be a normal evening.

There were also times when I shared a bed with the peasant women I visited or with whom I stayed overnight. These were good opportunities for the *kwentohan sa gabi,* and they became very trusting moments in which the women could pour out their stories openly. I found these occasions very personal and meaningful. A Westerner may not be used to sleeping with little privacy, but it was not foreign for me to sleep on a mat on the floor with two or three other women next to me, for I grew up in a poor family in the Philippines, and our house was small. My own class background and peasant origins thus helped me to adapt to the conditions in the village and to establish rapport with the peasant women.

Conducting research in natural settings also means being able to use different methods of gathering data where they are appropriate, rather than relying on a single method.[5] For example, I found that certain occasions were more conducive to group interviews than individual ones, and I used these times to talk to the women in groups. Some examples were meetings or training sessions, ongoing conversations I would join, and anytime I sensed women could talk to me most naturally with other women around. Sometimes I conducted semi-formal individual interviews, in which I would sit down with a woman primarily for the purpose of asking her some questions and would write down her responses if I saw that this activity did not threaten her, but I generally followed these with informal conversations, since the women felt more comfortable talking within this format.

Being Flexible by Letting Questions Emerge

Going to the field with an open methodology allows one to be responsive to what is emerging. Although I had clear objectives in my fieldwork, I chose not to test a predefined hypothesis. This allowed me to learn early in my fieldwork what the women frequently talked about: the militarization of their community (something I had thought they would be hesitant to discuss), their *paghihirap* (poverty), *tagkiriwi* (the season of the year when they are most poor), their exploitation ("we are just working to let the rich eat"), and how militarization affected their lives, work, organization, family, children, and community. I made these issues central to my inquiry. Why are the peasant women poor? In what ways are they exploited? How do they experience militarization? How does militarization affect their lives and their organization? How do development policies affect their lives? What forms of resistance have they attempted, and what has been the result? These questions became clear to me as a result of my interaction with the women. That I quickly got a sense of these questions can be partly attributed to my being "indigenous" to the culture I was studying, which placed me at an "indisputable advantage of being able to attach meanings to patterns . . . faster than a non-indigenous researcher who is unfamiliar with the culture" (Altorki and El-Sohl 1988, 7).

Seeking to Understand the Power Structures in which Women's Lives Are Enmeshed

Organic feminist inquiry seeks to understand the power structures in which women's lives are enmeshed and the women's struggle for empowerment.[6] The questions that quickly emerged in my fieldwork allowed me to see the complex, interlocking power structures that made the peasant women and their families poor, exploited, and repressed, as I have discussed in Chapter 3. To understand these structures more fully, it is important to examine the women's resistance. This allows us to see the dynamics of exploitation and resistance—how women challenge that which oppresses them (see Chapters 4 and 5). By examining their forms of resistance, we are able to let women give voice to their often repressed and suppressed thoughts, and to articulate their alternative vision of a better society and their strategies of empowerment. Thus, we can construct an image of women, not as passive victims of oppression, but as active agents of their own liberation. We can therefore conceive of power structures as dialectical processes of contending forces. An oppressed woman is not a willing victim. Structures of oppression devise ways to manage her consent. Organic feminist inquiry seeks ways to make visible and explain such dynamics of oppression, exploitation, and resistance.

Being Reflexive

The final element of organic feminist inquiry is being reflexive. The process of inquiry should allow us to reflect about ourselves as we contemplate the lives of the women we study. This should allow us to connect our own experiences with those of the women we encounter as we consider our commonalities and differences.[7] For example, my fieldwork made me more aware and appreciative of my peasant-class origin. I saw and understood more clearly the significant contribution of peasant women and of the peasantry as a whole to the economy of the Philippines as well as to the global political economy, despite the fact that they are devalued, exploited, and accorded very low prestige. I also became aware that my experiences differ from those of the peasant women because I have experienced upward social mobility in terms of education and occupational status. These women do not lack aspirations and goals for themselves and their children, but they have not had the opportunities that I had. I was able to get the higher education that my family could not afford because I received financial aid and scholarships. Such opportunities were not available to these women and their children.

Being reflexive in the process of organic feminist inquiry in turn allows us to treat the women we study not only as sources of "data," but also as fellow human beings. We develop an emphatic understanding and bonding, learning about ourselves and our place in the existing hierarchies as we come to understand the women's daily lives and the power structures that shape them.[8]

This empathic bonding and understanding, in turn, allows us to recognize the connection between research and our commitments to social justice.[9] What we choose to study and the choices we make concerning how to research what we choose to study already speak about what our commitments are: how much we want to engage with or maintain distance from the social reality that binds or divides us. For example, contrary to the positivist argument that we must leave our values behind, what influenced me to overcome the difficulties I encountered in my field was partly the personal commitment I have to social justice. It was this commitment that made me take the risk of doing fieldwork in a militarized zone. Seeking courage in my God, who calls people to respond to the demands of justice, I decided that I, as a sociologist doing research in a context of injustice, could not stand apart from the conflict injustice breeds and that I could not study peasant women's resistance without myself being part of that resistance.[10] By evolving a methodology that brought me into the village, I heard and saw things I would not have seen or heard if I had simply stayed in the city and invited the peasant women to be interviewed there (an option that tempted me at first because I feared entering a militarized zone).[11] I found the peasant women to be beautiful people, and while I admired their courage, I also cried at the sufferings militarization has brought them and their families. I felt humanized just by being with them and learning about their earnest attempts to create a culture of resistance.[12]

Appendix B.
Frontiers in Feminist Inquiry

This study opens doors to areas for further feminist research. First, there is a need to assess the impact of Philippines 2000 on all sectors of Filipino women in comparison to men. As a development program, Philippines 2000 is heavily dependent on transnational capital (foreign investments) and foreign loans. What are the places of gender and women in this process, and what policy alternatives can be proposed?

Second, how do massive land-use conversions affect women and their families in different regions of the country? What would a comparative study reveal? What forms of resistance are taking place in these regions, and how are conflicts resolved? What policy implications does this comparative study reveal?

Third, how do export of labor and feminization of migrant labor, which segregate Filipino women in domestic service work, affect the lives of Filipino women and their families? What is the situation of these migrant workers in foreign countries, and what happens to them when their contracts end? What government policies and agencies are there to protect the rights of these workers? Is the export of labor a good policy?

Fourth, how does the development policy of Philippines 2000 that continues to promote tourism in various parts of the country affect women, men, and children and transform their communities? Who are the beneficiaries and the exploited in this development process?

Fifth, what happens throughout the country to peasant women who are displaced from their communities or their farms by land-use conversions? What happens to women, men, and children in indigenous communities who are dislocated by land-use conversions?

Sixth, what is the impact of continuing militarization on women, men, and children in different sectors and in various regions of the Philippines? Is there a connection between militarization, land-use conversions, and transnational corporations' entry into different regions? How does militarization continue to affect peasant women's organizations throughout the country?

Seventh, what makes land occupation succeed or fail? What would a comparative study of land occupations in different parts of the country reveal? In successful land occupations, in which peasants are able to settle with their families, what happens to gender relations in communal production?

Eighth, what is the ecological impact of land-use conversions? How are women and men, children and the elderly affected by ecological and environmental changes?

Ninth, what specific policies in GATT and the Medium Term Agricultural Development Program under Philippines 2000 erode peasant women's struggle for genuine agrarian reform, control of biodiversity, and initiatives on sustainable agriculture? What alternative policies can be proposed and implemented?

Tenth, what are the positive and negative effects of NGOs on peasant women's organizations? How do NGOs set up policies in relation to their work with grassroots women's organizations? What are the different vantage points on which they base their work with peasant women? Where do they get their funding, and how does their relationship with foreign funding agencies constrain their support for peasant women's empowerment?

Last, in what ways would organic feminist inquiry be useful or not useful in researching these questions? What other elements can be added to organic feminist inquiry, as we apply it in different contexts and with different groups?

Notes

Introduction

1. I personally witnessed Marcos on television when he declared the whole Philippines a land reform area on the day he declared martial law in 1972; in reality his program affected only rice and corn land. My own view is that he announced this program at the same time that he declared martial law in order to cushion the impact of military rule. Some peasants believe his failed land reforms were meant to suppress revolutionary insurgency among the peasantry.

2. Interview by author with a national officer of AMIHAN on May 17, 1996. See also *Agrarian Directions*, no. 1 (June 1995).

3. Department of Agrarian Reform, *1993 Annual Report*; quoted in *Agrarian Directions*, no. 1 (June 1995): 10.

4. Kilusang Magbubukid ng Pilipinas, "Delivering the Death Blow to a Mangled Agrarian Reform Law: A Critique on Senate Bill 740 and House Bill 918," January 20, 1995; quoted in *Agrarian Directions*, no. 1 (June 1995): 8.

5. *Agrarian Directions*, no. 1 (June 1995): 9.

6. See Table 3, "Land Conversions in Relation to DTI's Regional Industrial Centers and Its Impact on Farmers, by Region," in *Laya: Feminist Quarterly* (January 1994): 14–16. Tess Oliveros, executive director of the national office of AMIHAN, also documents in her report, which she read at Oxfam America Partners' Dialogue, held at Binangonan, Rizal, June 26–28, 1995, that many AMIHAN members in Laguna had been displaced by the CALABARZON conversion program. Many migrated to Manila, some moved to neighboring villages and are working as laundrywomen and food vendors, and others clean soft-drink bottles for one peso a case. There are those who were hired to work on rotation (therefore with irregular income) on the "flower farms" in Cavite for eighty pesos a day, and some work as "caddy women" on the international golf courses in Tagaytay. Some of the children who are high school graduates managed to find jobs in the factories in the zone, although for some this was only because their parents promised they would prevent their children from engaging in unionizing work.

7. From informants I talked to when I visited Mindoro again in 1996.

8. Culled from "Children and Human Rights Violations: The Need for a More Relevant Perspective for Rehabilitation Work," (report presented by the Children's Rehabilitation Center at the UN Conference on Traumas of Youth and Children on Armed Conflict, Amsterdam, November 1995).

9. Interview by author with an AMIHAN national officer, Manila, May 17, 1996.

10. Kilusang Magbubukid ng Pilipinas-Mindanao; cited in *Agrarian Directions*, no. 1 (June 1995): 11.

11. See a TFDP leaflet entitled "Krimen ba ang Maglinkod sa Bayan?" December 1995. See also the "Report of the Philippines Alliance of Human Rights Advocates on Human Rights in the Philippines," fifty-second session of the United Nations Commission on Human Rights, March 18 to April 26, 1990, Geneva, Switzerland, prepared by Philippine Human Rights Information Center, the research and information arm of PAHRA.

12. Interview by author with an AMIHAN national officer, Manila, May 17, 1996.

13. Children's Rehabilitation Center, "Children and Human Rights Violations: The Need for a More Relevant Perspective for Rehabilitation Work" (report at the UN Conference on Traumas of Youth and Children on Armed Conflict, Amsterdam, November 1995), p. 2.

14. Center for Women's Resources, *Pilipinas 2000 sa Taong 1995: Aktwal na karanasan ng mamayan laban sa ilusyon ng pamahalaan*, (Quezon City, Philippines: Center for Women's Resources, 1996), 14.

15. Children's Rehabilitation Center, quoting an estimate of the Citizens' Disaster Response Network.

16. Quoted in *Pilipinas 2000 sa Taong 1995*, 15.

17. Interview by author with two AMIHAN national leaders and one local organizer, Manila, May 16, May 17, and June 1, 1996.

18. I gathered information about GABRIELA through my interviews with three key members, one of them the founder of this organization, during my fieldwork in the Philippines in 1989. I also knew about GABRIELA through the Friends of GABRIELA in Chicago, a women's support group for GABRIELA in the Philippines of which I was a founding member in 1988. This group is now called GABRIELA Network. See also GABRIELA, *Empowering Filipinas for Development* (Quezon City, Philippines: GABRIELA, 1987).

19. I gathered information about MAKIBAKA through interviews with two MAKIBAKA members, one in Manila on August 2, 1989, and another in Chicago in October 1990. See also Salome Ronquillo, "MAKIBAKA Remembered," in *Sourcebook on Philippine Women in Struggle*, ed. Sergy Floro and Nana Luz (Berkeley, Calif.: Philippine Resource Center, 1985), 124–28; Leonora Angeles, "The PKP and MAKIBAKA Revisited: Women's Liberation in Revolutionary Theory and Practice," *KASARINLAN* 3 (March 1988): 26–38.

20. Most historical accounts on the Philippines do not really discuss the experience of Filipino women, which gave me difficulty. Some feminists see the need to rewrite Philippine history from a feminist perspective. Elizabeth Eviota has done pioneering work in this area which was very useful in writing this chapter.

Chapter 2

1. There are inconsistencies in the historical record regarding the precolonial system of governing. Some say that the position of chief was inherited; others say that it was achieved through valuable service to the community. It could be possible that, in the early formation of the barangay, the chief was selected, and that this position could be inherited by male heirs. When the line of succession was broken, selection based on service may have come to the fore.

2. Ancestral lands were areas owned by tribal Filipino communities. Some of these communities resisted colonial intrusion or were pushed to the hinterlands,

in the process losing their lands to colonialists or other land grabbers. Their ownership of these lands was and still is based on their indigenous concept of land ownership: they or their ancestors were first to occupy the land. These tribal communities preserved most elements of their culture from Western colonial influence. They exist even to this day. Now they are considered ethnic minorities in Philippine society, although they are actually the indigenous Filipinos. Some Filipino scholars and educators refer to them as "cultural communities" rather than "tribal communities" because of the ethnocentric connotation of the term *tribal.* Examples of these cultural communities are the Muslims in Mindanao, the Mangyans of Mindoro, and the Igorots and Ifugaos of northern Luzon.

3. After the Filipinos gained independence from Spain, America bought the Philippines for 20 million pesos on December 10, 1898. Then, on February 4, 1899, following Emilio Aguinaldo's proclamation of the First Republic of the Philippines on January 23, the United States declared war against the Filipinos. This action was taken in order to secure the Philippines as a colony. See Volker Schult, *Mindoro: A Social History of a Philippine Island in the Twentieth Century* (Manila: Divine Word Publications, 1991), 35.

4. See Sylvia Chant and Cathy McIlwaine, *Women of a Lesser Cost: Female Labour, Foreign Exchange and Philippine Development* (Manila: Ateneo de Manila University Press, 1995), 55, quoting "RP Gets New $650m Loan," *Filipino* 6, no. 1 (February/March 1994): 3.

5. See Arnel de Guzman, "Philippines 2000: Vision or Ilusyon?" *Pinoy: Overseas Chronicle* 11, no. 2 (1993): 4–5, 34.

6. Free trade zones are areas designated primarily for foreign transnational corporations to build factories and industries for export commodities. Workers in free trade zones usually are not allowed to strike or unionize, and the government gives the transnational corporations privileges and incentives in order to attract foreign investment.

7. See Freedom from Debt Coalition, *The Philippine Debt Crisis* (Diliman, Quezon City: Freedom from Debt Coalition, 1989), 30, quoting IBON Data Bank, n.d.; Joseph Carabeo, Guest Editorial, *Tambalan* 2, no. 2 (Spring 1996): 1.

8. See Dale Hildebrand, *To Pay Is to Die* (Davao City, Philippines: Philippine International Forum, 1991), 77.

9. Ibid., 75.

10. *Philippine Daily Globe,* April 6, 1989; quoted in Aida Fulleros Santos and Lynn F. Lee, *The Treadmill of Poverty for Filipino Women* (Philippines: Kalayaan, 1989), 44.

11. Military Base Agreement, March 14, 1947, quoted in Daniel B. Schirmer and Stephen Rosskamm Shalom, eds., *The Philippines Reader: A History of Colonialism, Neocolonialism, Dictatorship and Resistance* (Boston: South End Press, 1987), 97–100.

12. *United States News and World Watch Report,* March 13, 1967, quoted in Roland G. Simbulan, *The Bases of Our Insecurity: A Study of the U.S. Bases in the Philippines* (Philippines: Balai Fellowship, 1985), 178. The Hukbalahap (sometimes referred to as the Huks) was formally established on March 22, 1942. Its official name was Hukbo ng Bayang Laban sa Hapon (Peoples Army to Fight Japan). Many of its leaders had been involved with the Communist party and leftist peasant groups. As a movement it fought for liberation from Japanese occupation and sought welfare for the common people, especially landless peasants.

13. Alliance for Philippine Concerns, "Statement on the U.S. Bases," June 12, 1988.

14. Synapses, *Synapses Messages* 8, no. 4 (July 1989).

15. Church Coalition for Human Rights in the Philippines, *Philippine Witness* (Summer 1989).

16. Forum for Rural Concerns Human Rights Desk, *The Philippine Human Rights Situationer* (Quezon City, Philippines: 1989), 21.

17. Constitution of the Republic of the Philippines, 1986, art. 2, sec. 8.

18. In this brief historical sketch I focused on the American neocolonial control of the economy because it is still the United States that exercises dominant control over the Philippine political economy. The flow of Japanese capital into the Philippines, although increasing, is much lower than it is in neighboring countries. For example, as of the later 1980s the "accumulated stock" of Japanese investment in the Philippines amounted to approximately $1 billion, compared to $10 billion in Indonesia and $2 billion each in Malaysia and Thailand. One reason for this is Japan's cautiousness in "encroaching on" what it has "historically recognized as an area of special interest for US firms." (Walden Bello, *People and Power in the Pacific: The Struggle for the Post–Cold War Order* [London and San Francisco: Pluto Press, with Food First and Transnational Institute, 1992], 95.) Japan's colonial occupation of the Philippines took place in 1941–45 as part of Japan's attempt to bring the Philippines, a major American outpost in Southeast Asia, into the East Asia Co-Prosperity Sphere; Japan would serve as the industrial power and the rest of Southeast Asia would supply the raw materials (Schult 1991).

Chapter 3

1. There are very few regional studies that deal specifically with the history of Mindoro. This subsection is based on some of the literature I found useful, including the following: (1) *Mindoro History* (n.d.), an unpublished historical account of Mindoro prepared by the Mindoro Institute for Development (MIND), which I obtained during my fieldwork in Mindoro in the summer of 1989. The Mindoro Institute for Development had a Research and Documentation Desk, which conducted research relevant to its support work for the peasantry in Mindoro; (2) *Occidental Mindoro: A Profile* (n.d.), which a staff member of MIND gave me during my second visit, in the summer of 1996; (3) a government document prepared by the Mindoro Integrated Rural Development Office, *Mindoro Integrated Development Plan* (Quezon City, 1980), which I was also given by a staff member of MIND during my revisit; and (4) Schult's *Mindoro: A Social History of a Philippine Island in the Twentieth Century*, the only comprehensive historical book on Mindoro that I found in the Filipiana collection of De La Salle University in Manila during my revisit to the Philippines in 1996.

2. See *Mindoro Integrated Development Plan*, 4–5; MIND, *Occidental Mindoro: A Profile* (n.d.), 1.

3. MIND, *Mindoro History* (n.d.), unpublished historical account.

4. Schult, *Mindoro: A Social History*, 28.

5. MIND, *Mindoro History*.

6. Schult, *Mindoro: A Social History*, 26.

7. Ibid., p. 31.

8. Based on my informal talk with some peasant women in Santa Cruz, a municipality of Mindoro, during my second visit in 1996.

9. Schult, *Mindoro: A Social History*, 35.

10. Ibid., 36, quoting the decree of June 18, 1898: Teodoro Agoncillo, *Malolos: The Crisis of the Republic* (Quezon City: University of the Philippines Press, 1960),

quoted in Schult, *Mindoro: A Social History*, 36, n.44; Amado Guerrero, "The Provincial and Municipal Elite in Luzon," in *Philippine Social History: Global Trade and Local Transformations*, edited by Alfred W. McCoy and Edilberto C. De Jesus (Honolulu: University Press of Hawaii, 1982), quoted in Schult, *Mindoro: A Social History*, 36, n.44.

11. Personal and Police History of Deputies to First Filipino Assembly, October 19, 1907, W. Cameron Forbes Papers, Houghton Library, Harvard University; quoted in Schult, *Mindoro: A Social History*, 53.

12. MIND, *Mindoro History*.

13. Benedict J. Kerkvliet, *The Huk Rebellion: A Study of Peasant Revolt in the Philippines* (Berkeley, Los Angeles, London: University of California Press, 1977); quoted in Schult, *Mindoro: A Social History*, 67.

14. See Schult, *Mindoro: A Social History*, 68, 78–81.

15. Macario Z. Landicho, *The Mindoro Yearbook* (Manila: Yearbook Publishers, 1952); Willem Wolters, *Politics and Class Conflict in Central Luzon*, Research Report Series no. 14 (The Hague: Institute of Social Studies, 1983), quoted in Schult, *Mindoro: A Social History*, 69.

16. Schult, *Mindoro: A Social History*, 65.

17. This finding supports what Cynthia Banzon-Bautista says in her "Capitalism and the Peasantry: A Review of the Empirical Literature," *Philippine Sociological Review* 31 (1983): 17–26. Here she cites Theodore Shanin's finding that peasants are exploited not only by landlords but also by moneylenders who extract a share from the peasants' produce through interest on loans.

18. "Para ba akong nangliliit kung nanghihiram ako ng pera." This statement, which cannot be literally translated into English, implies a feeling that one's dignity has been insulted.

19. A recipient of a CLT, under the Marcos land reform program, had to pay amortization to the landlord or to the Land Bank of the Philippines for fifteen years before he could claim ownership of the land specified in the certificate. A poor peasant could not afford this amortization and, unable to pay regularly, could lose his right to the land as well as forfeit his CLT and paid amortization. Most landlords opposed the transfer of their land to tenants. Ate Beni, for example, said that their landlord is resistant to the terms of the CLT.

20. See Mindoro regional file, table entitled "Palay Production Per Municipality, 1984–1989," National Food Authority, Mindoro Branch.

21. Lugaw, translated in English as porridge, is usually a meal that poor families resort to when they have very little rice with which to feed many family members.

22. I gathered the information about the Quedan Financing Scheme included here through an interview with someone who was working with Quedan. I learned about the existence of Quedan during my interviews with staff members of the National Food Authority, Mindoro Branch, one of whom mentioned Quedan but did not give much information about it. I then interviewed a staff member whose work is directly connected with the Quedan Financing Scheme.

23. I gathered information regarding the National Food Authority, a government bureau set up for the procurement and marketing of agricultural products, through interviews with five members of the National Food Authority, Mindoro Branch Office. I had never heard of this government agency until the peasant women mentioned the NFA several times in their conversations.

24. Not every peasant in Mindoro wanted to be a member of the Samahang Nayon (SN). A former member was very critical of this organization. He said he left it because it was useless (*walang kabuluhan*). Its leaders told members that the

organization would acquire tractors, but only the leaders ended up using them. He later joined KMP-Mindoro when it was still openly active before it was harassed by the military in 1987. The KMP (Peasant Movement of the Philippines) is a militant and progressive nongovernmental peasant organization, open to both men and women. It has chapters throughout the country, of which KMP-Mindoro was one.

25. I gathered information about Valiant through an interview with its manager in his office at the corporation's rice mill and warehouse in San Jose, Mindoro.

26. I learned about this corruption from an employee of NFA, whom I interviewed at the branch office in Mindoro.

27. At first I was unsure whether Ate Gansa was right, so during the group interview I asked if indeed the Philippines exports rice. Ate Gansa answered firmly, "Yes, that is certain." The other peasant women nodded their heads. My interviews of NFA personnnel confirmed the peasant women's perception and explanation.

28. Information culled from the NFA's document on Occidental Mindoro's dispersal plan for February–September 1989.

29. I have approximated this number from a document provided by the NFA regional file, "Rate of Absorption, Occidental Mindoro, 1980–1990."

30. I have computed the figures here from the table "Monthly Production, Occidental Mindoro" (1983–88) from the NFA regional file in Mindoro. I acquired this material during my interview of NFA personnel. The table did not specify the unit of measurement; I assume it is metric tons.

31. Data from the NFA regional file "Rate of Absorption, Occidental Mindoro, 1980–1990."

32. I have computed this average from a table in the NFA regional file, "Historical NFA Stocks, Rice Form, Occidental Mindoro, 1983–1990." Data for 1989–1990 had not yet been added to this table.

33. Ate Morina's analysis is supported by the findings of the Philippine Peasant Institute. Because of the massive use of agrochemicals in rice and corn production, fertilizer consumption rose from 101,198 metric tons in 1956 to 563,000 metric tons in 1972, 789,000 metric tons in 1975, and 1,153,600 metric tons in 1980. Importation of pesticides also increased from 1.53 million kilos in 1953 to 9.52 million kilos in 1972. Pesticide production increased as well, from 7,714 kilos in 1962 to 920,000 kilos in 1971. For a detailed discussion on the penetration of TNCs in the Green Revolution, see Mari Luz Tiongson et al., "Agriculture in the 70s and 80s: TNC's Boon, Peasants' Doom," in *Sowing the Seed: Proceedings of the International Conference for the Filipino Peasantry (ISCFP), October 11–21, 1986,* ed. Rodolfo Desuasido (Manila: KMP, 1988), 22–49.

34. A large portion of this section first appeared as "The Philippines: Peasant Women and Counter-Insurgency," *Race and Class: A Journal for Black and Third World Liberation* 34, no. 4 (April–June 1993): 1–11.

35. The Children's Rehabilitation Center (CRC) in the Philippines was set up in 1985 by a group of former political detainees who were aware of the psychological effects of militarization on children. That it received a tremendous number of requests for help indicates the extent of the impact of militarization on children. Because of the demand, it expanded operations from Metro-Manila to other critical regions in the Philippines, such as Bicol, Davao, Negros, and Panay. See "Children and Human Rights Violations," cited above in n. 8 of the Introduction.

36. In Benguet, the military looted people's kitchen utensils. See ibid., 2.

37. During my second visit to Mindoro, one member of KAMMI I talked to said that her work in the health program gives her visibility in the community. Because she relates health issues to broader political issues, she became suspected of revolutionary activity and was called a communist by some people in the local government. She said her parents are very worried when she leaves the house to do her work. A male peasant also told me that the military took a picture of him when he joined a demonstration protesting the destructive ecological impact that the Japanese multinational corporation's chromite mining will have in Mindoro.

38. There is other documentation of widespread human rights violations in the Philippines. See, for example, Marie Marciano, ed., *Let's Work Together for the Protection of Human Rights of Filipino Women: Documentation on the Human Rights Situation of Filipino Women* (Philippines: GABRIELA Women's Commission on Human Rights, 1989).

39. U.S. military aid to the Philippines was $50 million annually during the Marcos regime. This was raised to $100 million during the Aquino regime. *IBON Facts and Figures* 15, no. 16 (August 31, 1992) states that in 1990, the U.S. gave 4 billion pesos worth of military assistance.

40. See, for example, James Putzel and John Cunnington, *Gaining Ground: Agrarian Reform in the Philippines* (London: War on Want Campaigns, 1989), 43–44.

Chapter 4

1. Although KAMMI has maintained an organization distinct from the KMP, some of its local chapters, such as that in Calintaan, work closely with the male peasant organizations because they say they are concerned with the same issues and their working together facilitates action. Sometimes they hold meetings together and produce an agenda that includes KAMMI's concerns. They say that sometimes the men learn to be more supportive of the political work of women when they are involved in the same organization. I was given this information during my second visit to KAMMI in 1996.

2. When I revisited in 1996, some members of KAMMI I talked to said that while this approach might be true, care must be taken or people will come to meetings only when there is a project. They think that when organizing is solely project-centered, there is the danger that political awareness will fall by the wayside. This idea dawned on them because some women ceased coming to meetings when a nongovernmental organization in Mindoro discontinued financial support for their projects. This indicates that KAMMI continually learns from its experience. There is also a theoretical implication: principles and strategies of organizing evolve from concrete experiences. As grassroots organizers, peasant women have something to contribute to the construction of this theory, which non-peasant organizers supportive of the peasant women's movement can learn from.

3. In his study of class and status in San Ricardo (a pseudonym), a village in the central Luzon region of the Philippines, Benedict J. Tria presents a similar analysis of the consciousness of the poor villagers: they have their own perceptions of the class relations in their village. See *Everyday Politics in the Philippines* (Berkeley and Los Angeles: University of California Press, 1990).

4. Interview with a staff member of the Research and Documentation Desk of the Mindoro Institute for Development.

5. I have gathered information about land occupation from interviews with

two peasant leaders of KAMMI; a female member of KMP-Mindoro, who at the time of my fieldwork was holding a position in the organization that enabled her to know about the issue; and a researcher in the Mindoro Institute for Development (a nongovernmental organization providing support services to the peasants in Mindoro).

6. In May 1990, while writing this report, I received a letter from a researcher at the Mindoro Institute for Development along with documentation of the land occupations in Mamburao. My discussion of KAMMI's initiative on land occupation is based primarily on this letter and documentation.

7. Based on a letter to me from the Mindoro Institute for Development, April 6, 1990.

8. I obtained information about this land occupation when I visited Santa Cruz during my revisit to Mindoro in 1996. I talked to some women who were involved in the land occupation and received written documentation from one of the leaders of the local chapter.

9. The chapter of AMIHAN in the Bondoc Peninsula in Quezon Province also uses kakawati for a pesticide. The women boil the leaves and mix the sap with *sili* (red or green pepper). Then they spray the mixture on the fields (from my interview with an AMIHAN organizer from the Bondoc Peninsula, at the AMIHAN national office in Quezon City on May 16, 1996). Carmen Buena, the national chairperson of AMIHAN at the time of my visit in 1996, also received in 1994 the Resourceful Women Award for her massive dissemination of information, her campaign against harmful chemical pesticides (such as the banned Aquatin), and her involvement in developing alternatives to chemical fertilizers and pesticides. (This information is culled from AMIHAN documents I gathered during my revisit to AMIHAN.)

10. A grassroots initiative such as this deserves funding and support. When I revisited Calintaan in 1996 I learned that the women's rice marketing cooperative project had operated for three years but came to a standstill when the Mindoro Institute for Development withdrew its support. I also saw the foundation for a warehouse they had begun constructing for the rice marketing cooperative. They hope to be able to continue when funding becomes available again.

Chapter 5

1. During my revisit in 1996, AMIHAN was in the process of changing its structure in order to strengthen local organizing work. Learning from the past limitations of "NGOism"—in which professionals set up institutions to support peasant women's organizations without immersing themselves in the villages—AMIHAN attempts to develop and evolve leaders from its local groups, who are more integrated in peasant women's communities (from my personal interview of an AMIHAN national leader, May 17, 1996, Quezon City, Philippines).

2. See Niza R. Licuanan, "Factory Work and the Third World Woman: A Case Study of Filipina Workers in a Global Assembly Line" (paper presented at the annual meeting of the Midwest Sociological Society, Chicago, April 1996).

3. See Sylvia Chant and Cathy McIlwaine, *Women of a Lesser Cost: Female Labour, Foreign Exchange and Philippine Development* (Manila: Ateneo de Manila University Press, 1995).

4. Leticia Ramos-Shahani, Representative of the Government of the Philippines, Address to the United Nations Expert Group Meeting on Violence Against

Women Migrant Workers, Manila, May 27–31, 1996. I attended this meeting as an observer.

5. Bureau of Women and Young Workers, Department of Labor and Employment, *Facts and Figures on Women,* prepared by Romulo C. Brilliantes, OIC, Research Division, and Ferdinand M. Bacani, LEO 1, Research Division (Manila, March 1995).

6. Based on my research-in-progress, "The Global Political Economy of Domestic Service Work: The Experience of Filipino Women."

7. AMIHAN, "Their Failure Becomes Our Strength," *Conference Proceedings of Asian Peasant Women: Dialogue on the General Agreement on Trade and Tariffs (GATT) and Structural Adjustment Programs (SAPs)* (Quezon City, Philippines: AMIHAN, 1992), 59. The conference was held in Rizal, Philippines, November 9–18, 1992.

8. PUMALAG, "A Position Paper on the General Agreement on Tariff and Trade (GATT)," *Peasant Update Philippines* (June 1994): 14–16.

9. Ibid.

10. Ibid.

11. From documentation of the activities of a village chapter of KAMMI, given to me during my revisit in 1996.

Chapter 6

1. AMIHAN, *Pagsibol* 5 (January–March 1991): 6.

2. Ibid., 7.

Appendix A

1. See also Jeffrey Sluka, who points out the need to consider the problems and difficulties in conducting fieldwork in "violent social contexts," as in the Third World where "there is more need now for such research than there has ever been before," and to treat these issues as an "essential methodological concern" in the training of fieldworkers ("Participant Observation in Violent Social Contexts," *Human Organization* 49, no. 2 [1990]: 124).

2. Margery Wolf also thought of protecting the safety of her informants from the police when she did her fieldwork in Taiwan at a time when police confiscation of her notes was "a very real possibility." In writing field notes she did not use names but assigned numbers to her informants. (Margery Wolf, *A Thrice-told Tale: Feminism, Postmodernism, and Ethnographic Responsibility* [Stanford: Stanford University Press, 1992].)

3. See also Shulamit Reinharz, *Feminist Methods in Social Research* (New York: Oxford University Press, 1992), 151. In chapter 2 she talks about "feminist interview research," citing having a more personal relationship with the interviewee as an aspect of the feminist interview process. Theresa Balayon, a Filipina feminist, also points out that in feminist research, the process of data collection must be a "dialectical or interactive" relationship between the researcher and the researched ("Undertaking Feminist Research," in *Empowering Women Through Research Networking,* ed. R. Esguerra [Philippines: ABAY, n.d.]).

4. This is related to Shulamit Reinharz's idea that one of the aspects of feminist research is "openness to environment, immersion, being subject to and shaped by it" ("Experiential Analysis: A Contribution to Feminist Research," in *Theories*

of Women's Studies, ed. G. Bowles and A. D. Klein [London: Routledge and Kegan Paul, 1983]).

5. This is related to Reinharz's discussion on the use of multiple research methods in feminist research (*Feminist Methods*).

6. This is somewhat similar to what Dorothy Smith talks about in her concept of "institutional ethnography," a process of inquiry that allows a researcher to begin from what is problematic in women's everyday lives, attempting to find the causes and resolutions of these issues within the larger ruling structures in which women's lives are intricately woven (*The Everyday World as Problematic: A Feminist Sociology* [Boston: Northwestern University Press, 1987]). Gita Sen and Caren Grown also talk about beginning the analysis of development from the experience of Third World women, though she does not suggest a specific methodology (*Development, Crises, and Alternative Visions* [New York: Monthly Review Press, 1987]). Although Smith, Grown and Sen influenced me in viewing the concrete experiences of peasant women within the broader power structures of development and underdevelopment in the Philippines, I did not go to the field to test or implement Smith's "institutional ethnography," since she evolved the method in a Western setting and I wanted to allow what emerged to shape my methodology.

7. L. Stanley and S. Wise, in their discussion of how to understand intersubjectivity in feminist research, also point out the importance of recognizing shared or common experiences of the researcher and the researched in the theoretical descriptions of the social world that we produce ("Method, Methodology and Epistemology in Feminist Research Processes," in *Feminist Praxis: Research, Theory, and Epistemology in Feminist Sociology*, ed. Liz Stanley [London and New York: Routledge, 1990]).

8. Sandra Harding succinctly argues that the "best feminist analysis" is one that places the inquirer "in the same critical plane as the overt subject matter," such as situating her/his "class, race, culture and gender assumptions" within the "frame of the picture that she/he attempts to paint." She refers to this reflexivity of feminist research as the "new subject matter" to emphasize its strength and to make us ask the often-neglected question of how it shapes our inquiry ("Introduction: Is There a Feminist Method?" in *Feminism and Methodology*, ed. Sandra Harding [Bloomington and Stratford: Indiana University Press and Open University Press, 1987]).

9. Patti Lather also talks about the connection between research and social justice in her concept of emancipatory, praxis-oriented feminist research methodologies ("Feminist Perspectives on Empowering Research Methodologies," *Women's Studies International Forum* 11 [1988]; and *Getting Smart: Feminist Research and Pedagogy With/in the Postmodern* [New York: Routledge, 1991]).

10. In feminist research, Reinharz also describes the nature of the researcher-subject as one of involvement, "sense of commitment, participation, and sharing of fate" ("Experiential Analysis," 171).

11. Having grown up in a town, I had little knowledge of what militarization was like in a village before I did my fieldwork.

12. According to Reinharz, this is related to one of the expectations of the feminist research process: to bring some change in the researcher as a person, which must be "recorded, reported, and valued" ("Experiential Analysis," 171).

References

Agoncillo, Teodoro. 1960. *Malolos: The Crisis of the Republic*. Quezon City: University of the Philippines Press.

Aguilar, Delia. 1988. *The Feminist Challenge*. Manila: Asian Social Institute.

Alliance for Philippine Concerns. 1988. "Statement on the U.S. Bases." June 12.

Altorki, Soraya, and Camilla Fawzi El-Solh. 1988. *Arab Women in the Field: Studying Your Own Society*. New York: Syracuse University Press.

AMIHAN. 1991. *Pagsibol* 5 (January–March).

AMIHAN. 1992. "Their Failure Becomes Our Strength." *Conference Proceedings of Asian Peasant Women: Dialogue on the General Agreement on Trade and Tariffs (GATT) and Structural Adjustment Programs (SAPs)* (Quezon City, Philippines: AMIHAN).

AMIHAN. 1996. "Kababaihang Magbubukid Puspusang Makibaka Para Sa Tunay na Repormang Agraryo." June 6.

AMIHAN. n.d. *Pagsibol*, Special issue.

Anand, Anita. 1984. "Rethinking Development." In *Women and Development*, edited by ISIS International Information and Communication Service. Philadelphia: New Society Publishers.

Angeles, Leonora C. 1986. "Marxism and the 'Woman Question.'" *Praxis* 1 (January–December): 40–61.

Antrobus, Peggy. 1989. "The Empowerment of Women." in *Women and International Development Manual*, edited by Rita S. Gallin, Marilyn Aronoff, and Anne Ferguson. Boulder and San Francisco: Westview Press.

Ayupan, Loreng. "Life of Peasant Women." In *Empowering Filipinas for Development*, edited by GABRIELA. Quezon City: GABRIELA, 1987.

Babb, Florence. 1986. "Producers and Reproducers: Andean Market Women in the Economy." In *Women and Change in Latin America*, edited by June Nash and Helen Safa. South Hadley, Mass.: Bergin and Garvey Publishers.

Balayon, Theresa. n.d. "Undertaking Feminist Research." In *Empowering Women Through Research Networking*, edited by R. Esguerra. Philippines: ABAY.

Banzon-Bautista, Cynthia. 1983. "Capitalism and the Peasantry: A Review of the Empirical Literature." *Philippine Sociological Review* 31:17–26.

Bauzon, Kenneth E. 1991. "Knowledge and Ideology in Philippine Setting." *Philippine Quarterly of Culture and Society* 19:20–234.

———. 1992. "Social Knowledge and the Legitimation of the State: The Philippine Experience in Historical Perspective." *Political Communication* 9:173–89.

Becker, Howard. 1963. *The Outsiders*. New York: The Free Press of Glencoe.

———. 1967. "Whose Side Are We On?" *Social Problems* 14(3): 239–47.

Bello, Walden, David Kinley, and Elaine Elinson. 1982. *Development Debacle: The World Bank and the Philippines.* San Francisco: Institute for Food and Development Policy.

———. 1987. *U.S.-Sponsored Low-Intensity Conflict in the Philippines.* San Francisco: The Institute for Food and Development Policy.

———. 1992. *People and Power in the Pacific: The Struggle for the Post–Cold War Order.* London and San Francisco: Pluto Press, with Food First and Transnational Institute.

Bello, Walden, and Severina Rivera, eds. 1977. *The Logistics of Repression and Other Essays.* Washington, D.C.: Friends of the Filipino People. Quoted in Roland Simbulan, *The Bases of Our Insecurity: A Study of the U.S. Military Bases in the Philippines.* Philippines: Balai Fellowship, 1985, 176–77.

Beneria, Lourdes. 1979. "Production, Reproduction, and the Sexual Division of Labor." *Cambridge Journal of Economics* 3 : 203–25.

Beneria, Lourdes, and Gita Sen. 1986. "Accumulation, Reproduction, and Women's Role in Economic Development: Boserup Revisited." In *Women's Work: Development and the Division by Labor by Gender,* edited by Eleanor Leacock and Helen Safa. South Hadley, Mass.: Bergin and Garvey Publishers.

Bisilliat, Jeane, and Michele Fieloux. 1987. *Women of the Third World.* Translated by Enne Amann and Peter Amann. London: Associated University Press.

Blomstrom, Magnus, and Bjorn Hettne. 1984. *Development Theory in Transition: The Dependency Debate and Beyond Third World Responses.* London: Zed Books.

Bolles, Lynn A. 1986. "Economic Crisis and Female-Headed Households in Urban Jamaica." In *Women and Change in Latin America,* edited by June Nash and Helen Safa. South Hadley, Mass.: Bergin and Garvey Publishers.

Boserup, Ester. 1970. *The Woman's Role in Economic Development.* London: George Allen and Unwin.

Brewer, Anthony. 1980. *Marxist Theories of Imperialism.* New York: Routledge and Kegan Paul.

Brilliantes, Alex B. 1986. "Capitalism: The World Bank's Ideological Straightjacket." *Praxis* 1 (January–December): 62–93.

Bronstein, Audrey. 1982. *The Triple Struggle: Latin American Peasant Women.* Boston: South End Press.

Brown, Elwood. 1917. Letter of Elmwood Brown, athletic director of the YMCA, to Mrs. Saleeby, president of the Manila Women's Club. *Manila Times,* July 24. Quoted in Elizabeth Eviota, "Women, Work, and Sex: Gender Relations and Social Transformation in the Philippines" (Ph.D. diss., Rutgers University, 1985).

Bulmer, Martin. 1984. *The Chicago School of Sociology.* Chicago: The University of Chicago Press.

Bunster-Burroto, Ximena. 1985. "Surviving Beyond Fear: Women and Torture in Latin America." In *Women and Change in Latin America,* edited by June Nash and Helen Safa. South Hadley, Mass.: Bergin and Garvey Publishers.

Bureau of the Census (BOC). 1954. *1948 Census of the Population and Agriculture: Summary and General Report.* Vol. 3. Manila. Quoted in Elizabeth Eviota, "Women, Work, and Sex: Gender Relations and Social Transformation in the Philippines," (Ph.D. diss., Rutgers University, 1985), 86–87.

Bureau of Women and Young Workers. 1995. *Facts and Figures on Women.* Prepared by Romulo C. Brillantes, OIC, Research Division, and Ferdinand M. Bacani, LEO 1, Research Division. Manila: Philippine Department of Labor, March.

Camagay, Maria Luisa. n.d. "Doing Historical Research." In *Empowering Women Through Research Networking,* edited by Ricky Esguerra. Philippines: ABAY.

Cancian, Francesca. 1991. "Feminism and Participatory Research." Talk presented at the Annual Social Science Mellon Award Symposium, Loyola University, Chicago, Illinois, May 1.

Carabeo, Joseph. 1996. Guest Editorial. *Tambalan* 2, no. 2 (Spring).

Center for Women's Resources. 1996. *Pilipinas 2000 sa Taong 1995.* Quezon City, Philippines: Center for Women's Resources.

Chant, Sylvia, and Cathy McIlwaine. 1995. *Women of a Lesser Cost: Female Labor, Foreign Exchange and Philippine Development.* Manila: Ateneo de Manila University Press.

Chilcote, Ronald H. 1984. *Theories of Economic Development and Underdevelopment.* Boulder, Colo.: Westview Press.

Children's Rehabilitation Center. 1995. "Children and Human Rights Violations: The Need for a More Relevant Perspective for Rehabilitation Work." Paper presented at the U.N. Conference on Traumas of Youth and Children in Armed Conflict. Amsterdam, Netherlands, November.

Chirino, Pedro. 1903. "The Philippines in 1600." In *The Philippine Islands, 1493–1898*, edited by E. Blair and J. Robertson. Cleveland: A. H. Clark. Cited in Elizabeth Eviota, "Women, Work, and Sex: Gender Relations and Social Transformation in the Philippines" (Ph.D. diss., Rutgers University, 1985), 31.

Church Coalition for Human Rights in the Philippines. 1989. *Philippine Witness,* Summer.

Clark, Ramsey, Gerald Horne, Ralph McGehee, Sr. Catherine Pinkerton, Lester Edwin J. Ruiz, and Leonard Weinglass. 1987. *Report of the U.S.-Philippine Fact Finding Mission to the Philippines.* May 20–30. n.p.

Colin, Francisco. 1903. "Native Races and Their Customs (1663)." In *The Philippine Islands, 1493–1898*, vol. 40, edited by E. Blair and J. Robertson. Cleveland: A. H. Clark. Cited in Elizabeth Eviota, "Women, Work, and Sex: Gender Relations and Social Transformation in the Philippines" (Ph.D. diss., Rutgers University, 1985), 32.

Commission of the Census (COC). 1941. *Census of the Philippines, 1939.* Vol. 2. Manila. Cited in Elizabeth Eviota, "Women, Work, and Sex: Gender Relations and Social Transformation in the Philippines" (Ph.D. diss., Rutgers University, 1985), 86–87.

Constantino, Renato. 1975. *The Philippines: A Past Revisited.* Manila: By the author.

———. 1966. "The Miseducation of the Filipino." In *The Filipinos in the Philippines and Other Essays.* Quezon City: Malaya Books.

Constitution of the Republic of the Philippines. 1986. Article 2, Declaration of Principles and State Policies, Section 8.

Croll, Elizabeth. 1986. "Rural Production and Reproduction: Socialist Development Experiences." In *Women's Work: Development and the Division of Labor by Gender,* edited by Eleanor Leacock and Helen Safa. South Hadley, Mass.: Bergin and Garvey Publishers.

Deere, Carmen Diana, and Magdalena Leon de Leal. 1982. "Peasant Production, Proletarianization, and the Sexual Division of Labor in the Andes." In *Women and Development,* edited by Lourdes Beneria. New York: Praeger.

de la Costa, Horacio. 1965. *Readings in Philippine History.* Manila: Bookmark. Quoted in Renato Constantino, *The Philippines: A Past Revisited.* Manila: Self-published, 1975, 53.

Edholm, Felicity, Olivia Harris, and Kate Young. 1981. "Conceptualizing Women." *Critique of Anthropology,* 101–31.

Enloe, Cynthia. 1980. *Sex and Levi's: The International Sexual Division of Labor.* Worcester, Mass.: Department of Government, Clark University.

————. 1983a. *Does Khaki Become You? The Militarization of Women's Lives.* London: Pluto Press.

————. 1983b. "Women Textile Workers in the Militarization of Southeast Asia." In *Women, Men, and the International Division of Labor,* edited by June Nash and Maria Patricia Fernandez-Kelly. Albany, N.Y.: SUNY Press.

————. 1985. "Bananas, Bases, and Patriarchy: Some Feminist Questions About the Militarization of Central America." *Radical America* 19, no. 4: 7–23.

————. 1989. *Bananas, Beaches and Bases: Making Feminist Sense of International Politics.* London: Pandora Press, 1989.

Eviota, Elizabeth U. 1985. "Women, Work, and Sex: Gender Relations and Social Transformation in the Philippines." Ph.D. diss., Rutgers University; Ann Arbor, Mich.: University Microfilms International.

————. 1986. "The Articulation of Gender and Class in the Philippines." In *Women's Work: Development and the Division of Labor by Gender,* edited by Eleanor Leacock and Helen Safa. South Hadley, Mass.: Bergin and Garvey Publishers.

————. 1992. *The Political Economy of Gender: Women and the Sexual Division of Labour in the Philippines.* London and Atlantic Highlands, N.J.: Zed Books.

Fanon, Frantz. 1968. *The Wretched of the Earth.* New York: Grove Press.

Forum For Rural Concerns Human Rights Desk. 1989. *The Philippine Human Rights Situationer.* Quezon City, Philippines.

Frank, Andre Gunder. 1974. *Lumpenbourgeosie: Lumpendevelopment.* New York: Monthly Review Press.

————. 1981. *Crisis in the Third World.* New York: Holmes and Meir Publishers.

Freedom from Debt Coalition. 1989. *The Philippine Debt Crisis.* Diliman, Quezon City: Freedom from Debt Coalition.

Freire, Paolo. 1970. *Pedagogy of the Oppressed.* London: Penguin Books.

Fuentes, Annette, and Barbara Ehrenreich. 1984. *Women in the Global Factory.* Boston: South End Press.

GABRIELA. 1987. *Empowering Filipinas For Development.* Quezon City: GABRIELA.

Golden, Renny. 1991. *The Hour of the Poor, The Hour of Women: Salvadoran Women Speak.* New York: Crossroad.

Grossman, Rachel. 1979. "Women's Place in the Integrated Circuit. The Global Assembly Line and the Social Manipulation of Women on the Job." *Southeast Asia Chronicle* 9 (66), nos. 5–6.

Guerrero, Amado. 1983. "The Provincial and Municipal Elite in Luzon." In *Philippine Social History: Global Trade and Local Transformations,* edited by Alfred W. McCoy and Edilberto C. de Jesus. Honolulu: University of Hawaii Press.

Guzman, Arnel de. 1993. "Philippines 2000: Vision o Ilusyon?" *Pinoy: Overseas Chronicle* 11, no. 2: 4–5, 34.

Harding, Sandra. 1987. "Introduction: Is There a Feminist Method?" In *Feminism and Methodology,* edited by Sandra Harding. Bloomington and Stratford: Indiana University Press and Open University Press.

Hartendorp, A. V. H. 1958. *Short History of Industry and Trade in the Philippines.* Vol. 3. Manila: American Chamber of Commerce in the Philippines, 1958. Quoted in Pedro Salgado, *The Philippine Economy: History and Analysis.* Quezon City, Philippines: R. P. Garcia Publishing Co., 22.

Heyzer, Noeleen. 1986. *Working Women in South-East Asia: Development, Subordination and Emancipation.* Philadelphia: Open University Press.

Hildebrand, Dale. 1991. *To Pay Is to Die.* Davao City, Philippines: Philippine International Forum.

IBON Data Bank, Philippines. 1988. *Land Reform in the Philippines.* Metro-Manila, Philippines: IBON Data Bank.

IBON Data Bank. n.d. Quoted in *The Philippine Debt Crisis*. Diliman, Quezon City: Freedom From Debt Coalition, 1989, 30.

IBON Facts and Figures, no. 191, July 31, 1986.

IBON Facts and Figures, vol. 15, no. 16, August 31, 1992.

Johnson, Cheryl. 1986. "Class and Gender: A Consideration of the Yoruba Women During the Colonial Period." In *Women and Class in Africa*, edited by Claire Robertson and Iris Berger. London: Africana Publishing.

Karl, Marilee. 1984a. "Integrating Women into Multinational Development?" In *Women in Development*, edited by ISIS Women's International Information and Communication Service. Philadelphia: New Society Publishers.

———. 1984b. "Women and Rural Development: An Overview." In *Women in Development*, edited by ISIS Women's International Information and Communication Service. Philadelphia: New Society Publishers.

———. 1984c. "Women, Land, Food Production." In *Women in Development*, edited by ISIS Women's International Information and Communication Service. Philadelphia: New Society Publishers.

———. 1984d. "Appropriate Technology." In *Women in Development*, edited by ISIS Women's International Information and Communication Service. Philadelphia: New Society Publishers.

———. 1984e. "Income Generation for Women." In *Women in Development*, ISIS Women's International Information and Communication Service. Philadelphia: New Society Publishers.

Kelly, Maria Patricia Fernandez. 1986. Introduction to *Women's Work: Development and the Division of Labor by Gender*, edited by Eleanor Leacock and Helen I. Safa. South Hadley, Mass.: Bergin and Garvey Publishers.

Kerkvliet, Benedict J. Tria. 1990. *Everyday Politics in the Philippines*. Berkeley and Los Angeles: University of California Press.

Kessler, Richard J. 1986. "Marcos and the Americas." *Foreign Policy* (Summer): 52. Quoted in *The Philippines Reader*, edited by Daniel Schirmer and Stephen Rosskam Shalom. Boston: South End Press, 1987, 225.

KMP (Kilusang Magbubukid ng Pilipinas). 1989. *Philippine Peasant Update*, no. 16 (July–August).

Kurihara, Kenneth K. 1945. *Labor in the Philippine Economy*. Stanford: Stanford University Press. Quoted in Elizabeth Eviota, "Women, Work, and Sex: Gender Relations and Social Transformation in the Philippines" (Ph.D. diss., Rutgers University, 1985).

Lachica, Eduardo. 1963. "The Age of Awakening." Part 2. *Historical Bulletin* (December). Quoted in Renato Constantino, *A Past Revisited*. Manila: Self-published, 1975, 142.

Lather, Patti. 1988. "Feminist Perspectives on Empowering Research Methodologies." *Women's Studies International Forum* 11: 567–81.

———. 1991. *Getting Smart: Feminist Research and Pedagogy with/in the Postmodern*. New York: Routledge.

Leacock, Eleanor, and Helen Safa, eds. 1986. *Women's Work: Development and the Division of Labor by Gender*. South Hadley, Mass.: Bergin and Garvey Publishers.

Leon, Rosario. 1990. "Bartolina Sisa: The Peasant Women's Organization in Bolivia." In *Women and Social Change in Latin America*, edited by Elizabeth Jelin, translated by J. Ann Zammit and Marilyn Thomson. London and Atlantic Highlands, N.J.: Zed Books.

Lewis, Oscar. 1959. *Five Families: Mexican Studies in the Culture of Poverty*. New York: Basic Books.

Licuanan, Niza R. 1995. "Factory Work and the Third World Woman: A Case

Study of Filipina Workers in a Global Assembly Line." Paper presented at the annual meeting of the Midwest Sociological Society, Chicago, April.

Lim, Linda. 1983. "Capitalism, Imperialism, and Patriarchy: The Dilemma of Third World Women Workers in Multinational Development." In *Women, Men and the International Division of Labor*, edited by June Nash and Maria Patricia Fernandez-Kelly. Albany: SUNY Press.

Lindio, Ligaya M. 1979. "An Exploratory Study Toward the Development of a Possible Method for Folk Research." Master's thesis, Asian Social Institute.

Mackintosh, Maureen. 1990. "Abstract Markets and Real Needs." In *The Food Question: Profits Versus People?* edited by Henry Berstein, Ben Crow, Maureen MacKintosh, and Charlotte Martin. New York: Monthly Review Press.

Mangahas, Fe. 1987. "The Status of Filipino Women From Pre-Colonial Times to Early American Period." In *Kamalayan: Feminist Writings in the Philippines*, edited by Pennie Azarcon. Quezon City: Pilipina.

Marciano, Marie, ed. 1989. *Let's Work Together for the Protection Human Rights of Filipino Women: Documentation on the Human Rights Situation of Filipino Women*. Manila: GABRIELA Women's Commission on Human Rights.

Mason, Beverly J. 1985. "The Continuing Modernization of Underdevelopment: Jamaican Women as Producers and Reproducers." Ph.D. diss., Brandeis University.

McCall, Michal. 1991. "Why I Am Not a Running Dog PostModernist and How I Hope to Become One." Paper presented at the Annual Midwest Sociological Conference, Des Moines, Iowa, April 11–16.

McCoy, Alfred W., and Edilberto C. de Jesus, eds. 1982. *Philippine Social History: Global Trade and Local Transformations*. Honolulu: University of Hawaii Press.

McGovern, Ligaya. 1993. "The Philippines: Counter-Insurgency and Peasant Women." *Race and Class: A Journal for Black and Third World Liberation* 34, no. 4: 1–11.

Meis, Maria. 1982. "The Dynamics of the Sexual Division of Labor and the Integration of Rural Women into the World Market." In *Women and Development*, edited by Lourdes Beneria. New York: Praeger and Meir Publishers.

Miliband, Ralph. 1969. *The State in Capitalist Society*. New York: Basic Books.

"Military Base Agreement." March 14, 1947. Quoted in Daniel E. Schirmer and Stephen Rosskamm Shalom, eds., *The Philippines Reader: A History of Colonialism, Neo-Colonialism, Dictatorship, and Resistance*, ed. Daniel B. Schirmer and Stephen Rosskamm Shalom. Boston: South End Press, 1987, 97–100.

Mindoro Institute for Development. n.d. "Occidental Mindoro: A Profile." Mindoro, Philippines: Photocopy.

Mindoro Integrated Rural Development Office. 1980. *Mindoro Integrated Development Plan*. Quezon City, Philippines.

Moselina, Leopoldo M. 1981. "Olongapo's R and R Industry: A Sociological Analysis of Institutionalized Prostitution." *Makatao: An Interdisciplinary Journal for Students and Practitioners of the Social Sciences* 1 (January–June): 10. Manila: Asian Social Institute. Quoted in Cynthia Enloe, *Does Khaki Become You? The Militarization of Women's Lives*. London: Pluto Press, 1983, 39.

Nash, June. 1983. "The Impact of the Changing International Division of Labor on the Different Sectors of the Labor Force." In *Women, Men, and the International Division of Labor*, edited by June Nash and Maria Patricia Fernandez-Kelly. Albany: SUNY Press.

National Census and Statistics. n.d. Quoted in *IBON Facts and Figures* (July 31, 1986), 8.

Nera-Lauron, Tetet. 1994. "Philippines 2000: A Woman's Worst Nightmare." *Laya: Feminist Quarterly* 3, no. 1: 4–25.

Oliveros, Tess. 1995. "Walang Katapusang Kayod at Hirap, Wala Pa Ring Pag-unlad." Report presented at Oxfam America Philippine Partners' Dialogue, Lake Island Resort, Binangonan, Rizal, Philippines, April 26–28.

Ong, Sihwa. 1979. "Industrialization and Prostitution in Southeast Asia." In *Beyond Stereotypes: Asian Women in Development,* Southeast Asia Chronicle, no. 96.

Paez, Patricia Ann. 1985. *The Bases Factor: Realpolitic of RP-US Relations.* Manila, Philippines: Dispatch Press and Center for Strategic and International Studies in the Philippines.

Payer, Cheryl. 1974. *The Debt Trap: The IMF and the Third World.* New York: Monthly Review Press.

Peasant Education and Development Center. 1995. "Fiefdom 2000." *Agrarian Directions,* no. 1 (June).

Pelzer, Karl. n.d. *Pioneer Settlement in the Asiatic Tropics.* Quoted in Pedro Salgado, *The Philippine Economy: History and Analysis.* Quezon City, Philippines: R. P. Garcia Publishing Co., 1985, 25.

Perpiñan, Sr. Mary Soledad. 1986. "Philippine Women and Transnational Corporations." In *The Philippine Reader: A History of Colonialism, Dictatorship and Resistance,* edited by Daniel B. Schirmer and Stephan Rosskam Shalom. Boston: South End Press.

Philippine Daily Globe. 1989. April 6. Quoted in *The Treadmill of Poverty for Filipino Women,* by Aida Fulleros Santos and Lynn F. Lee (Philippines: Kalayaan, 1989), 44.

Philippine Human Rights Information Center [research and information arm of the Philippine Alliance of Human Rights Advocates). 1996. "Report of the Philippine Alliance of Human Rights Advocates on Human Rights in the Philippines." Report presented to the Fifty-second Session of the United Nations Commission on Human Rights, Geneva, Switzerland, 18 March–26 April.

Philippine Peasant Institute. 1989. *Farm News and Views* 2, no. 1 (March–April).

PUMALAG. 1994. "A Position Paper on the General Agreement on Tariffs and Trade (GATT)." *Peasant Update Philippines,* June.

Putzel, James, and John Cunnington. 1989. *Gaining Ground: Agrarian Reform in the Philippines.* London: War on Want Campaigns.

Ramos-Shahani, Leticia. 1996. Address representing the Philippine government to the United Nations Expert Group Meeting on Violence Against Women Migrant Workers, Division for the Advancement of Women, Manila, Philippines, May 27–31.

Ranger, Terence. 1989. "Peasant Consciousness: Culture and Conflict in Zimbabwe." In *Peasant and Peasant Societies,* 2d ed., edited by Theodore Shanin. Oxford and New York: Basil Blackwell.

Reinharz, Shulamit. 1983. "Experiential Analysis: A Contribution to Feminist Research." In *Theories of Women's Studies,* edited by G. Bowles and R. D. Klein. London and Boston: Routledge and Kegan Paul.

———. 1992. *Feminist Methods in Social Research.* New York: Oxford University Press.

Research and Policy Studies Desk, Philippine Peasant Institute, 1989. "The Debt Trap in CARP." Unpublished research paper. Quezon City: Philippine Peasant Institute.

Rodriquez, Joel L. 1987. *Genuine Agrarian Reform.* Quezon City, Philippines: Urban Rural Mission.

Roodkowsky, Mary. 1984. "Women and Development: A Survey of the Literature." In *Women in Development,* edited by ISIS Women's International Information Service. Philadelphia: New Society Publishers.

Russel, Diana E. H. 1989. *Lives of Courage: Women for a New South Africa.* New York: Basic Books.

Rutten, Rosanne. 1982. *Women Workers of Hacienda Milagros: Wage Labor and Household Subsistence on a Philippine Sugarcane Plantation.* Amsterdam: University of Amsterdam.

Safa, Helen. 1986. "Runaway Shops and Female Unemployment: The Search for Cheap Labor." In *Women's Work: Development and the Division of Labor by Gender,* edited by Eleanor Leacock and Helen Safa. South Hadley, Mass.: Bergin and Garvey Publishing.

Salgado, Pedro V., O.P. 1985. *The Philippine Economy: History and Analysis.* Quezon City, Philippines: R. P. Garcia Publishing Co.

Sandoval, Romulo A., ed. 1986. *Prospects of Agrarian Reform Under the New Order.* Philippines: NCCP-URM and REAPS.

San Juan, E., Jr. 1992. *Racial Formations/Critical Transformations.* Atlantic Heights, N.J. and London: Humanities Press.

Santos, Aida, and Lynn F. Lee. 1989. *The Debt Crisis: A Treadmill of Poverty for Filipino Women.* Philippines: Kalayaan.

Schirmer, Daniel B., and Stephan Rosskamm Shalom. 1987. *The Philippines Reader: A History of Colonialism, Neocolonialism, Dictatorship, and Resistance.* Boston: South End Press.

Schult, Volker. 1991. *Mindoro: A Social History of a Philippine Island in the Twentieth Century (A Case Study of a Delayed Developmental Process).* Manila: Divine Word Publications.

Schutte, Gerhard. 1991. "Racial Oppression and Social Research: Field Work Under Racial Conflict in South Africa." *Qualitative Sociology* 14, no. 2: 127–46.

Scott, James C. 1985. *Weapons of the Weak.* London: Yale University Press.

Sen, Gita, and Caren Grown. 1987. *Development, Crises, and Alternative Visions.* New York: Monthly Review Press.

Shanin, Theodore. 1973. "The Nature and Logic of the Peasant Economy." *Journal of Peasant Studies* 1: 63–80. Quoted in Cynthia Banzon-Bautista, "Capitalism and the Peasantry: A Review of the Literature," *Philippine Sociological Review* 31 (1983): 21.

Shiva, Vandana. 1992. "GATT, Agriculture and Third World Women." In *Their Failure Becomes Our Strength.* Philippines: AMIHAN.

Siegel, Lenny. 1979. "Orchestrating Dependency." *Southeast Asia Chronicle* 9, no. 5.

Simbulan, Roland G. 1985. *The Bases of Our Insecurity: A Study of the U.S. Military Bases in the Philippines.* Manila: Balai Fellowship.

Sluka, Jeffrey. 1990. "Participant Observation in Violent Social Contexts." *Human Organization* 49, no. 2: 114–26.

Smith, Dorothy. 1987. *The Everyday World as Problematic: A Feminist Sociology.* Boston: Northwestern University Press.

———. 1990. *Texts, Facts, and Femininity: Exploring the Relations of Ruling.* New York and London: Routledge.

Stamp, Patricia. 1986. "Kikuyu Women's Self-Help Groups: Toward an Understanding of the Relation Between Sex-Gender System and Mode of Production in Africa." In *Women and Class in Africa,* edited by Claire Robertson and Iris Berger. London: Africana Publishing Company.

Stanley, L., and S. Wise. 1990. "Method, Methodology and Epistemology in Feminist Research Processes." In *Feminist Praxis: Research, Theory and Epistemology in Feminist Sociology*, edited by Liz Stanley. London and New York: Routledge.

Synapses. 1989. *Synapses Messages* 8, no. 4 (July).

Takaki, Ronald. 1993. *A Different Mirror: A History of Multicultural America.* New York: Little, Brown and Company.

Tangcangco, Luz. n.d. "Women Undertaking Academic Research." In *Empowering Women Through Academic Research*, edited by Ricky Esguerra. Philippines: ABAY.

Task Force Detainees of the Philippines. 1995. *"Krimen ba ang maglingkod sa bayan?"* December.

Tiongson, Mari Luz, Aurora Regalado, and Ramon San Pascual. 1988. "Agriculture in the 70s and 80s; TNC's Boon, Peasants' Doom." In *Sowing the Seed: Proceedings of the International Solidarity Conference for the Filipino Peasantry (ISCFP), October 11–21, 1986*, edited by Rodolfo Desuasido. Manila: Kilusang Mangbubukid ng Pilipinas.

Tungcul, Catarina. 1996. "The Impact of World Trade on Peasant Women and Women Farm Workers in the Philippines." Paper presented at the WIDE Conference on Women and Trade, Bonn, Germany, May 30–31.

Urdang, Stephanie. 1989. *And Still They Dance: Women, War, and the Struggle for Change in Mozambique.* New York: Monthly Review Press.

United States Bureau of the Census (USBOC). 1905. *Census of the Philippine Islands.* Taken under the direction of the Philippine Commission in the year 1903. 4 vols. Washington, D.C. Quoted in Elizabeth Eviota, "Women, Work, and Sex: Gender Relations and Social Transformation in the Philippines" (Ph.D. diss., Rutgers University, 1985), 86–87.

United States News and World Watch Report. 1967. March 13. Quoted in Roland G. Simbulan, *The Bases of Our Insecurity: A Study of the U.S. Bases in the Philippines.* Philippines: Balai Fellowship, 1985, 178.

Wolf, Margery. 1992. *A Thrice-told Tale: Feminism, Postmodernism, and Ethnographic Responsibility.* Stanford: Stanford University Press.

Wurfel, David. 1988. *Filipino Politics: Development and Decay.* London: Cornell University Press.

Youssef, Nadia. 1976. "Women in Development: Urban Life and Labor." In *Women and World Development*, edited by Irene Tinker and Michele Ramsen. Washington, D.C.: Overseas Development Council.

Index

problems of peasant women, ix–x, 46–50, 114–15, 121, 135; poverty, 35, 53, 60, 64, 104, 108, 122, 129, 143, 205 n.21; landlessness, 46–47; lack of funds for collective projects, 103–4, 108; lack of government subsidy, 47; usury, 47–48, 103, 111; lack of production capital, 50, 93; lack of recognition for economic contribution, 54; lack of government subsidy of irrigation, 54–55; lack of government subsidy for rice production, natural calamities, 55, 103; privatization of food production, 54–55; lack of health care services, 104–7; inadequate income, 107; inadequate access to education, 129. *See also* Militarization; Repression; Rice; Exploitation
proletarianization of the peasantry, 20
PUMALAG (Pambansang Ugnayan ng Mamamayan Laban sa GATT; Philippine Network of Citizens' Action Against GATT), 180

Quedan Financing Scheme, 56–57; rice traders control of, 57–59, 185

Ramos, Fidel, 1; regime/government, 1–6, 35, 68
repression, 78, 118. *See also* Militarization; Military repression; Military rape
resistance: of KAMMI, ix, x, xiii (*see also* KAMMI); of AMIHAN, x, xiii (*see also* AMIHAN); of indigenous Filipinos, 4–5 (*see also* Indigenous Filipinos)
rice: artificial scarcity of, import of from U.S., 61; capitalist penetration in production of, 64; commercialization, importation, production of, 29; control of traders, commercialization, monopoly in marketing, 56–59; exchange value of, 59; export of, 45, 56, 158; impact of fertilizers and pesticides on production of, 100–101; impact of price increase of, 58–59; politics of, 59–61; production in Mindoro, 60; shortage/scarcity of, 5, 45; traditional variety, high-yielding variety, 62–63, 99, 100
ruling elite/class, 40, 61, 66, 67, 78

Samahang Nayon, 58, 205 n.24
SAMAKANA (organization of urban poor women), 171

Samar, 6
sexual division of labor, 46, 50, 132, 184
social change, xii
Southeast Asian women: nongovernmental organizations (NGOs), 17; women's movement, 17
statistics: on farm work of peasant women, 9; U.S. military aid, 38; on level of poverty, 122; on foreign debt, 155; on use of agrochemicals, fertilizers, and pesticides in rice and corn production, 206 n.33
stereotypes about Third World women, xiii
subsistence production, 21, 23

tax measure, 5
tenancy, 45; system of, 47; sharecropping system in, 85
tenants, 47, 84, 89; displacement of, 4
Third World, concept of, 7, 137
Third World women: in Africa, 21, 125; in capitalist world market, 18; and colonization, 20; empowerment, politicization, triple oppression, 22; in India, 20; in informal sector, 20; in Latin America, 22; in transnational corporations, 19; in national liberation movements, 124
tourism, and prostitution, 33
traditional politics, 39–40; patronage, 127, 128; nepotism, 128
transnational corporations, 5, 19, 62, 63, 105. *See also* Multinational corporations

underdevelopment, concept of, 7
United States, xii, 7; exports to, 30; migrant labor to, 32; enlistment of Filipinos in U.S. army, 34; military bases, CIA covert operations, interventionism in Philippine internal politics, 37; military aid to Philippines/repression, 38, 78; use of military bases for intervention in other countries, 38; military bases, prostitution in, 143
usury/usurers, 45, 58

village economy, linked to global economy, 187

women: in socialist countries, 18; and debt, 25
Women's International Day, 80
women's studies, xii, xiv